GARLAND MEDIEVAL CASEBOOKS
VOL. 9

SAINT AUGUSTINE
THE BISHOP

GARLAND REFERENCE LIBRARY
OF THE HUMANITIES
VOL. 1830

GARLAND MEDIEVAL CASEBOOKS

JOYCE E. SALISBURY AND CHRISTOPHER KLEINHENZ
Series Editors

SAINT AUGUSTINE THE BISHOP

A Book of Essays

edited by

Fannie LeMoine
Christopher Kleinhenz

GARLAND PUBLISHING, Inc.
New York & London / 1994

Library of Congress Cataloging-in-Publication Data

Saint Augustine the bishop : a book of essays / edited by
Fannie LeMoine, Christopher Kleinhenz.
    p.   cm. — (Garland reference library of the
humanities ; vol. 1830. Garland medieval casebooks ;
vol. 9)
    Proceedings of a conference held in Madison, Wis.,
Sept. 22–25, 1991, sponsored by the Commission for
Lutheran-Anglican-Roman Catholic Relationships in
Wisconsin and Upper Michigan.
    Includes bibliographical references and index.
    ISBN 0–8153–1639–9 (alk. paper)
    1. Augustine, Saint, Bishop of Hippo—Congresses.
2. Church history—Primitive and early church, ca. 30–
600—Congresses. I. LeMoine, Fannie. II. Kleinhenz,
Christopher. III. Commission for Lutheran-Anglican-
Roman Catholic Relationships in Wisconsin and Upper
Michigan. IV. Series: Garland reference library of the
humanities ; vol. 1830. V. Series: Garland reference
library of the humanities. Garland medieval casebooks ;
vol. 9.
BR65.A9S313   1994
270.2'092—dc20   94–7258
                                             CIP

Composition of this book by Ruth Anne Semmerling,
Madison, Wisconsin.

Printed on acid-free, 250-year-life paper
Manufactured in the United States of America

Contents

Part 3: Workshops

Illustrations

Acknowledgments

The conference on "Augustine: His Influence on the Church and the World" was sponsored by the Commission for Lutheran-Anglican-Roman Catholic Relationships in Wisconsin and Upper Michigan (LARC), and by the Medieval Studies Program at the University of Wisconsin-Madison. It was funded in part by the Wisconsin Humanities Committee, serving on behalf of the National Endowment for the Humanities, with assistance from the Anonymous Fund, University of Wisconsin-Madison. Additional support was received from Luther Memorial Church; St. John's Lutheran Church Foundation, Madison; St. Patrick's Catholic Church; the Roman Catholic Diocese of Madison; St. Mary of the Snows Episcopal Church in Eagle River, Wisconsin; St. John's Episcopal Church in Wisconsin Rapids, Wisconsin; St. Augustine of Hippo Episcopal Church in Rhinelander, Wisconsin; and the Department of History and the Department of Classics at the UW-Madison.

Thanks should be given to Chair Rhoda Braunschweig and to members of the Augustine Celebration Planning Committee as well as to others who generously volunteered their assistance at the conference: James Bartelt, Bruce Bengston, Gerald Born, Gennie Bostian, Kathy Boyd, Patrick W. Carey, William Courtenay, Paul R. Dicks, John B. Dillon, Francis G. Gentry, Clarence Harms, Jane Henning, Christopher Kleinhenz, H. Gerard Knoche, Fannie J. LeMoine, David Lindberg, Bernard McGarty, Elaine Meyer, Connie Ott, Harvey Peters, Maureen Rodgers, Fran Schlimgen, Bonnie Schmidt, Ruth Semmerling, Ralph J. Stanwise, Mary Stolz, John Tedeschi, Dawn von Wiegand, and George Wirz.

Audio-cassettes of the lectures by the ten principal participants are available for purchase through "The Audio Store," a non-profit division of Wisconsin Public Radio, 821 University Avenue, Madison, Wisconsin 53706, Telephone 1-800-972-8346.

PLATE 1. Augustine, in seated position, supports the church and bears
the characteristic signs of sixteenth-century episcopal office. Alonso
de Orozco (1500–1591), *Recopilación de todas las obras* (Valladolid:
Sebastian Martinez, 1554).

Introduction

Christopher Kleinhenz and Fannie LeMoine

In the spring of A.D. 391 Augustine visited the small African seaport of Hippo Regius. While standing in the Catholic church's unimpressive nave, he first listened to Bishop Valerius pleading the urgent needs of the church. Augustine then heard the congregation shouting as they surrounded him, forced him to the altar, and witnessed both his reluctant consent to ordination and his tears.

Augustine recalls the circumstances of this enforced draft into clerical orders vividly in a sermon he delivered to his congregation some thirty-five years after the event (*Serm.* 355.2). Such forced ordinations were not unusual in the African church of the period. For example, in a well-known letter written in A.D. 411 Augustine gives a strong sense of the tumult and violence which could erupt in a congregation bent on gaining a clerical prize. In that letter to Albina (*Epist.* 126) Augustine describes the congregation of Hippo's attempt to capture her son-in-law, the wealthy and devout patrician, Pinianus, as a priest for their church. His words underline the volatility of the parishioners and the dangers a notable man could encounter from an excited and determined congregation. Although the letter is written in part as a defence against the charge that the congregation of Hippo and its clergy (including Augustine) had wanted Pinianus for his money, the vivid description of events shows how quickly a situation could spin out of control in the crowded heat of a congregation's passion (126.1):

> Ego autem post primos eorum clamores cum eis dixissem de illo invito non ordinando, qua iam promissione detinerer, atque adiecissem quod, si mea fide violata illum haberent presbyterum, me episcopum non haberent, ad nostra subsellia relicta turba redieram. Tum illi aliquantulum inopinata mea responsione cunctati atque turbati velut flamma vento paululum pressa, deinde coeperunt multo ardentius excitari, existimantes fieri posse, ut vel

mihi extorqueretur illud non servare promissum vel me tenente promissi fidem ab alio episcopo ordinaretur. . . . Multitudo vero pro gradibus constituta horrendo et perseverantissimo clamorum fremitu in eadem voluntate persistens incertos animi consiliique faciebant. Tunc illa in fratrem meum indigna clamabantur, tunc a nobis graviora timebantur.

Moreover, I myself, after their first shouts, had stressed that I could not ordain him when he was unwilling. I said I was prevented from doing this by the promise I had made; and, I added that, if my pledge were violated and they had him as presbyter, they would not have me as bishop. Then I left the crowd and went back to my seat in the apse [i.e., the raised seats reserved for clergy in the apse of the church]. Then they hesitated because of my unexpected response and they milled about in confusion for a little while, just like a fire that has been pressed back a little bit by the wind. Then they began to burn even more hotly in their excitement, thinking that it would be possible to force me not to keep my promise or, if I kept my promise, to have him ordained by another bishop. . . . But the multitude were planted in front of the steps and, persevering in the same desire with horrible and very persistent shouting, they made them [the more distinguished and steady members of the congregation] uncertain what to think or to do. Then disgraceful things were yelled at my brother, then I was afraid of worse to come.

Closer in time to Augustine's ordination as a presbyter is a letter he wrote in 391 to Bishop Valerius in order to request a short time for praying, reading Scripture, and repenting before he embarked upon his new ministry. His profound sense of chagrin at his own inadequacies underlies much of the language. In the opening paragraph, for example (*Epist.* 21.1), he describes himself as an inexperienced sailor who has been given the second place at the helm, when he does not even know how to hold an oar:

> . . . *ut secundus locus gubernaculorum mihi traderetur, qui remum tenere non noveram.*

By becoming a priest, Augustine left the quiet life of ascetic and philosophical contemplation he had planned and embarked upon a round of liturgical duties and irksome lawsuits which were the characteristic occupations and responsibilities of priests and even more of bishops in the small provincial towns of fourth- and fifth-century North Africa. When he first arrived in Hippo, he was seeking a place in which to establish a monastery. He had come to meet a new recruit who had expressed an interest in the contemplative life.

Yet, the Lord's design as well as that of His unwitting human agents added a new dimension to that intention. Augustine did, in fact, establish a monastic community at Hippo; but, through his ordination, he also assumed precisely the type of responsibilities which would challenge his mind, discipline his heart, and sharpen his talent for *ex situ* and *ex tempore* reasoning and speech.

Augustine's work as a bishop made him a saint.[1] His work as a bishop also defined and conditioned his work as a theologian and as a rhetorician. The sense of immediacy still conveyed by Augustine's words often arises from the reader's recognition of a mind wrestling with parochial issues which he has transformed into universal concerns of humankind. After his ordination Augustine embarked on the period of his life in which he composed his most important works, delivered well over four-hundred sermons, served as judge in countless small and large cases, maintained a voluminous correspondence with people all over the Mediterranean world, and articulated a philosophy of self, time, and history which was to influence profoundly the intellectual underpinnings of the Western World.

The moment in which Augustine accepted ordination was clearly as significant as any of the moments in his earlier life so vividly recalled for us by the ordained Bishop Augustine some ten years later in the *Confessions*. The vividness of these recollected events takes its particular hue from an Augustinian sense of time and the self which we, as subsequent readers of his words, have come to acknowledge as our own. No one before Augustine so forcefully articulated the fragmentary moments by which we humans live in time and pass from one instant of incomplete and insufficient self-awareness to another. Few have also possessed the ability to express thoughts of astonishing originality with a simplicity and emotional directness which makes them unforgettable.

---

[1] Archbishop Runcie, in his homily opening the 1991 conference on Augustine, repeats this apt phrase.

Augustine's ordination was a pivotal moment in his life and an event of extraordinary significance for subsequent history. It was therefore appropriate for us to recall the life and work of Augustine some 1600 years later and to organize a conference in 1991 which would reflect some of the best and most informed modern insights into aspects of Augustine's thought and influence on the church and the world.

From September 22–25, 1991, over one thousand people—scholars, homemakers, theologians, carpenters, and students, among others—attended the international conference in Madison, Wisconsin, commemorating the 1600th anniversary of Augustine's ordination. The conference included lectures, workshops, an exhibit of books and textiles in the Memorial Library, and specially arranged musical programs. The invited participants were asked to address themselves to one or more aspects of the general theme, "Augustine: His Influence on the Church and the World." Distinguished scholars and theologians from England, Italy, and the United States participated in this major ecumenical event. The conference opened with an evensong conducted by the former Archbishop of Canterbury, Lord Robert A. K. Runcie. Bruce Bengston, the music director of Luther Memorial Church, arranged the music for the evensong and the performances given before each evening lecture.

The conference was a joint venture, sponsored by the Commission for Lutheran-Anglican-Roman Catholic Relationships in Wisconsin and Upper Michigan (LARC) and the Medieval Studies Program of the University of Wisconsin–Madison. It was funded by the Commission, the Wisconsin Humanities Committee serving on behalf of the National Endowment for the Humanities, and the Anonymous Fund of the University of Wisconsin, and by private donations from a number of individuals and groups. These are all listed in the Acknowledgments.

The Department of Special Collections in the University of Wisconsin–Madison Memorial Library exhibited library materials relating to Saint Augustine and his teachings. The exhibit also included some fine examples of Coptic textiles dating from the fourth through the eighth centuries from the Helen Allen Textile Collection. A catalogue of the exhibit "Augustine and the Augustinian Tradition" was prepared for this occasion by John B. Dillon, European Humanities Bibliographer in Memorial Library. The first illustration of this volume of essays (Plate 1) reproduces the catalogue's cover illustration from Alonzo de Orozco (1500–1591), *Recopilación de todas las obras* (Valladolid: Sebastian Martinez, 1554). It shows Augustine seated, supporting the church and bearing the characteristic signs of sixteenth-century episcopal office.

The iconographic tradition of Augustine in his *cathedra* reinforces our image of him as defender of the church and forceful preacher against heretics. The sixteenth-century illustration has considerably augmented and aggrandized the Augustinian figure. When Augustine preached in his small three-naved church in Hippo, he sat in his chair without ring or mitre or splendid vestments. In his usual rough and dark colored cloak (*birrus*) he would certainly have seemed a small, sharp-featured and rather unimpressive figure when set beside the robust man in the frontispiece illustration. Although the frontispiece is an inaccurate portrayal of the actual historical bishop, it is an appropriate illustration of the ways in which the words of Augustine and his presence have come to be seen. In a similar way, much of the dynamic energy of the conference arose from the intellectual excitement that accompanies the opportunity to see a familiar figure within new and differing frames and to appreciate the "newness" of insights first articulated long ago.

The other illustrations reproduced in this volume have been selected from the seventy-two items listed in the aforementioned exhibition catalogue, which was prepared for the conference. We have deliberately limited our selection to material from the University of Wisconsin–Madison Memorial Library, Department of Special Collections. The three woodcuts (Plates 2–4) from the *Recopilación de todas las obras* are examples of illustrations that appear frequently in that text. Like the frontispiece, they present Augustine very prominently in his role as bishop and protector of the Church (Plate 2) and as a penitent and confessor (Plate 3). His own experience is presented in the background, his priestly role in the foreground. The same iconography is used in the woodcut of Saint Monica. Her anguish over her son's departure for Italy serves as a backdrop to the serene Monica kneeling in meditation before the (sixteenth-century) altar (Plate 4). These woodcuts reveal a simultaneous vision of Augustine as an immutable defender of the Church in contrast to the changing history of the individual person. Personal meditation of the reader is the focus of two woodcuts (Plates 3–4), while the public image of the defender is the focus of the other (Plate 2).

Augustinian influence may be seen in many popular manuals of devotion attributed to the saint. The *Soliloquies of the Soul with God* and the *Manual* were among the most widely read of all the pseudo-Augustinian apocrypha. These compilations of eleventh- and twelfth-century spirituality were apparently put together at different times in the thirteenth and fifteenth centuries. The 1577 volume of *Certaine Select Prayers* (Plates 5–6) presents an anonymous Elizabethan translation of the *Soliloquies* and the *Manual* published by the zealous reformer John Day (1522–1584).

Plate 7 comes from a seventeenth-century French translation of the *Confessions* done by Robert Arnauld d'Andilly (1588–1674), brother of the great Jansenist Antoine Arnauld (1612–1694). This illustration shows how strongly the experience of Augustine's conversion in the garden has been influenced by representations of Christ's agony in Gethsemane. The arcaded structures in the background demonstrate a growing contemporary interest in the classical past. The figure of Augustine leans on a tombstone whose epitaph suggests the burial of the past life and the acceptance of the command "Tolle, Lege."

The continuing vitality of Augustine's writings is attested by the final two plates in this volume, one illustrating the widespread use of his sermons (Plate 8) and the other his continuing authority as a major voice against heresy (Plate 9). The Italian translator of the *Varii sermoni* is Galeazzo Florimonte (1484–1567), a noted south Italian Christian humanist. This volume of sermons testifies to Augustine's continued importance as a spiritual guide and guarantor of traditional orthodoxy in counter-Reformation Italy. The work against heresy, *Historia pelagiana,* is by the distinguished Augustinian scholar Enrico Noris, who was at once a theologian and an ancient historian. His chief theological writings are the *Pelagian History and Dissertation on the Fifth Ecumenical Synod* and the *Augustinian Vindications.* These works attempt to refute protestant and Jansenist interpretations of Augustine by presenting more historically authentic accounts of his soteriology. Noris was accused of both Baianism and Jansenism, and in the 1740s the *Pelagian History* was briefly placed on the Index of the Spanish Inquisition.

* * *

The open and friendly atmosphere during the conference was conducive to the exchange of ideas and encouraged interaction among participants. In the workshops, in particular, participants eagerly contributed to the animated discussions, and the mix of people from various backgrounds was remarkable: in one session active participants included retired business executives, members of the clergy, graduate students, and a butcher from Kenosha, Wisconsin.

In the homily—"Amor Dei"—that opened the conference, Robert A.K. Runcie spoke on Augustine's understanding of the "love of God." He concentrated on the incompleteness of this love and its movement toward the arts of perception and justice that help human beings see things not just as they appear but as they may be. On the subsequent days of the conference nine major scholars presented lectures on Augustine and the Augustinian tradition. The present volume contains seven[2] of these lectures, as well as abstracts of the nine workshops given as part of the conference.

Although the Bishop of Hippo is better known today as a polemicist and literary author than as a preacher, his sermons unveil his concern for the daily, often passionate, struggles of pagans, Jews and Christians in a world of unrest, violence and political upheaval. Augustine's motivation for preaching, his formal theory of preaching, and his advice to preachers form the basis for George Lawless's essay, "Augustine of Hippo as Preacher." As the author notes in his essay: "Although the reader is sixteen centuries removed from the original texts, they have the ring of genuine crystal. We are in the presence of an artist, a seasoned practitioner who exhibits acute sensitivity both to the issues at hand and to his congregation, the fruit of extraordinary intelligence, personal holiness, prayer, and firsthand experience as a pastor of souls."

In "Augustine's Understanding of the Church as a Eucharistic Community," Gerald Bonner highlights a central Augustinian doctrine, that Christ is the true minister of any sacrament and that the essence of the Church is the offering of the Eucharist. In this great sacrament of unity, Christ offers His Body—the company of the faithful—to the Father. The Eucharist thus provides, in time, a momentary participation in eternity. This sacramental ecclesiology is typical of

---

[2] Professor Martin Marty and Professor Krister Stendahl participated in the symposium, but declined this opportunity to publish their lectures.

Augustine and is enlightening for those contemporary Christians who are seeking visible unity in and through Christ.

In examining "Augustine on the Resurrection" Gerald O'Collins demonstrates how belief in Jesus' resurrection defines the identity of Christians and shapes the Christian way of life. According to Augustine, this Easter faith correlates existentially with humankind's internal hunger for happiness. Among the points he addresses are "Augustine's principle of continuity between the earthly and the risen body" and the way in which Augustine "holds together Easter faith and Easter life . . . the redemption and revelation that reached their climax with the paschal mystery."

In "Augustine on Nature and Human Nature"[3] Elaine Hiesey Pagels focuses on Augustine's view of human powerlessness because of original sin. She contrasts the Augustinian view with that of Julian of Eclanum's emphasis on human control and causality in the moral realm and challenges readers to reexamine Augustine's views.

Paula Fredriksen, in her essay "Augustine on History, the Church, and the Flesh," examines how Augustine reshapes the dualistic view of the universe current in antiquity and redefines the nature of man. In so doing, he radically rehabilitates the flesh, which then becomes definitive of human nature and of final redemption. This rehabilitation allows Augustine to reaffirm a simple understanding of the "resurrection of the dead." It necessarily complicates the eschatological value of the church as the "communion of saints" and of history as "saving events."

"Art, Wisdom and Bliss: Their Interplay in Saint Augustine" is the title of Robert J. O'Connell's essay. In it he notes how Augustine sees in the beauty of mathematics and geometry (proportion, balance, symmetry, and measure) a reflection of the reality of the Logos, the higher world pattern of all things. When Augustine writes about "art" as distinct from the *artes,* he supposes a view of the human which differs from his usual perspective. When confronting "art" in its peculiarity, Augustine adopts a less Neoplatonic position in favor of a more "incarnate" stance. This is especially true in the early work *De*

---

[3] In her lecture Professor Pagels covered many of the points she had already elaborated in her chapter, "The Nature of Nature" (in *Adam, Eve, and the Serpent*). Because of the similarity of the oral presentation and her published essay, she prefers to include the latter in this volume.

pulchro et apto. He believes that if Augustine had pursued that stance consistently, he might have made some welcome changes in his notion of the pursuit of wisdom and its relationship to the quest for human bliss.

Henry Chadwick's lecture "On Re-reading the *Confessions*" concluded the symposium. Many consider this prose poem addressed to God and overheard by anxious Christian readers as Augustine's finest work. In it Augustine both confesses his faults and offers a subtle self-vindication. As Augustine himself noted, the book is about his good as well as his bad points. In the account of his life before baptism, Augustine makes the reader aware that the narrator has undergone a great change, a consequence of his ordination.

The symposium featured a series of workshops in which scholars engaged interested participants from a variety of backgrounds in discussion of a particular topic relating to Augustine, his writings, and their influence on subsequent ages. An abstract for each of these appears in Part 3 of this volume.

In the workshop on "Augustine: Bishop and Theologian" the group led by Agnes Cunningham examined how Augustine succeeded in integrating the different offices of bishop and theologian, ministries frequently perceived to be mutually exclusive.

Gillian Rosemary Evans analyzed the contradictions present in Augustine's doctrine of the Church. She observed that "In his controversy with the Donatists Augustine was obliged to work out an ecclesiology in which there remained, despite his best efforts, a number of paradoxes and imperfectly resolved dilemmas." A clearer understanding of these contradictions emerged from the workshop.

Robert Booth Fowler's workshop on "Augustine's Political Theory: 'Realism Revisited'" concentrated on the revival of Augustine after World War II in Western political thought. It examined how this revival was closely connected with the ascendency of political "realism." The group considered the degree of Augustine's appeal in the current political climate.

In "Augustine and Calvin" Robert M. Kingdon investigated the pervasive influence of Augustine's theology on the Protestant Reformation of the sixteenth century. So great was this influence that the age could be termed a revival of Augustinianism. The workshop considered in particular the impact of Augustine on Calvin, the single most influential theologian of the Protestant movement in its second generation and outside Germany.

Fannie LeMoine focused her workshop, "Augustine on Education and the Liberal Arts," on his views of teaching and study of the liberal arts, especially in his work *On the Teacher* and in the *Confessions.* Augustine was a teacher of grammar and rhetoric and became a harsh critic of the educational aims and practices to which he himself had subscribed and which he observed in others.

In the workshop on "Augustine on Grace: The Early Years" Joseph T. Lienhard examined Augustine's doctrine on grace, free choice, original sin, and predestination, up to the writing of the work *De spiritu et littera* in 412. Lienhard considers in particular the influence of a new interpretation of Saint Paul's works in the West and suggests that Simplician may have been a significant figure in this revival of interest and reinterpretation.

In "Augustine and the Scientific Tradition" David C. Lindberg took as his point of departure the view of Augustine as a symbol of Christian opposition to the scientific movement. He reconsidered this traditional judgment through a wider review of the scientific movement in Augustine's day and his response to it.

In the workshop devoted to "Deus Caritas Est" Jill Raitt used selections from Augustine's works to consider the multi-dimensional nature of Charity. Charity is identified with the Holy Spirit, acts as the bond uniting Christ and Christians, serves as crown of all the infused virtues, and works in human life. The group also considered ways of reconciling Augustine the theologian of the love of God in Christ with the person most responsible for the doctrine of Original Sin.

Graham Walker's workshop, "Antique Modernity: Augustine's 'Liberalism' and the Impasses of Modern Politics," investigated the notion in modern Western thought that the state should be limited, a neutral arbiter among competing "value systems." Walker asked whether this notion is limited to the twentieth-century view of the universe as value-neutral, value-empty. On the contrary, Augustine propounds a limited and quasi-neutral state, but not because the universe is empty. He subtly connects political power to inescapable ontological tensions. This approach may suggest ways to deal with the moral justification of difficult contemporary public policy choices.

Over the centuries few figures in the Western tradition have been as influential as Augustine, and even fewer could command the interest of such a diverse group of interested participants today. We hope this volume reflects the depth and intensity of that interest and demonstrates why modern readers still listen to his words.

Madison, Wisconsin
November 1993

PLATE 2. Augustine as bishop and protector of the Church. Alonso de Orozco (1500–1591), *Recopilación de todas las obras* (Valladolid: Sebastian Martinez, 1554).

Abbreviations

PART 1

Homily

Amor Dei

The Right Honorable Robert Runcie
Archbishop of Canterbury, Retired

When, in 1938, a relatively unknown Cambridge Classics scholar offered to the world of Augustinian scholarship, under the title *Amor Dei,* his study of the religion of Saint Augustine, he chose unerringly as a text for the book the words which in all the Augustinian writings could be said to have been written in the Saint's lifeblood:

> *Sero te amavi, pulchritudo tam nova, tam antiqua.*

> [Late have I loved you, Beauty so old and so new.]

At long last, in 1991, that book of John Burnaby has been reprinted.[1] The last paragraph of its original preface deserves quotation. The reason for repeating the quotation is surely the same as that which has inspired the summoning of this ecumenical conference. The pupil has made the *desiderium,* the longing, the yearning, the ache of his master his own. It is an ache not only for another world, but an ache for this present world. It is the longing that this world of men and women, finding the God who made it and redeemed it and loves it still, should at last find peace.

These are the words, the date is 1938:

> The years in which this book has been written have been a time in which pride, hatred and violence have seemed the rulers of this world, and the meditation of an ancient ideal has been too easily oppressed by a sense of futility. St. Augustine stands for the faith that an advancing knowledge and an increasing love of the Eternal God is the only foundation upon which frail humanity can build the love of one another and learn to live together in peace. *Sero te amavi, pulchritudo tam nova, tam antiqua.* It may be that at long last a broken world will come back to the love of that Beauty which is old, but ever new. (p. xi)

3

That there are signs of such a longing stirring in the hearts of serious-minded men and women with a new urgency surely comes through the events of this momentous year of 1991. It was a central theme of an early encyclical of Pope John Paul II, *Dives in Misericordia.* "God rich in mercy." *Misericordia* is a word that resounds through the pages of the *Confessions* of Saint Augustine. The rueful irony of Saint Augustine's most widely remembered sentence, "Give me chastity but not yet" [*da mihi castitatem et continentiam, sed noli modo, Conf.* 8.17], has given the superficial impression of a document of guilt. It is not so. It is of God rich in mercy.

The encyclical puts its finger on what is called the uneasiness felt by contemporary man with regard to our world, a gigantic remorse at the hunger of the poor when the world is so rich, or what the greed of our culture has been doing, sometimes irreversibly to the face of the earth, and confronted by this a deep uneasiness about the future of humankind.

In other words, it is as though for those with ears to hear a great cry wells up for our time. So there is an immediacy of Saint Augustine for our day.

More to me than any of the Church Fathers and because he knew his own precariousness and the precariousness of his world—the classical world threatened by the paganism that would engulf it—he knows what the cry of longing means. And reading him today, it is surely as though he has come into his own.

> *Da amantem et sentit quod dico. Da desiderantem, da esurientem, da in ista solitudine peregrinantem et sitientem, et fontem aeternae patriae suspirientem, da talem et scit quid dicam.* (*Trac. Joh.* 26.4)

> [Give me one who loves and he feels what I am saying—give me one who desires, give me one who hungers, give me one travelling and thirsting in this solitude and sighing for the fountain of an eternal homeland, give me such a one, and he knows what I am talking about.]

Among those who in their writing reveal they know what Augustine is talking about, I prize the poetry of the Lutheran pastor and martyr Dietrich Bonhoeffer. In a powerful poem he reveals the mixture of desires behind the front he presents in the prison camp. The poem is called "Who am I?" [*Wer bin ich?*]

> They say I come out of my cell like a squire coming out of his country house. Is that the real me or is the real me the one I meet when I cannot sleep at night pining for freedom, just hanging on—a pathetic figure with my conflicting desires. Is that the real me? Or is the real me something between the two?

The above summary gives a sense of the poem before its dramatic final lines:[2]

> Who am I? they mock me, these lonely questions of mine.
> Whoever I am, Thou knowest, O God, I am Thine.

> Wer bin ich? Einsames Fragen treibt mit mir Spott.
> Wer ich auch bin, Du kennst mich, Dein bin ich, o Gott!

Augustine belongs to all our traditions—Lutheran, Catholic, Episcopalian. Certainly he belongs to the world of Western learning, and indeed after his conversion in the garden Augustine planned for himself a scholarly withdrawal to draw close to the perfection of God in congenial company and peaceful surroundings.

Yet the world was not so easily kept at bay. North African congregations knew the value of clever scholars like himself and were forever trying to headhunt them for their churches. Fully aware of the problem, he kept away from any place that had a vacancy for a bishop. But as we know it was no good. An aged bishop, who was less of a fool than he looked, incited his congregation into a piece of consecrated hijacking. They pushed Augustine forward to the altar to secure his promise for ordination. Augustine, more realistic than many ordination candidates, burst into tears at the prospect. For his ordination would push him rudely back from his scholarly withdrawal into the world. He would serve a church struggling for life against aggressive and self-confident rivals. He would be faced with a host of practical problems. He would end his ministry in a besieged city awaiting final disaster for his people. So we can see that Augustine's ordination in 391 was as significant for his Christian Witness as his conversion in the garden. Indeed it was more so. Because what we might justifiably call his ordination retreat was the real beginning for the philosopher of that deep and serious pondering and standing under the Scriptures which we know through his sermons on the psalms and on Saint John. They reveal the heart of his faith as related to his people. It is right that we should celebrate that ordination and that episcopate, and thank God for this imaginative Ecumenical Commission which has brought us together here. It is a tremendous achievement.

A biographer, Professor Van der Meer, says that the debates of the day made Augustine the philosopher and the theologian, but the diocese of Hippo made him a saint.[3]

I wish to draw attention out of many things to just three facets of Augustine's discussion of love which, for me, need to be heard by the churches we represent. I state them fairly succinctly, I hope not too obscurely.

First, our love is always desire incomplete, always unfulfilled. Even in the tranquil years of withdrawal Augustine had bitter reminders of how fragile human desires can be; for it was then he lost his mother, then his only son, and one of his closest friends. The philosopher's quest for perfection proved no defense against death and bereavement. Yet he tells us this very incompleteness is a road to God. "It is yearning," he says, "that makes the heart deep." That is why he so fiercely fought the doctrines of Pelagius, which many have seen as a kindly view of the human condition. Far from it, said Augustine. For him, Pelagius's terrifying mistake was to suppose that human beings could create perfection in their lives by their own efforts. In our century we have seen what horrors totalitarian systems can create in Nazism and in Stalinism: how millions of lives can be wrecked by the quest for human perfection. Augustine would soon have seen what all these creeds were about. It is an unhappy type of humanity which earthbound utopias can create because the final solution lies in the designs of men rather than in the love of God.

And then secondly, because our love is incomplete and fractured it involves compromise. We not only compromise as we relate to other people, we are compromised by our relationships. Again we see the importance of his ordination. Suddenly he found himself immersed in all the mess of ecclesiastical and civic business. Henceforth he could not abide versions of Christianity which sought to opt out of worldly affairs just because they were impure and liable to soil the pious believer. He denounced the Donatists who said that only the uncompromised—those who stood apart—were worthy members of the church. He insisted that the church was the home of those who were trying their muddled best to be loveable, not the home of those who were expert at it. The church is the place for making mistakes because there is always the possibility of being forgiven. As long as we live, that door is open. There is a remarkable passage in a sermon where Saint Augustine says that Saint Peter did not stop being an apostle when he betrayed Christ.

Third and last: our love which is the incomplete yearning of desire is active. It moves toward its goal. It cannot accept injustice, stagnation, pain. There is that remarkable image he employed of a carpenter, seeing a piece of timber lying just as it had been cut down in the forest. The carpenter loves the timber, but the reason for his love is not that it may always remain as it is; he loves it for what it can be, what he can make out of it. Still more remarkable is that Augustine makes this image a picture not just of God's love for us but also of our love for our own enemies. Our active love should see what people can be, not what they are. We are called to change the world in which we find ourselves, to challenge all that is loveless or stands in the way of love, and we do this as members of the church obeying God's command.

The goal of the Christian life is always around the corner, over the hills, beyond the horizon. It is never where we are at present. Of course, there was danger there. It is easy for us to decide which way the timber will be cut, and there can be few people today who can feel very comfortable about Augustine's use of our Lord's command, "compel them to come in." But John Burnaby warns us that "in these days we are more likely . . . to reproach him for the errors which his authority made calamitous, rather than to honour him for the measure of truth which he was worthy to attain" (21).

Augustine made mistakes. He lost his temper. He played politics. In his old age he was sometimes harsh and pessimistic. But he challenges every temptation to take the church out of history into some fabulous realm where purity and stability are institutionally certified. And the positive side of this is that we live in what he calls "the happiness of hope." Our lives with God are never exhausted, never sealed off. We go on being re-created by God and each other in the *communio sancti spiritus*—in active *caritas.*

He worked all of his life in the light of promises made at his ordination. His first biographer, Possidius, assessing his pastoral impact as his most important legacy, more important than all the books of theology which Possidius himself had cataloged, says: "Yet I think that those who gained most from him were those who had been able actually to see and hear him as he spoke in church and most of all those who had some contact with the quality of his life among people." That is the greatest tribute any ordained minister can enjoy. Truly it could be said of him as of his Lord and master as we heard in the reading: "He sanctified himself that they also might be sanctified in the truth." The words of the prayer of the Good Shepherd have become those of the Shepherd's apprentice, and through his ministry he will speak to us all again during the coming week of papers and discussion.

For we live in days which have shown again that it is a terrible fact that, when men ignore God, they cease to be human. It is a terrible fact that, when they deny eternity, they cannot find contentment in time. It is a terrible fact that, when they will have none of the heavenly city, they cannot build a tolerable society on earth.

So may that love of God, which held him and yet set him free, continue to draw us together as individuals and churches, enabling us to work more selflessly and more patiently for this beautiful world of ours; and to do so by turning ourselves toward that heavenly city where we shall rest and we shall see, we shall see and we shall love, we shall love and we shall praise, for its builder and maker is God, Father, Son, and Holy Spirit to whom be the Glory through all the ages. Amen.

Notes

1. John Burnaby, *Amor Dei: A Study of the Religion of St. Augustine,* The Hulsean Lectures for 1938, foreword by Professor Oliver O'Donovan (Norwich: Canterbury Press, 1991; orig. pub. London: Hodder & Stoughton, 1938).

2. Dietrich Bonhoeffer, *Widerstand und Ergebung: Briefe und Aufzeichnungen aus der Haft,* ed. Eberhard Bethge (Munich: Kaiser, 1970), 381–382. The translation is by Reginald H. Fuller, in Dietrich Bonhoeffer, *Letters and Papers from Prison,* ed. Eberhard Bethge (London: SCM Press, 1953), 165.

3. F. Van der Meer, *Augustine the Bishop: Religion and Society at the Dawn of the Middle Ages,* tr. Brian Battershaw and G.R. Lamb (London: Sheed & Ward, 1961).

PART 2

Essays

Augustine of Hippo as Preacher[*]

George P. Lawless, OSA

When we speak about the sermons of Saint Augustine, we are speaking about more than one-third of his voluminous writings. In his own lifetime the actual number of sermons composed by him far exceeded that amount. The French Benedictines of Saint Maur in the seventeenth century judged 398 sermons and fragments of Augustine to be authentic (Verbraken 1990:166), and they classified them along the following lines: (1) on texts from the Old Testament; (2) on texts from the New Testament; (3) for liturgical seasons and feasts (such as Christmas, Epiphany, Easter and Ascension); (4) for feasts of the saints (for example, Peter and Paul, Lawrence, Cyprian, Perpetua and Felicity, Stephen, John the Baptist); (5) for specific occasions (such as the dedication of a church, the presentation of the Creed to catechumens, the occasion of an episcopal ordination); and (6) on specific themes (such as avarice, love, peace, almsgiving, and pilgrimage).

Since the late seventeenth century nearly two hundred authentic sermons and fragments of Augustine have been added to the list. The most recent addition occurred in 1990 when a French scholar, François Dolbeau, of the École Pratique des Hautes Études in Paris, made an extraordinary discovery in the Municipal Library at Mainz, Germany. He examined an unedited manuscript which dates from the second half of the fifteenth century (Mainz I 9). According to his judgment, the manuscript is noteworthy for three reasons: (1) it contains the texts of nineteen new sermons of Augustine, hitherto unknown; (2) it provides evidence for establishing a superior text for about a dozen sermons of Augustine already extant; and (3) in at least

---

[*] For Reverend Dr. Jordan Aumann, OP, faithful friend, teacher and preacher of God's word for many years, now Emeritus Professor of Theology at the University of Saint Thomas Aquinas (Angelicum), Rome, Italy, on the occasion of his seventy-fifth birthday.

five instances, it furnishes a fuller text of some Augustinian fragments which had already been identified and preserved in their truncated forms by John the Deacon, Florus and the Venerable Bede (Dolbeau 1990).

Authenticity of this unedited manuscript is guaranteed by multiple evidence from the *Indiculum,* which is a rather comprehensive listing of Augustine's writings by Possidius, his friend of some forty years and his first biographer. In addition, the manuscript brings together into three groups of sermons two subsequent inventories of the bishop's sermons dating from the ninth and sixteenth centuries, respectively, and it links them with the uncontested evidence from Possidius's *Indiculum.* These inventories are: (1) a Carolingian catalogue dating from the ninth century then housed in the cathedral library of Saint-Nazaire at Lorsch, and (2) another inventory of sermons which dates from the sixteenth century and takes its name from an ancient manuscript belonging to the monastery of Grande-Chartreuse.

As a result of this discovery at Mainz, Augustinian studies will be enriched and enlarged. We shall learn more about Augustine's Bible, specifically the Synoptics, John, Paul and the Book of Psalms. Thanks to this fortunate find by François Dolbeau we are now able to read in a homiletic medium (Mainz 27) Augustine's interpretation of Paul's rebuke to Peter in Galatians 2:11–14, thereby furnishing us with another optic on these verses and the famous exegetical controversy which extended over many years in a bristling exchange of several letters between Augustine, the busy bishop, responding to the queries of his North African congregation and Jerome, the isolated biblical scholar, working tirelessly in his monastery at Bethlehem.

In another of the Dolbeau sermons (Mainz 40), Augustine's lapidary Latin: *Amandi deum modus est sine modo* anticipates by several centuries Bernard of Clairvaux's well-known words: "The measure with which to love God is to love God without measure." Before the end of yet another sermon (Mainz 61) the stenographers faithfully record the moment at which pagan members of the congregation left the Basilica of Peace so that the Christian assembly could continue with celebration of the eucharist.

In another sermon (Mainz 15) Augustine stands in at the request of a local bishop whose unpleasant task it was to resist the importunate pleas of a bereaved and influential family who were insisting that the deceased, in this case a catechumen, be permitted the rite of Christian burial and subsequent interment alongside those who were baptized.

These new sermons yield detailed information about the lives of both pagans and Christians, while augmenting still further our amply documented knowledge about the Donatists. As of the first of May 1992 seven of the nineteen new sermons have been published (Dolbeau 1991). One does not hesitate to predict for this manuscript of new and unedited sermons of Augustine a propitious fate similar to the publication of the twenty-nine new letters of Augustine, published in Vienna ten years ago (Divjak 1981).

The latest count, then, of Augustine's authentic sermons is now 568. If it is true that the bishop preached about 8,000 times over a period of thirty-nine years (I see no reason to dispute Pierre-Patrick Verbraken in this matter), this is another way of saying that one in fourteen of his sermons has come down to us (Verbraken 1987:106). Tradition has assigned them the title, "Sermons to the People," *Sermones ad Populum.*

Add to these more than 200 *Commentaries on the Psalms,* 124 *Tractates on the Gospel of John* and 10 *Tractates on the First Letter of John,* and we have the grand total of more than 900 authentic sermons. Together with those of John Chrysostom, Augustine's sermons constitute more than one-half the homiletic material which has survived from the patristic age (Hamman 1986:23).

The Preacher's Audience

What kind of people were these North Africans? To whom were the sermons addressed? Within a year of his ordination to the presbyterate, Augustine set out to combat alcoholism, which had become a national health problem in North Africa. No longer limited to infrequent occasions such as feast days or the commemoration of the local martyr named Leontius, disorderly and drunken behavior were lapses which happened on a daily basis. Overseas churches in Milan and Rome had adopted stern measures to curtail such abuses. It was high time for North Africa to do the same (*Epist.* 22).

In this regard, the many difficulties experienced by women, particularly nuns, concerned Augustine. Referring to this problem in an evocative account of identity of Christians, whether laity, clerics, monks or nuns, the bishop mentions nuns "who occasionally had too much to drink" (*Enarr.* 99.13). Evidently the convent provided no immunity against a national health problem of this magnitude.

At one time when he was giving a sermon, some women staged a walkout. Either the sermon was too long, the summer heat was intolerable, or they had to prepare dinner at home. Whatever the reasons for their sudden departure, Augustine was obviously nettled by the experience, for he twice took notice of it after their departure (*Serm.* 32.23 and 25). By no means, however, was Augustine ever caustic in his remarks about women. At the age of seventy-two, he wrote the following words in reference to Ephesians 1:22ff and Psalm 112:1,

> . . . there is nothing to prevent us from applying to women what is expressly stated of man, since *vir*, man, often means *homo*, human being. Similarly, the verse, "Blessed is the man, *vir*, who fears the Lord," obviously applies to women who fear the Lord (*Civ. Dei* 22.18).

A fifth-century bishop, Augustine of Hippo, thus ranks in the forefront of those twentieth-century critics who nowadays champion the cause of women by pointing out to us the shortcomings of exclusive language in the Bible.

"It is more difficult," he tells us, "to correct a person who insists upon tapping the ground with his bare foot for eight days in a row than it is (to correct) one who drowns his mind in drink" (*Epist.* 55.19.34). In his usual forthright manner Augustine chided his congregation: "Many of you have possibly come here today to celebrate the feast, not to hear the sermon" (*Trac. Joh.* 8.13). "I hate to say it, yet I must; you know it is true that a clown makes greater appeal to you than God does" (*Enarr.* 32.s.2.1).

Of those people (and there were many) who claimed to have penetrated the obscurities of the Bible, Augustine says that this boast is tantamount to understanding the universe, the moon and the stars, without ever having consulted a book on astronomy (*De doctr. christ.*, Prologue 3). Bible-thumping fundamentalists among the Donatist sect insisted that the Greek loanword, *agonistici,* had a biblical base in 2 Timothy 4:7, whereas the Catholic word for monks, *monachi,* was nowhere to be found in the Scriptures. According to them, "monks," therefore, have no place within the economy of salvation. (The *agonistici,* a word which Peter Brown translates as "prize-fighters of the Lord," were a subset of the "Circumcellions," a right-wing group of Donatists, whose belligerent maneuvers compare with the brutality of the Irish Republican Army or the guerrilla warfare tactics of the *Sendero Luminoso,* the Shining Path currently plaguing Peru.)

The fact that the Egyptian monk, Antony, had reputedly memorized the Scriptures simply by hearing them with no formal training whatsoever (since, as the tradition goes, he had never learned to read) and that, furthermore, he had grasped their contents is no guarantee that such a charism is automatically transferable to others. At any rate, Augustine did not contest the veracity of the story that no one ever taught Antony how to read (*De doctr. christ.,* Prologue 5).

Although Marcus Terentius Varro (116–27 B.C.) had long ago repudiated pagan superstitions, they did not completely disappear from the Christian community (*De doctr. christ.* 2.17.27). Still the practice persisted of telling people with hiccups to hold their left thumb in their right hand in order to stop the hiccups (*De doctr. christ.* 2.20.30). Some of Augustine's flock (whether they were churchgoers is unclear) wore jewelry of all kinds, for example, rings suspended from the top of each ear and little rings of ostrich bones worn on the fingers, as if to ward off evil spirits and demons (ibid.). Some people would never leave the front door of their houses without consciously stepping on the threshold. Others went back to bed if they sneezed while putting on their shoes. Many people believed that should mice gnaw at one's shoes during the night (recall the scene in *De ordine* where field mice entered the bedroom), this was a surefire sign of imminent personal disaster. Cato had long since noted that the real marvel would have occurred in the event that the shoes had gnawed the mice (*De doctr. christ.* 2.20.31).

These remnants of paganism recall Books 8–10 of *The City of God* where Augustine refutes the world of astral bodies, divination by means of auguries, sorcery, the examination of animal entrails, the wearing of talismans and amulets. In the same work, he exposes astrology as a pseudo-science, and he denounces the reading of horoscopes and the magical arts of persuading semidivine intermediaries to intercede for personal petitions (*Ss.* 9.3 and 15A.4; *De doctr. christ.* 2.21.32).

SELECT IMAGES OF THE PREACHER

How did Augustine view the profile of a preacher? From his writings, I have sorted out appreciably more than fifty images which depict people from all walks of life, derivations from many aspects of human anatomy and physiology, characteristic behavior of birds and animals, resemblances from both nature and inanimate objects and, finally, varieties of food and drink. In every instance, Augustine's vivid descriptions of the preacher are taken from the Bible.

The drudgery and hard work of preaching, for example, are emphasized by the choice of oxen, horses and beasts of burden to cultivate the Lord's fields (*Enarr.* 103.s.3.10; *Civ. Dei* 18.32). Preaching is an untidy and messy ministry, which the bishop further characterizes by the image of "dirty feet." Fortunately for preachers, the Lord continues to bathe their feet and the feet of their listeners in the sacraments of baptism, eucharist and reconciliation (*Trac. Joh.* 57 on John 13:10).

In unflattering language unworthy preachers are described by Augustine as the spout of a watering can. Nevertheless, he notes that light still filters through and so does water. Both the water and the light represent Christ (*Trac. Joh.* 5.15). While echoing Ezechiel, Augustine portrays preachers as watchmen or sentries in a North African vineyard and in the imagery the vineyard belongs to the Lord. Unworthy watchmen, that is, bishops and preachers, deserve to be compared to scarecrows in the vineyard so that birds will not peck the grapes (Guelf. 32.6 in *Miscellanea Agostiniana* 1.568).

Enlisting the story of Gideon's victory over Midian with an army of three hundred men, Augustine likens preachers to dogs faithful to their master, as though barking for Christ. Gideon pitched camp near the "Spring of Fright" (*Enharod*), where the victors lapped water with their tongues, like dogs, rather than like human beings who cup their hands (Judges 7:5; *Enarr.* 67.32). In a twentieth-century update, the preacher might be portrayed either as a pop singer or as a member of a musical group where the zither with its ten strings, made of sheep intestines, would be replaced by the ubiquitous electric guitar (*Serm.* 9.5 and 6).

There are many instances in Augustine where he uses the Latin words *eructare/ructare* and their cognates to express the function of the preacher. Crudely put, the great preacher is one who belches

(*Serm.* 34.2). Like Martin Luther, Augustine could be very visceral in responding to the earthiness of his people. The ancients were evidently more comfortable with their bodies than we moderns. Literally, "to belch" means "to expel gas suddenly from the stomach through the mouth." Figuratively, the above Latin words express a transition from the depths of the human soul by bringing its contents to the surface and uttering audible sounds. Augustine preached the Bible all the time. Augustine's preaching consequently was so glutted or surfeited with the Bible that its savor bursts forth spontaneously from his lips. In this connection one recalls the psalm-verse: *Eructavit cor meum verbum bonum,* which means something like "my heart belched forth the good word" (Ps. 44:2). Invariably Augustine relates his use of *eructare/ructare* to the first three verses in the Prologue to John's Gospel and the fundamental mysteries of the Christian faith (*Serm.* 20A.8; 119.1 and 2; *Trac. Joh.* 36.1 and 124.7).

In another context, the bishop's preoccupation with the dynamics of knowing and willing feeds his exposition of the psalm-verse (Ps. 41:8):

> Deep calls to deep in the roar of your cataracts
> and all your waves, all your breakers pass over me.

Augustine offers four interpretations of this verse, which are by no means mutually exclusive. "Deep" or "abyss," a late Latin loanword from Greek signifies, first of all, self-understanding or knowledge-of-oneself in the tradition of the Delphic oracle and Aristotle's concept of *notitia sui,* that is, self-knowledge, self-consciousness. "A human being is a mighty deep," the bishop says elsewhere (*Conf.* 4.14.22). Secondly, the word "deep" implies an understanding of other people, an elusive task for individuals who are a mystery or a question mark to themselves (*Conf.* 10.33.50; 5.2.2). Thirdly, we may construe "deep" as an understanding of God, an impossible feat, surely. Augustine himself assures us: "If you have understood what you want to say, it is not God. If you have been able to understand, you have understood something other than God" (*Serm.* 52.6.16). The bishop's fourth interpretation of "deep calls to deep" correlates this biblical phrase with "the preachers of God's word" (*Enarr.* 41.8). Both listeners and preachers are an "abyss" in the sense of "a mighty deep," most especially when addressing "any point of faith, any point of truth as it relates to eternal life" (ibid.). Who, after all, can penetrate the secrets of the human heart which discloses a depth deeper than the ocean or any unfathomable void? For example, who would presume to predict Peter's weakness as he swore to stand by Jesus the night before the crucifixion? Life is teeming with rash promises; only God's promises guarantee fulfillment. Recalling the original context of Psalm 41 with its pervasive theme of yearning or longing for God (*desiderium*), Augustine depicts humanity as sinking, swamped, indeed, submerged beneath the waves of this world. Yet, Augustine insists that both preachers and their listeners keep on swimming.

His comparison of the preacher to the pelican, the owl and the sparrow reveals one of Augustine's more imaginative samples of biblical exegesis (*Enarr.* 101.s.1.7 and 8).[1] He would be the first to decry the perspective which virtually eliminates poetic imagination from the narrow lens of historical criticism. Here the bishop is preaching on the psalm-verse (Ps. 101:7–8):

> I am like a pelican in the wilderness,
> an owl that lives among ruins,
> like a sparrow perched alone on the housetop.

We are told that pelicans dwell along the desolate banks of the Nile river. It is well-known that owls favor night over day and that their favorite haunt is the walls of dilapidated buildings with no roof. Sparrows ordinarily perch as solitaries on the rooftop of a house with high visibility on all sides.

With a slightly different optic, these three birds further suggest to Augustine the basic posture and comportment of preachers. To save their young, pelicans pour out their blood; preachers, accordingly, must exhibit compassion for weak individuals. Owls seek out crumbling walls of derelict buildings; the stripe of any bona fide preacher indicates an outreach to others for the sake of Christ. As so often in Augustine, an eschatological twist is marked by the preacher's anticipation of the Lord's return, somewhat elusively hinted at by the sparrow on the housetop. To buttress his case, the bishop ingeniously recalls the admonition of Matthew 24:17 to stay on the roof without retrieving any possessions inside the house and of Matthew 10:27 to proclaim from the rooftops what you hear in private. A single preacher is encouraged, therefore, to assimilate the habits of all three birds, or three preachers are invited to cultivate and to accentuate distinctive traits of one or another of the birds, as the pastoral situation requires.

Pressing into service still further the amateur knowledge of ornithology which he learned, probably, from the Elder Pliny's *Natural History,* Augustine tells his congregation that the environs or habitat of these three birds represents several people. Non-Christians roam the deserted banks of the Nile; the empty ruined houses without a roof characterize the collapse and debris of Judaism; many Jewish people refuse to enter these ramshackle dwellings and, in like manner, lapsed Christians have forsaken and abandoned them. On the other hand, the house with a roof enshrines nominal and lukewarm Christians. All such people have a special claim upon the ministry of preachers.

Our kaleidoscope now turns, however so slightly, away from preachers, their basic qualities and their respective audiences, toward Christ. We learn that the three birds now represent Christ. Allowing for the extreme reserve with which he accepts the myth of the pelican (*fortasse falsum sit*), Augustine links Deuteronomy 32:39 (the same God who brings life and death both wounds and heals), with the body of Jesus, who was born of a virgin and whose blood was shed for his assailants and for others. By killing its offspring and afterwards pecking at its maternal breast, thereby pouring its blood over its young and then reviving them in three days, the pelican hints at the dimension of the redeeming sacrifice which nestles at the heart of the Christian mystery.[2] In this way Saul was thus transformed into Paul. Like the Apostle to the Gentiles, all preachers are in a special way beneficiaries of Jesus' shedding his blood at the hands of his enemies.[3]

Jesus, in turn resembling the owl, suffers in the darkness of rejection by the Jewish people, who sinned during the night in the darkness of their ignorance. Crucified by people who could not accept the church as sequel to the synagogue, Jesus continues to forgive Jewish people and all enemies who refuse to enter the house and the many lapsed Christians who have abandoned it to the open sky.[4] From its lofty perch on the housetop the sparrow also signifies Christ as "head," while the mourning-dove raises its plaintive lament as it builds its nest, that is to say, the "body" of Christ from the wood of the cross (*nidus ex lignis crucis*). The church is conceived of as a nest. Its painfully slow construction is symbolized by the gentle and loving activity of the turtledove.

Images of the turtledove building its nest and of a mother hen with her chicks make the point that, like the apostle Paul, preachers are mothers (Matt. 23:37) and fathers as well (1 Cor. 4:15). Feminine and masculine components are the lot of every preacher, and this complementarity felicitously harmonizes in both a human and in a practical way the traits of affection, love and authority.

Deserted areas inundated by the Nile river, a house with crumbling walls and an open sky for its roof, a lonely perch on a housetop are hardly desirable places to live. As suggested by the imagery in all three instances, preachers seemingly stand alone and solitude appears to be their predicament. This is true to a point, says Augustine, but the housing situation and the loneliness are both alleviated by the presence of Christ. Significantly, the pelican, the owl and the sparrow simultaneously symbolize Christ and preacher and people. Augustine, as we know, was fond of thinking in triads. Yet the profile of a corporate personality with its intimate connection between head and body (which he had learned from ancient Judaism and from Saint Paul, respectively) evoked an inherent unity, and it furnished the bishop with an anvil upon which he forged his theology of the "whole Christ," the *totus Christus,* with which I shall conclude this essay.

AUGUSTINE ON AUGUSTINE

With respect to the ministry of preaching, the *Sermons* are no less revelatory than are the *Soliloquies,* the *Confessions* and the *Reconsiderations* revelatory in other areas of Augustine's life and thought. Preaching was always considered to be both a priority and a heavy responsibility; "burden" was his favorite word to describe it (*Serm.* 82.15; *Serm.* 339.3.4; *Epist.* 29.7).

Augustine laments the shortage of preachers, *inopia praedicatorum* (*Trac. Joh.* 57.5), and he complains that the clergy of Hippo were deficient in their knowledge of Latin (*Epist.* 84.2; *Bapt.* 6.25.47). A conciliar document of 401 (Bishop Aurelius of Carthage was the speaker) deplores the fact that "many churches have no clergy at all, not even an illiterate deacon" (C. Murnier, *Concilia Africae* a. 345-a. 525; CCL 149, 194). The ordination of Augustine to the presbyterate was itself an event which we owe to the limited proficiency of Bishop Valerius in the Latin language. This limitation had put Valerius, who was an ethnic-Greek, at a disadvantage with the Latin-speaking congregation at Hippo (*Vita Augustini* 5). To preach as a presbyter, in Augustine's case, for example, was clearly "contrary to the practice and custom of the African churches" (ibid.). Gradually both Augustine and Aurelius extended the task of preaching to their presbyters. Custom, however, required the bishop to speak first (*Serm.* 20.5; Hill 1990, III/2, p. 19, n. 1). A recently discovered letter addressed by Augustine probably to Possidius refers to six tractates on the Gospel according to John which were posted from Hippo for public use in the church at Carthage (*Epist.* 23 A*.3.6–7). Within Augustine's lifetime there was a market for the bishop's sermons, which subsequently became a black market, where Augustine's name was falsely associated with myriad sermons whose doubtful authenticity has taxed to the utmost the astute skills of generations of textual critics in their elusive task of distinguishing an authentic text from a spurious one.

Augustine never, it seems, wrote out a sermon; he preached extempore. The sermons were recorded by secretaries on the spot, with all the imperfections which such a style of delivery admits. Basically they are exegetical pieces expressed in a homiletic medium. We possess them today in a form which reflects as closely as is humanly possible their original delivery, the *sermo cottidianus* of everyday speech. The fact that Augustine was prevented by death from polishing the sermons or revising them, as he had planned, adds to, rather than subtracts from, their intimate and lively rapport with his listeners.

Most of the sermons were actually preached before a congregation in the presence of shorthand writers, who by all accounts did a marvelous job of reproducing them. Faithfully they noted disturbing shouts from the nearby amphitheater as well as applause and vocal approval of the preacher. Very few sermons were dictated in the presence of an *amanuensis* in the quiet of the bishop's study (*Enarr.* 118, *Proemium: partim sermocinando in populis, partim dictando exposui*; *Serm.* 10; Hill 1990, III/1, pp. 289–290, n. 1). In a manner reminiscent of his teaching years as a *grammaticus,* the bishop would break up piecemeal the sacred text of the Bible, as the eucharistic bread was broken, and he would nourish the people with

words, which he frequently described as their "dishes" (*Serm.* 339.4;
Conf. 5.3.3; Frangipane 2.4 in *Miscellanea Agostiniana* 1.193). The
extemporaneous character of the sermons was sometimes pushed to
the limit when the lector read the wrong lesson or the cantor chanted
the wrong psalm, and Augustine gracefully accommodated himself to
their mistake (*Enarr.* 138.1).

Augustine gladly risks criticism from teachers of grammar rather
than forfeit clarity of expression (*Enarr.* 36.s.3.6 and 138.20), which
he regards as far more desirable an accomplishment than either hollow
eloquence or inane elegance (*De doctr. christ.* 4.9.23). A golden key
may not open the door, he tells us; there is no objection to a wooden
key, if it can (*De doctr. christ.* 4.11.26). The "pedantic exactitude" of
the lecture hall is out of place in the cathedra of a local bishop
(*Enarr.* 36.s.3.6). "Popular speech is generally more useful for
expressing the meaning than correct and antiquated speech" (*De doctr.
christ.* 3.3.7). For this reason, Augustine sometimes preferred Punic
and Greek words, which were evidently intelligible to his listeners
(*Enarr.* 123.8).

Whether the letter "h" in *homo* was aspirated or not was of
much less concern to Augustine than the respect which was inherently
due to every human being (*Conf.* 1.18.29). With a mere three syllables
the Latin word *peccavi* expresses the warmth of a contrite heart
(*Serm.* 393). Whether *ignoscere* is pronounced with a long or short
syllable, belonging to either the second or third conjugation, is
irrelevant to a penitent who is asking God for forgiveness (*De doctr.
christ.* 2.13.19). In a well-known passage Augustine tells us:

> My own speech almost always displeases me. . . . I lament that
> my tongue cannot do justice to my heart. I wish those who hear
> me to understand exactly what I had understood, and I am aware
> of speaking in such a way that I fail in this. . . . My utterance,
> however, is slow and long-drawn and totally unlike my thoughts
> (*CR* 2.3; tr. Christopher; see also *Trac. Joh.* 5.10).

Sophisticated residents of Milan had long ago made fun of Augustine
with his rustic North African accent (*De ordine* 2.17.45).

A conversation at table in the monastery of clerics reveals in
Augustine a rare glimpse of personal satisfaction. Augustine remarked
how he had strayed far from the subject and had digressed instead on
the errors of Manicheism, which were farthermost from his thoughts

at the time. A businessman named Firmus who had been listening to the sermon came to the monastery "a day or two later" to tell the bishop how he had been won over by the strengths of the preacher's arguments. Firmus disposed of his business interests, cultivated an ascetic life and was eventually ordained a presbyter in a foreign country (*Vita Augustini* 15).

In a long sermon with at least ten minutes to go Augustine requests the "closest attention" of his hearers who had been noisy and restless from the start (*Serm.* 37.1 and 27). In Carthage at the Shrine of Saint Cyprian, Augustine acknowledges what he regarded as the undue length of a sermon on the previous Sunday. Its actual length hardly exceeded twenty minutes, a short sermon by Augustinian standards. Here the bishop's sensitivity might be attributed to his poor health and age; he was about sixty-five years at the time (*Serm.* 48). "An old man's sermon ought to be both serious and short," he tells us (*Serm.* 350.3), and he reproaches himself for his "talkative old age" (*loquax senectus, Serm.* 355.7). In marked contrast to sermons which lasted anywhere from a half hour to an hour-and-a-half (sometimes two hours), one of Augustine's shortest sermons amounts to thirty-nine lines in Migne (*Patrologia Latina* 38.580), preached at the dedication of a shrine at Hippo in honor of Saint Stephen during which he chides the visiting bishops for refusing to preach in his stead. Augustine was then over seventy years of age (*Serm.* 94). On another occasion he asked the lector to repeat Sunday's reading on Monday because the church had been filled to capacity and his feeble voice could not be heard above the muttering crowd except in complete silence (*Serm.* 68.1 = Mai 126.1 in *Miscellanea Agostiniana* 1.356).

That Augustine's cathedral church should be designated Basilica of Peace is somewhat ironic, for its bishop was ever so embroiled in controversy. The designation *Basilica Maior* ought not to mislead us. Its length measured a mere 126 feet (with apse 147 feet), and its width 60 feet, comparable in size, I suspect, to many country churches.

That Augustine cited a chest ailment (*dolor stomachi*) as one reason among others for resignation from his teaching post in Milan is well-known. Such chest pains, it is true, might reasonably be explained as symptoms of stress. Nevertheless, Augustine did not enjoy sound physical health; he was never robust. He detested the winter months for he was highly susceptible to colds. Though much more congenial, the summer months brought tiredness and profuse perspiration, particularly when he was preaching (*Serm.* 183.13, *Enarr.* 41.13). The exertion was sometimes too much for him, and we must recall that in those days the preacher sat, while the congregation was standing. Chronic hoarseness plagued him (*Serm.* 37.1; *Serm.* 68.1). As the turtledove seeks a nest for her chicks, so Augustine urges his listeners to be absolutely quiet in order to provide a nest for his sermon (*Serm.* 37.1).

From the time of his episcopal consecration, he suffered from hemorrhoids (*Epist.* 38.1). His physical condition completely collapsed during the summer of 410 when he retired to the country at the insistence of a physician (*Epist.* 122.1). At the best of times his health was problematic (*Epist.* 151.13). One may ask whether the cumulative evidence in this matter of health points in the direction of either acute laryngitis or possibly pleurisy. A Bossuet or a Lacordaire with robust and resonant voice Augustine was not. And so the tribute paid him by Possidius, his biographer, is all the more remarkable. (In Possidius's case I am strongly inclined to discount literary artifice or hagiographic adulation.) In contrast to the many people who had read Augustine's writings during his lifetime Possidius tells us: "I believe, however, that they profited even more who were able to hear him preaching in church" (*Vita Augustini* 31.4 and 9).

THE ART OF PREACHING

Augustine's approach to preaching is found in Book 4 of *De doctrina christiana*. Scholars have variously translated *doctrina* to mean "doctrine," "education," "culture," and "rhetoric." In fact, all four features figure in the title of this book, which was addressed to a large segment of interested Christians. Although eminently suited for the purpose, *De doctrina christiana* ought not to be regarded exclusively as a manual for training the clergy. Book 1 outlines the essentials of Christianity; Books 2 and 3 constitute a treatise on biblical hermeneutics. These three books were written in A.D. 396/7, shortly after Augustine's episcopal consecration. Book 4, a treatise on homiletics written some thirty years later, A.D. 426/7, reflects the bishop's incredibly wide range of experience as a preacher.

Summarily expressed, Book 1 articulates the *res* of Christianity, its sum and substance, its fundamental message, *regula fidei et praecepta vivendi.* Books 2 and 3 help us to decode this message, to interpret it, to grasp its meaning by an understanding of signs and words, *signa et verba.* How to communicate this message to others is the task Augustine sets before himself in Book 4. During the Middle Ages, Book 4 became detached from the rest of the work and circulated independently under the title *De arte praedicandi* as evidence of its widespread popularity.

"An individual speaks more or less wisely," Augustine observes, "to the extent that he has made more or less progress in the Scriptures" (*De doctr. christ.* 4.5.7). The preacher must never tire of listening to the biblical text. Cicero had long ago argued that, if wisdom was wanting, then eloquence was worthless (*De Inventione* 1.1.1). From Augustine's perspective, wisdom consists in worship of God and in knowledge of the Scriptures. For learning to preach models are more fruitful than rules of rhetoric. Augustine cites passages from the prophet Amos, Saint Paul, Saints Cyprian and Ambrose as deserving of imitation. Know the subject matter and the words will follow. Words are subordinate to the preacher, not the preacher to words (*De doctr. christ.* 4.28.61).

In miniature, Book 4 reflects the trajectory of Augustine's life: from his early interest in rhetoric (Cicero's *Hortensius*), to philosophy ("the books of the Platonists"), to pastoral ministry (Christ and His church as the basis for the sacraments and the Scriptures). In the bishop's theory and practice of preaching, one encounters the confluence of two ancient traditions, the ethical-philosophical (*vir probus*) and the rhetorical (*peritus dicendi*), with the Neoplatonists as representatives of the former and with Isocrates, Cicero and Quintilian, to a lesser extent, as representatives of the latter.

Graeco-Roman education aimed to cultivate both wisdom (*vir sapiens*) and eloquence (*vir eloquens*). But its goal was inherently deficient by reason of its failure to worship the one true God and Jesus Christ whom God had sent. Augustine was no despiser of culture; indeed his chief concern appears to have been rather with the cultivation of holiness (*vir sanctus*), without prejudice to either rhetoric or philosophy. This was not to suggest that piety was a presupposition for learning, or vice versa, for the bishop bluntly observes: "Many holy people know little about the liberal arts and some who do know (the liberal arts) are not holy" (*Retract.* 1.3).

This is not the forum to elaborate upon Augustine's many debts to Graeco-Roman oratory, notably Cicero's delineation of the orator's tasks, the three genres of oratory and the effective blend of Attic and Asian styles of speech. The life-style of the preacher, says Augustine, is an eloquent sermon in itself, *copia dicendi forma vivendi* (*De doctr. christ.* 4.29.61). In the interpretation of the Scriptures, the moral life of the preacher has greater influence than the most sublime eloquence (*De doctr. christ.* 4.27.59). With the aid of a marvelous *double-entendre* which echoes the titles of two of Cicero's principal works, *De oratore* and *Orator,* Augustine urges: "one ought to pray before one speaks," *sit orator antequam dictor* (*De doctr. christ.* 4.15.32). Six references to prayer form a major consideration for effective preaching in the penultimate paragraph of Book 4 (*De doctr. christ.* 4.30.63), which then proceeds to conclude with a prayer.

CHRIST AS PREACHER

"We are ministers of the word," says Augustine, "not ours, but God's (word) and our Lord's" (*Serm.* 114.1; *Epist.* 21.3 and 228.2; *C. Cresc.* 2.11.13). The bifurcation of word and sacrament which exists today would have been unthinkable in late antiquity. Had Augustine been present at the Council of Trent, I hazard the conjecture that he would have strongly urged recognition of preaching as the eighth sacrament. The preacher interposes himself between the subjective dispositions of a human being and the providential activity of God. This is clearly as it should be: Human dignity would have been lowered if God seemed to be unwilling to have human beings minister the divine word to human beings "*si per homines hominibus Deus verbum suum ministrare nolle videretur*" (*De doctr. christ.* Proemium 6). Mediation by Jesus Christ and his church, the communion of saints, Scriptures and sacraments, preaching—all these indispensable elements constituted, for Augustine, efficacious forces in the cultivation of holiness.

His basic approach to preaching is elucidated thus: "Even though people listen to human speech, understanding of the words comes about in an interior manner; there is an interior illumination; there is an interior revelation" (*Trac. Joh.* 26.7). The original Latin is all the more striking with its ringing anaphora: *quod intellegunt, intus datur, intus coruscat, intus revelatur* (*Trac. Joh.* 26.7). "When people announce the good news," he asks, "what is happening externally? What am I doing right now as I preach? I am pouring a clatter of words into your ears. But my words are meaningless, my sermon is senseless, unless he who dwells within (*ille qui intus est*) reveals their sense to you" (ibid.).

In his Christmas and Epiphany sermons Augustine repeatedly expressed the fundamental paradox of the incarnation as "the speechless Word," *infans Verbum, ineffabile Verbum.* While gesticulating, crying, raging in a temper, remonstrating, an infant is unable to articulate meaningful speech, all of which is suggested by the etymology of the word "infant," where the negative prefix *in-* is followed by the present participle, *fans* (from the deponent Latin verb *for, fari, fatus sum,* "to speak").

To assert that God became a human being was utterly preposterous, as if to describe an individual as a married bachelor. Christ alone, argues Augustine, unlocks the mystery of human life and death, and language too. In Christ, as both the preëxisting Word and the Word incarnate, all human speech is redeemed. Here one finds genuine meaning, authentic signification, the silent and unutterable Word without whom there are no words, the Word incarnate without whom all human speech is speechless (*Serm.* 188.2).

Preaching must always be subservient to the ministry of the incarnate Word of God. To teach or instruct (*docere*), to sustain attention in order to persuade (*placere*), regularly fall within the limited competence of a human agent. To bend the human will, however (*movere, flectere*), pertains to divine agency and the generous promptings of grace. All words (*verba*) in the world, and most especially the incarnate Word, Jesus Christ, are signposts (*signa*) along the way of the pilgrim pointing to the only reality (*res*) that truly matters, the triune God of love (*De doctr. christ.* 1.5.5).

A certain diffidence on the part of Augustine had long ago been adumbrated in his treatise, *On the Teacher.* Composed at Thagaste before his ordination to the presbyterate at Hippo in 391, it consists of a conversation with his son, Adeodatus. In this rudimentary work the Platonic theory of teaching and learning was consciously displaced by the role of Christ as the "Interior Teacher," *Magister Interior,* who presides within an individual. From that time on, Augustine assigned to Christ the dual role of teaching and of imparting understanding, a function that many theologians subsequently accorded to the activity of the Holy Spirit. Throughout his busy pastorate, the bishop leaned heavily on the biblical text: "Avoid being called teachers. Only one is your teacher, the Messiah" (Matt. 23:10), which echoes the earlier verse, "One among you is your teacher, the rest are learners" (Matt. 23:8).

> You ask what sort of God Christ is?
> Listen to me,
> or better, listen *with* me.
> Let us listen together,
> let us learn together.
> It is not a matter
> of my speaking and your listening
> and, on that account,
> I have reason for not listening with you . . .
> In this school we are disciples together,
> all of us; heaven is the chair of our teacher.
> (*Serm.* 261.2; see also 23.2 and 278.11.)

There is no separation between the preëxisting Word of God, the historical Jesus and the church, head and body (to invoke a Pauline metaphor), the totality and fullness of Christ. This latter dimension, namely the eternal Word incarnate in both Jesus and the church, Augustine describes as a third way of understanding Christ (*tertius modus est, Serm.* 341.9.11). To elaborate on this matter would take us too far afield. It needs to be said, however, that we do not understand Augustine, if we insist upon separating this ecclesial character of Christ and his members, head and body, from the truth of the incarnation. At the same time, Augustine forcefully distinguishes between *potestas* and *ministerium* (*Trac. Joh.* 5.11).

There are many Pauline echoes in the bishop's writings where the preacher's task is to plant the seed and to water it, but the grace of God alone makes it grow (1 Cor. 3:6). Twice within a single paragraph, an arresting Latin word order catches both the ear and the eye; twice the bishop tells his people that "Christ actually preaches Christ," *Christum ipse praedicat Christus / praedicat ergo Christus Christum* (*Serm.* 354.1). One of the clearest expressions of this cardinal principle of Augustine's thought is found in his explication of Psalm 49, verse 3: "God will come openly, our God, and he will not keep silent."

> He did not keep silent through the patriarchs, he did not keep silent through the prophets, he did not keep silent through the mouth of his own body.
> And if he were silent now, he would still be speaking through the Scriptures, wouldn't he? The reader goes to the lectern, but it is Christ who is not silent. The preacher explains the text; if he says what is true, it is Christ speaking. If Christ were silent, I myself wouldn't be saying all this to you now. Nor has he been keeping silent through your mouths. When you were singing, he was speaking. He's not silent. What we have to do is hear him—but with the ears of the heart, because it's easy to hear him with (ears) of cartilage (*Serm.* 17.1; tr. Hill 1990, III/1, 366).

AUGUSTINE'S SERMONS TODAY

Good sermons, we are told, are designed for the listener, not for the reader. They necessarily possess an ephemeral quality. When written down, their impact is dulled. I firmly disagree. At the same time, one must always heed the Italian adage, *traduttore traditore.* For example, instances of the Latin *Christus passus* portraying the Passion of Christ, echo the earlier image of Christ as the roasted fish, *piscis assus,* on the shore of Lake Tiberias in a sermon where sheep overtake and eventually supplant fish as the dominant symbol (*Trac. Joh.* 123). While necessarily suppressing strikingly similar sounds of so elegant a Latin wordplay in an English translation and allowing further for the uneven character of Augustine's preaching as originally crafted oral compositions, it is a singular tribute to the artistry of the bishop that so many of his sermons resonate loud and clear on the printed page of a Latin text and in English translation. Many sermons reject classification as period pieces or antiquated art forms dating from the first quarter of the fifth century. Their appeal to fifth-century *hearers* is by no means lost upon twentieth-century *readers* (as testified by many devout Christians who pray the *Roman Breviary*). In fact, the human eye offers many advantages which often escape the human ear. Both listening to classical (and medieval) texts and reading them aloud with their full range of audiovisual materials brings pleasure which surpasses the sense of hearing.

Although the reader is sixteen centuries removed from the original texts, they have the ring of genuine crystal. We are in the presence of an artist, a seasoned practitioner who exhibits acute sensitivity both to the issues at hand and to his congregation, the fruit of extraordinary intelligence, personal holiness, prayer, and firsthand experience as a pastor of souls. Frequently the rapid-fire succession of ideas permits little or no time for nuance or detailed explanation. Perhaps this was unnecessary for a congregation long accustomed (some thirty-nine years) to the bishop's exegetical and homiletic method.

While reading the sermons one frequently gets the impression of watching a video game or listening to a soundtrack. Does either the image or the soundtrack erase easily? I think not. Their overall impact and coherence are convincing.

People with a sense of history are painfully aware of the disastrous effects occasioned by the long-standing rupture between Scripture and tradition which occurred in the sixteenth century. No less painful is the memory of the eighteenth-century Enlightenment which carved two distinctly subjective spheres between reason and revelation. The French word *spiritualité,* a post-Enlightenment word, whose current meaning is shot through with slippery imprecisions, straddles these two overlapping sectors of divine/human activity, which cannot be separated at all, except as artificial constructs of the mind by individuals who possess an Enlightenment mentality. In still another retrograde step, theology has tended to become a narrowly academic discipline, in the interests of scientific objectivity, with enormous loss of meaning to any bona fide definition of authentic spirituality. Herein lies the strength of Augustine's sermons (and writings) as they bridge the gap between the two spheres of spirituality and theology, thereby enabling the reader of Augustine to overcome the cognitive dissonance of recent centuries by examining firsthand the truly remarkable congruence which necessarily exists between theology and spirituality, doctrine and life, Scripture and tradition, text and the interpreting community.

I wish to conclude by making four brief observations:

• As an antidote to widespread theories of self-actualization and self-sufficiency, Americans particularly need to be reminded that conversion, in the main, is essentially God's work. From an Augustinian perspective it is sheer arrogance for a preacher to claim a Master of Divinity during a lifelong struggle to master one's humanity.

• At the outset of his treatise on hermeneutics and homiletics Augustine remarks: "In this battle of words one ought to maintain a discreet silence rather than to settle the score with speech" (*De doctr. christ.* 1.5.5). He was speaking about the triune God of love as the goal of human existence. There is somewhat of an anomaly in this reflection by a man whose written legacy appreciably exceeds five-million words now stored in a data base at Würzburg University in Germany and Villanova University in eastern Pennsylvania. "The super-eminence of God," Augustine tells us, "surpasses the powers of everyday speech" (*Trin.* 7.4.7). By his own reckoning his fifteen books on *The Trinity* failed conspicuously to articulate adequately the mystery of God. This apophatic undercurrent in Augustine's sermons issues many warnings to preachers who think that they somehow have God in their pocket.

• Augustine's sermons likewise provide a stimulus to ecumen-ical consciousness. Schism, for Augustine, was fundamentally the failure to love. This theme is the chief focus of his ten *Tractates on the First Letter of John.* In another sermon the bishop tells us: "When they cease to pray the Our Father, only then will they cease to be our brothers (and sisters)" (*Enarr.* 32.2.29).

• Never an armchair theologian, Augustine had, after more than a decade, abandoned the podium of the professor for the priedieu and cathedra of a bishop. We have been reminded by Hans Urs von Balthasar that ever since the Reformation, doctrine has become all bone without flesh, while spirituality and pastoral theology have become all flesh without bone. In helping us to cross this wide gulf in contemporary post-Reformation thought, Augustine's sermons are powerfully suggestive. Augustine stands for both flesh and bones. That is why we continue to read

him. He has buried all his undertakers. Permit him, therefore, to
have the last word:

> What, after all, do I want?
> What do I desire?
> What am I longing for?
> Why am I preaching?
> Why am I sitting here?
> What do I live for,
> if not with this intention,
> that we should all live together with Christ?
> That is my desire, that's my honor,
> that's my most treasured possession,
> that's my joy, that's my pride and glory.
> But if you don't listen to me,
> and yet I have not kept silent,
> then I have at least saved my soul.
> But I don't wish to be saved without you.
> (*Serm.* 17.2; tr. Hill/1990, III/1, 367)

Notes

1. It is important to keep in mind that Augustine is extremely tentative
    about his exegesis. Plotinus gave good advice in this regard:
    "Everywhere we must read 'so to speak'" (*Enneades* 6.8.13). No one
    realized this better than the bishop of Hippo. God's activities far
    transcend human comprehension (*De vera relig.* 36.67). We can say all
    sorts of things about God, but everything we say is wide of the mark
    (*Trac. Joh.* 13.5). In his prayerful reading of the Scriptures, Augustine
    felt compelled to seek multiple meanings other than the one which
    suggested itself to the reader firsthand (*Conf.* 12.18.27; 12.26.36;
    12.31.42 and 12.32.43). Only in this way could human speech convey
    more fittingly the mysteries which the Scriptures intend to reveal.

2. That the Christian moment basically transpires between Good Friday
    and Easter Sunday is expressed in an unmistakable Augustinian
    anaphora: *nascendo, moriendo, resurgendo,* "birth, death and
    resurrection."

3. The sacrificial and redeeming blood of Christ is a controlling image
    throughout. Here we learn that the blood of Christ brings essential

vitality to both preacher and his congregation. In another sermon, the bishop suggests that Jesus spilled his blood on the ground in order to mark a steadfast path for preachers (*Trac. Joh.* 55.7).

4. Thus, in this sermon (*Enarr.* 101.s.1), Augustine identifies the first serious ecumenical hurdle both historically and also in degree of difficulty: the relationship between Judaism and Christianity.

References

Divjak, Johannes. 1981. *Epistolae ex duobus codicibus nuper in lucem prolatae. Sancti Aureli Augustini Opera. CSEL* 88 (Vienna). Eng. tr. Robert B. Eno, *St. Augustine Letters* 1*-29*. *The Fathers of the Church,* vol. 81 (Washington, D.C.: 1989).

Dolbeau, François. 1990. "Sermons inédits de S. Augustin dans un manuscrit de Mayence (Stadtbibliothek, I 9)," *Revue des études augustiniennes* 36 (1990), 355–359.

Hamman, Adalbert. 1986. "The Turnabout of the Fourth Century," *Patrology* 4, ed. Angelo di Berardino, intr. Johannes Quasten (Westminster).

Verbraken, Pierre-Patrick. 1987. "Saint Augustine's Sermons: Why and How to Read Them Today," *Augustinian Heritage* 33 (1987), 105–116.

——. 1990. "Les éditions successives des 'Sermons' de saint Augustin," *Troisième Centenaire de l'Edition Mauriste de Saint Augustin. Communications présentées au colloque de 19 et 20 avril 1990* (Paris), 157–167.

Latin Texts of the Sermons

Enarrationes in Psalmos, CCSL, vols. 38, 39, and 40 (Turnhout, 1956).

In Johannis Evangelium Tractatus CXXIV, CCSL, vol. 36 (Turnhout, 1954).

In Epistulam Iohannis ad Parthos tractatus decem., ed. J.-P. Migne, *Patrologia Latina,* vol. 35 (Paris, 1861).

Sermones ad Populum, ed. J.-P. Migne, *Patrologia Latina,* vols. 38–39 (Paris, 1865).

Sancti Augustini sermones post Maurinos reperti, vol. 1, *Miscellanea Agostiniana* (Rome, 1930).

> [Octavius Fraja Frangipane = Frangipane]
> [Codex Guelferbytanus 4096 = Guelf.]
> [Angelo Mai = Mai]

Patrologiae Cursus Completus, ser. lat., *Supplementum,* ed. A. Hamman, vol. 2 (Paris, 1960), 398–840.

English Translations

Howe, Quincy, ed. and tr., *Selected Sermons of St. Augustine* (New York, 1966).

Saint Augustine, *The First Catechetical Instruction.* Tr. Joseph P. Christopher. *Ancient Christian Writers* 2 (New York, 1946).

——. *Sermons for Christmas and Epiphany.* Tr. Thomas C. Lawler, *Ancient Christian Writers* 15 (Westminster, 1952).

——. *Sermons on the Liturgical Seasons.* Tr. Mary Sarah Muldowney, *The Fathers of the Church* 38 (New York, 1959).

The Works of Saint Augustine. A Translation for the 21st Century. Part 3—*Sermons,* vol. 1: *Sermons 1–19.* Intr. by Cardinal Michele Pellegrino. Tr. and notes by Edmund Hill, OP. Ed. by John E. Rotelle, OSA (Brooklyn, N.Y.: New City Press, 1990).

——. Vol. 2: *Sermons 20–50 on the Old Testament* (Brooklyn, N.Y.: 1990).

——. Vol. 3: *Sermons 51–94 on the New Testament* (Brooklyn, N.Y.: 1991).

Weller, Philip T., *Selected Easter Sermons of St. Augustine* (St. Louis and London, 1959).

New Sermons of Augustine
Discovered by François Dolbeau

Dolbeau, François. "Nouveaux sermons de saint Augustin pour la conversion des païens et des donatistes," *Revue des études augustiniennes* 37 (1991), 37–78.

——. "Nouveaux sermons d'Augustin pour la conversion des païens et des donatistes (II)," *Revue des études augustiniennes* 37 (1991), 261–306.

——. "Sermons inédits de saint Augustin prêchés en 397 (à suivre)," *Revue bénédictine* 101 (1991), 240–256.

Select Bibliography

Doyle, G. Wright, "Augustine's Sermonic Method," *Westminster Theological Journal* 39 (1976–77), 213–238.

Mohrmann, Christine, *Études sur le latin des chrétiens* 1 (Rome: Edizioni di Storia e Letteratura, 1958); 2 (Rome: Edizioni di Storia e Letteratura, 1961).

Pontet, Maurice, *L'exégèse de saint Augustin prédicateur.* Théologie 7 (Paris: Aubier, 1946).

Poque, Susanne, ed., *Augustin d'Hippone, Sermons pour la Pâque. Sources Chrétiennes* 116 (Paris, 1966).

Press, Gerald A., "The Content and Argument of Augustine's *De Doctrina Christiana,*" *Augustiniana* 31 (1981), 165–182.

Rowe, Trevor, *St. Augustine, Pastoral Theologian* (London: Epworth Press, 1974), chap. 2, "On Preaching," pp. 24–56.

Van der Meer, F., *Augustine the Bishop,* tr. Brian Battershaw and G.R. Lamb (New York: Harper & Row, 1961; repr. 1983), 405–467.

Verbraken, Pierre-Patrick, *Études critiques sur les sermons authentiques de saint Augustin. Instrumenta Patristica* 12 (Steenbrugge, 1976).

PLATE 3. Augustine as a penitent and confessor. Alonso de Orozco (1500–1591), *Recopilación de todas las obras* (Valladolid: Sebastian Martinez, 1554).

Augustine's Understanding of the Church as a Eucharistic Community

Gerald Bonner

It is a misfortune of Augustine of Hippo that consideration of his doctrine of the Church tends to neglect that pastoral aspect with which he was concerned from his ordination as a presbyter of Hippo to his death as bishop of that city thirty-nine years later.[1] We commonly discuss Augustine's ecclesiology within the context of his debate with the schismatic Donatist Church, when he was concerned to maintain that the unworthiness of the minister does not invalidate the efficacy of the sacrament, and to argue that the Church Militant here on earth must of necessity be composed of both saints and sinners, who will only be separated at the end of the world. The same theme is an important element in *The City of God,* designed to refute those pagans who claimed that Christianity had ruined the Roman Empire, and to reassure anxious Christians who could not understand why God had not protected Christian Rome against the Goths. Earthly misfortune, says Augustine, befalls good and wicked men alike, and no conclusions may safely be drawn in this life from material suffering. In the sack of Rome good and bad Christians were equally afflicted with the pagans, although for the Christian elect, tribulation may have an educative and reformatory value.

Yet, in *The City of God,* we also find another element of Augustine's ecclesiology: although perfection is possible only in the future in the Church Triumphant, in a certain fashion this future hope is already realized in the Church Militant which, in an eschatological sense, is even now the Kingdom of God on earth. These notions were developed and deepened in Augustine's last years, in his controversy with the Pelagians, when he was careful first to maintain that while salvation is possible only for those who have been incorporated within the Church by baptism, baptism is not, in itself, an automatic passport to salvation. He was careful, secondly, to deny that salvation is obtained by post-baptismal good works, as Pelagian theology seemed to him to imply. In his last years Augustine became increasingly concerned with the inscrutability of God's judgments and the apparent arbitrariness of the divine choice. Nevertheless, in his pastoral dealings, the Bishop of Hippo never despaired of anyone, as long as breath remained in the body. For him, every Christian was a potential member of the City of God and every pagan a potential Christian. Like other pastors at all times in Christian history, Augustine's parochial policy seems to have run counter to his theological dogma, and he was as assiduous as the Pelagians in commending good works, even though he did not believe them to avail for salvation.

These pastoral considerations may help us to understand Augustine himself, as a man called to pastoral ministry. I would like to suggest that, as an event in his life, his ordination represented a conversion-experience hardly less decisive than that which occurred at Milan in 386. In some ways, indeed, it was even more decisive, since the conversion at Milan involved a decision on his part, while that at Hippo was involuntary. Augustine's ordination at Hippo was unforeseen and undesired—he burst into tears, which the congregation supposed to be due to chagrin at not having been immediately made a bishop. In fact, of course, Augustine no more desired a bishopric than he did priest's orders. He had reached a stage in his religious development when he wanted to consolidate the monastic life which he had embraced on his return to Africa in 388 and to devote himself to Christian learning, which would generally be on a high intellectual level. The last thing he wanted was responsibility for a congregation which, if not unintelligent—and my impression is that congregations in the patristic age were in no way inferior to those of today in native wit—had nothing of the academic training and intellectual formation which he found in friends like Alypius and Evodius. Augustine's letter to Bishop Valerius,[2] asking for some delay before assuming pastoral responsibility, so that he might engage in a systematic study of the Scriptures, bears witness to the dismay which his enforced ordination inspired in his soul. Saul, son of Kish, went seeking his father's asses and found a kingdom. Augustine went to church and found himself saddled with a curacy.

Nevertheless, it is possible to think that Augustine's unwanted ordination was a blessing, both for him and for the people of Hippo. Their gain is obvious: one of the outstanding theological minds of the patristic or, indeed, of any age. However, Augustine gained as well, in that he found himself constrained to minister to all sorts of conditions of men and women without any choice, as opposed to enjoying the society of congenial minds. It seems to me that during the first half of his life Augustine was both self-centered and selfish. He had friends, but they were friends of his own choosing. We know, from the way that he treated his concubine, and even his mother, when he fled to Italy and left her on the African seashore lamenting,[3] that unswerving loyalty was not a mark of his character. Augustine, until his conversion, was a clever man on the make. Like other clever men on the make, he was not unduly concerned if he broke a few hearts in the process. Becoming a Christian revealed a different scale of values, but he still continued to choose his friends for himself and to live in a congenial society. Ordination altered all that. From then on Augustine had to accept all who came his way and to recognize them as children of God and potential heirs of the Kingdom of Heaven—a recognition made clear in the closing chapter of Book 9 of the *Confessions,* where Augustine asks God to inspire "Thy servants my brethren, Thy sons and my masters, whom I serve with heart and voice and writings."[4] We talk about the grace of Holy Orders. For Augustine it was a grace which came not far short of the grace received in baptism, in that in his case it extended love of his neighbor from a few chosen friends to a whole range of ordinary Christian souls, some good, some not so good, none indifferent in Augustine's eyes. It was such a gathering of ordinary Christian souls which confronted Augustine in church Sunday after Sunday, assembled to hear him preach, and to participate in the eucharist.[5] It was such as these who constituted the Body of Christ in the not very distinguished port of Hippo Regius, the modern Annaba in Algeria.

The Christian congregation of Hippo, then, represented the focal point of Augustine's conception of the Church of Christ, but it did not distract his gaze from the whole Catholic Church, spread from East to West. On the contrary, no Christian thinker has been more aware of the universality, of the catholicity of the Church than Augustine. In a sense his notion of catholicity was forced upon him by his dispute with the Donatists, who gloried in the notion that true faith had perished throughout the rest of the Christian world and remained only among themselves in Africa. Even without their challenge, Augustine would have been unable to rest content with a self-satisfied parochialism like theirs. By the spread of the Gospel a "multitude of believers" had been drawn together;[6] there existed a Christian unity of the whole world,[7] to which all who called themselves Christian must adhere. Unlike pagan philosophy, which was the concern only of an élite, Christianity appealed to all, without any distinction of learning and ignorance. In his treatise *On True Religion,* written in 390, before his ordination, Augustine could declare:

> . . . multitudes enter upon this way of life from every race, forsaking the riches and honours of this present world, desirous of dedicating their whole life to the One Most High God. Islands once deserted and many lands formerly left in solitude are filled [with monks]. In cities and towns, settlements and villages, country places and private estates, there is openly preached and practised such a renunciation of earthly things and conversion to the One True God that daily throughout the entire world with almost one voice the human race makes response: *Lift up your hearts to the Lord.*[8]

Augustine was not original here. Tertullian had made a similar claim, two centuries earlier.[9] Yet, Augustine's language makes clear his conviction of the catholicity of the Christian Church.

There was therefore no possibility that Augustine's immediate concern with his community at Hippo would cause him to neglect the wider fellowship of the whole Catholic Church throughout the world. But there was another consideration: Augustine's understanding of the Church was not limited by time. Departed Christians were members of the Church no less than the living. In the *Confessions* Augustine records how, at his mother's funeral at Ostia, "the sacrifice of our redemption"[10]—the eucharist—had been offered at the graveside, as it would be offered at Augustine's funeral, when his time came, in 430.[11] Just as, in pagan times, the rites of the *parentalia* had shown the solidarity of the dead with their living descendants, so now in Christianity the offering of bread and wine by Christ through His minister unites the people of God, both living and departed, and the departed may benefit from the offering as well as the living. "It cannot be denied," says Augustine, in his *Enchiridion* or *Handbook of Christian Doctrine,* composed about 420, that the souls of the departed obtain relief through the pious service of their living friends, when the Mediator's sacrifice is offered for them, or alms are given in the Church.[12]

Indeed, it was the fact of such eucharistic commemoration which furnished Augustine with proof that departed Christians are members of the Church. So in Book 20 of *The City of God,* composed toward the end of his life, in about 427, he writes:

> . . . the souls of the faithful departed are not separated from the Church, which is even now the Kingdom of Christ; for otherwise no mention would be made of them at God's altar at the communion of the Body of Christ. . . . Why are such things done, unless it is because the faithful, even after death, are still members of [Christ's] Body?[13]

Saint Monica, it will be remembered, exhorted Augustine and his brother Navigius not to have any concern with regard to her place of burial, but to remember her at God's altar.[14] In her request, she comprehended a whole ecclesiology, which her son would subsequently develop.

For Augustine, Christ's Church is not limited to human members, but includes the angels. "The Church," he says in the *Enchiridion,*

> must here be understood in its wholeness, not only in respect of that part which is a pilgrim upon earth, *from the rising up of the sun until its going down, praising the name of the Lord* (Ps. 112[113]:3) and after the end of its ancient captivity *singing a new song* (Ps. 32[33]:3), but also in that part which has always in heaven adhered to God and has not experienced any fall to its hurt. . . . This Church, therefore, which is the Church among the holy angels and virtues of God, will become known to us as it is when we have become joined to it at the last, to possess everlasting beatitude in its company.[15]

The Church, then, is made up of both angels and human beings. However, in the present age there is an important difference between the two classes of its members, not only in their natures—the angels are pure spirits, human beings are a compound of body and spirit—but also in their potentialities. The good angels cannot fall,[16] and the evil angels, it may be observed in passing, cannot be redeemed.[17] Human beings, however, in the present age, are divided into the Elect and the Reprobate, both known to God alone, and their destinies will be made manifest only at the Day of Judgment. Both the Elect and the Reprobate are to be found within the Church Militant.

> The Kingdom of Heaven must be understood in one sense as a kingdom which contains both the man who fails to practise what he teaches, and the man who does so, though the one is least and the other great in that kingdom. Yet, in another sense it is a kingdom only for the man who practises what he teaches. Accordingly, where both kinds of men are to be found, there is the Church as she now is; but where only the one sort is found, there is the Church as she will be, when no evil persons will be found in her. Therefore, the Church is *even now* the Kingdom of Christ and the Kingdom of Heaven.[18]

This passage from *The City of God* is of great significance, because it shows that, for Augustine, even the Church Militant, which includes sinners who will have no place with the saints in the eternal Jerusalem, is in some way to be identified with the Church Triumphant. In this particular chapter of *The City of God* Augustine was concerned to do away with the old Christian idea of the Millennium—a literal thousand-year reign of Christ with the saints before the Last Judgment, described in Revelation 20:6.[19] In earlier Christian centuries such an understanding had been entertained by luminaries of the Church like Saint Irenaeus. Augustine wished to dispense with it, not because he considered it to be grievously wrong, but because of the danger that the Thousand Years would be understood in a materialistic and carnal fashion. Accordingly, although Augustine saw humanity as currently living in the Sixth Age of the world—an age which extended from the Incarnation to the Last Judgment—he thought of the Church as already, in some way, living in the Seventh Age, the age of the Kingdom of God. It was this thinking which, in my view, enabled Augustine to see the Church both as a *corpus permixtum*—a thoroughly mixed body, in which good and bad live side by side until the close of the age—and also as the Body of Christ which, by definition, can only be pure.

To speak of the Church as the Body of Christ, as Augustine so frequently does, is to remind ourselves of the Christocentricity of his theology. If by Christocentricity we understand that devotion to the name of Jesus which has been characteristic of Western Christianity since the twelfth century, then Augustine is not Christocentric—he will be a disappointment to anyone whose religious sense has been fired by Bernard of Clairvaux or Julian of Norwich or Herrnhut or Methodism. If, however, we understand Christocentricity in a doctrinal sense, then Augustine is among the most Christocentric of theologians. The mediation of Christ, the God-man, is the foundation of his thinking. It is only the unity of the divine and human natures in the person of Jesus Christ which can bridge the gulf which the Fall opened between God and man. It is only by incorporation in Christ's humanity that humankind may participate in His divinity and become, in a certain sense, divinized. "To make those gods who were men, He was made man who is God."[20] These words of Augustine, which echo a famous sentence of Saint Athanasius,[21] express in the strongest form Augustine's understanding of mediation, and decisively separate him from the Neoplatonist philosophers, from whom he derived so large a part of his Christian philosophy.

In the *Confessions* Augustine described the effect of the Neoplatonic ecstasies which he experienced at Milan on the eve of his conversion: ascents of the mind by contemplation, initially from the senses and subsequently from the interpretation of sensory evidence by the mind until, by a sudden intuitive apprehension, it comes to the vision of reality, of THAT WHICH IS.[22] There is no good reason to question the Neoplatonic character of these ecstasies. When, however, Augustine came to write the *Confessions,* some ten years after the experiences, he recognized their limitations.

> I looked for a way of gaining sufficient strength for enjoying You, my God, but I did not find it until I embraced *the mediator between God and man, the man Christ Jesus, who is above all things, God blessed for ever* (Rom. 9:5; 1 Tim. 2:5), calling to me and saying: *I am the way and the truth and the life* (John 14:6). He mingled that food [the divine nature] which I was incapable of receiving with our flesh (*for the Word was made flesh*) (John 1:14), so that Your Wisdom, by which You created all things, might give milk to our infancy. I did not then cleave to Jesus my God, humbly clinging to Him who was humble, nor did I know

what thing His lowliness would teach me. For Your Word, the
eternal Truth, towering above the highest parts of Your creation,
has raised up those who had been brought low to Himself.[23]

This passage I find immensely important, not only in itself, but
for the consideration of the Church as a eucharistic community.
Although the Church is not mentioned, and the eucharist only implied
in the reference to the food which Augustine was unable to receive
(and the phrase could bear a wholly figurative interpretation),
Augustine, by his emphasis on the Incarnation as the sign of the
divine humility, makes clear the gulf which divided him, as a Catholic
Christian, from Neoplatonism, which rejected the notion of spirit
taking flesh. Some ten years after writing the *Confessions,* in Book 10
of *The City of God,* Augustine was to take issue with the Neoplatonist
philosopher Porphyry. According to Augustine, Porphyry had
contended that only the chief deities, whom he called "principles"
(*principia*), could purify men from sins; however, he declined to
recognize Christ as such a principle. "The fact is," says Augustine,

> that [Porphyry] despised Christ for the very flesh which He
> assumed to offer the sacrifice of our purification. It was because
> of his pride that Porphyry failed to understand this great mystery,
> that pride which our true and gracious Mediator overthrew by His
> humility, revealing Himself to mortals as a mortal. It was because
> they were immortal that the malignant and deceiving mediators
> [i.e., the fallen angels, masquerading as pagan gods] vaunted their
> supposed superiority, and deluded wretched men with false
> promises of help, as if they were immortals coming to the aid of
> mortals. And so the good and true Mediator has shown that it is
> sin which is evil, not the substance or the nature of flesh, since
> that flesh and a human soul could be taken and preserved from
> sin, and could be laid aside in death, and changed into a better
> condition by resurrection.[24]

This passage amplifies the previous quotation from the
Confessions. By His flesh-taking Christ has made possible an
encounter between man and God without any other mediation. He has
also removed any claim to angelic superiority over humanity by
reason of their purely spiritual nature. Moreover, although the good
angels are superior to humanity in that they cannot fall, this
superiority is, in the most literal sense, a temporary one. At the end

of the age, in the glorified body of the resurrection, men and women will be equal with the angels, "because both [parts of the Church, sc. angels and human beings] are destined to be one fellowship in eternity, as [the Church] is already one in the bond of charity, seeing that it was founded in its wholeness for the worship of the one God."[25]

It is perhaps because of this sense of the equality of angels and men that Augustine, unlike later theologians such as Pseudo-Dionysius, is not greatly interested in angelic hierarchies.[26] Rather, he sees the angels essentially as ministers of God who may, on occasion, aid humanity at God's direction, but who have no authority of their own over human beings. They are part of

> the temple of God—that is, of the whole supreme Trinity—which
> is Holy Church, the Church universal in heaven and earth,[27]

but not a superior part. It is therefore understandable that Augustine, when he treats of the Church, should start from the human element. He sees this element incorporated into the Church by the sacrament of baptism and united by the eucharist which, by its elements of bread, made from many grains of wheat, and wine, made from the juice of many grapes, represents the unity of the faithful in the one Body of Christ.

> *We being many are one body.* Remember that the bread is not
> made of one grain of wheat but of many. . . . Many grapes hang
> in a cluster, but their juice is mixed in unity. So the Lord has set
> His mark on us, wished us to belong to Him, has consecrated on
> His table the mystery of our peace and unity.[28]

But the bread and wine, after consecration—a consecration effected by the words of the Lord, who is the true minister of the sacrament—become the sacrament of the Body and Blood of Christ.

> What is seen has a physical appearance. What is understood, a
> spiritual. If, therefore, you wish to understand the Body of Christ,
> hear the Apostle speaking to the faithful: *You are the Body of
> Christ and the members* (1 Cor. 12:27). If you are *the Body of
> Christ and the members,* your own mystery has been placed on
> the Lord's table; you receive your own mystery. You answer
> "Amen" to what you are, and by answering you affirm; for you

hear: "The Body of Christ" and you answer: "Amen." Be a
member of the Body of Christ, so that your "Amen" may be a
true one.[29]

Much energy has been expended in the past in debate as to
whether Augustine holds a realist or figurative doctrine of the
eucharist—too much, perhaps. If one reads him with no particular
theological axe to grind, it is clear that both doctrines are
expressed—though not necessarily understood by Augustine in quite
the way that later controversialists understood them. The doctrinal
approach of the sermon just quoted is both different and in some ways
much bolder. In a mystery—and Augustine specifically employs the
word *mysterium,* with all its implications, pagan as well as
Christian—the grains of wheat and the individual grapes represent
individual Christian believers; they are ground and pressed to make
the eucharistic bread and wine. By consecration, again in a mystery,
they become the sacrament of the Body and Blood of Christ, by
partaking of which the believer is made part of the one bread and of
the one Body.[30]

Sermon 272, which I have just quoted, would have been
preached on the morning of Easter Sunday to the newly baptized, who
would already have communicated at the post-baptismal dawn liturgy
and were about to do it again. Another such sermon (227) expresses
the same doctrine.

> I have not forgotten my promise; for I promised those of you that
> have been baptised a sermon in which I would explain the
> sacrament of the Lord's table, which you now see once more, and
> of which you were made partakers last night. You ought to know
> what you have received, what you are about to receive, and what
> you ought to receive daily. This bread which you see on the altar,
> when sanctified by the word of God, is the Body of Christ. This
> cup—or, rather, what this cup contains—being sanctified by the
> word of God, is the Blood of Christ. Through these our Lord
> Jesus Christ has willed to entrust to us His Body and Blood,
> which He poured out for us for the remission of sins. If you have
> received them in good faith (*si bene accepistis*), you are what you
> have received. . . . What you see passes away, but the invisible
> reality which is signified does not pass away, but endures. Here
> the visible sign is received, is eaten, is consumed. Is Christ's
> Body consumed? Is Christ's Church consumed? Are Christ's

members consumed? By no means! *Here* they are cleansed; *there*
on high they are crowned. Therefore, what is signified will abide,
although the sign may seem to pass away.[31]

The idea of the many grains making one loaf and many grapes
making wine as a symbol of eucharistic unity is not an invention of
Augustine's. A century and a half before his day Saint Cyprian had
expressed a similar doctrine, as had Saint Irenaeus at an earlier date.[32]
Nor is Augustine original in his understanding of Christ as the true
celebrant at every offering of the eucharist. Before him, Saint Cyprian
had written:

> . . . if Jesus Christ, our Lord and God, is himself the great High
> Priest of God the Father, and first offered Himself as a sacrifice
> to the Father, and commanded this to be done in remembrance of
> Himself, then surely the priest truly acts in Christ's place who
> imitates what Christ did; and he then offers a true and full
> sacrifice in the Church to God the Father when he begins to offer
> it as he sees Christ Himself offered it.[33]

Nevertheless, Augustine was able to develop this notion of
Christ the High Priest. He does this particularly in Book 10 of *The
City of God,* when he had to attack the Neoplatonic endorsement of
the offering of sacrifices to the pagan gods who were, for Augustine
as for other Fathers of the Church, demons, fallen angels pretending
to be beneficent deities.[34] Augustine had to take account of the fact
that sacrifices had been offered to God, by His command, in the Old
Testament, and that in Africa the term sacrifice had long been applied
to the eucharist. He had to find an understanding of the notion of
sacrifice which would justify the Christian use, discredit the pagan,
and explain why the sacrifices of the Old Testament had become
unnecessary in the light of New Testament revelation.

Augustine clears the ground for this exercise by first asserting
that sacrifice is due only to God[35] (at a later date in the *Enchiridion*
he was to emphasize that the angels are not to be worshipped[36]), and
then that God has no need of sacrifices, quoting the psalm: *Thou art
my God, my goods are nothing unto thee* (Ps. 15[16]:2).[37]
Accordingly, "a true sacrifice is offered in every act which is
designed to unite us to God in holy fellowship."[38] Every act; for the
Apostle exhorts us to offer our *bodies as a living sacrifice, holy and*

acceptable to God (Rom. 12:1) and goes on to declare that *just as we have many members in one body, and all members have not the same functions; so we are many, but we make up one body in Christ* (Rom. 12:4–5). But this Body—Himself—is offered by Christ, as the Mediator, to the Father.

> . . . the whole redeemed City [of God], that is the congregation and fellowship of the saints, is offered to God as a universal sacrifice, through the great High Priest who offered Himself for us in His Passion in *the form of a servant* (Phil. 2:7), so that we might be the Body of so great a Head. In this form He offered, in this form He was offered, because in this form He is the Mediator, the Priest, and the Sacrifice. . . . This is the sacrifice of Christians who are *many, making up one body in Christ.* This sacrifice the Church continually celebrates in the sacrament of the altar, well-known to the faithful, in which it is shown to the Church that in the offering which she makes to God, she herself is offered.[39]

These views of Book 10 of *The City of God,* written about 417, are repeated some ten years later in Book 19.

> . . . We ourselves, His City, are His best and most glorious sacrifice, whose mystery we celebrate in our oblations, well-known to the faithful, as we have argued in earlier books. The sacrificial victims which the Jews offered as a shadow of future things were destined to come to an end, as was declared by the divine oracles of the Hebrew prophets, saying that the nations from the rising of the sun unto its going down would offer one sacrifice, as we now see happening.[40]

Here, Augustine speaks of the Christians as "His City," thus identifying the Church Militant with the City of God. Yet he is emphatic that, in her daily life, the Church Militant is composed of both saints and sinners. "The evil are mixed with the good, not only in the world, but even within the Church herself," he says in one of his sermons,[41] and again: "The Church has evil members mingled with the good. After the Judgement, she will have all the good without the evil."[42] It would seem then that, for Augustine, time intersects with eternity in the action of the eucharist. In the eucharist we experience, in some measure, the holy fellowship which we hope to enjoy forever in the Kingdom of Heaven and thus have a foretaste of eternity while still in the body.

This is, clearly, a bold understanding of the eucharistic mystery, and it is worth considering what caused it to develop in Augustine's mind. The thoughts underlying it were not, as we have seen, original. The notion of the loaf made of individual grains of wheat and the wine made from the juice of many grapes is found in Irenaeus and Cyprian, while the latter teaches the doctrine of Christ the great High Priest, for whom the local minister acts as representative (*sacerdos uice Christi uere fungitur*).[43] Even the doctrine of the two Cities—one of God, the other of the devil—seems to have been derived by Augustine from the Donatist theologian Tyconius, and may well have been something of a theological cliché in Roman Africa. What caused Augustine to develop these ideas into the remarkable sacramental doctrine which he offers, in which the eucharistic worship of the Church becomes a foretaste of eternity?

Some possible explanations are easily ruled out. Augustine was certainly not inspired by the sort of aesthetic emotion which is said to have persuaded the embassy of King Vladimir of Kiev to commend the Greek liturgy in the tenth century, after a visit to Hagia Sophia at Constantinople: "And we did not know whether we were in heaven or upon earth; for on earth there is no such splendour or such beauty and we are at a loss to describe it. We only know that God dwells there among men, . . . for we cannot forget that beauty."[44] No such verdict could have been passed on Augustine's church at Hippo, where the decoration and ceremonial would have been of the simplest and plainest, with the bishop in his black *birrus* (a kind of cassock), his clergy similarly attired, and the liturgical emphasis upon dignity rather than emotion and visual splendor.

Again, with the best will in the world, it would have been difficult for Augustine to have been carried away by any prayerful devotion on the part of his congregation, even if he had not been restrained by his grim doctrine of predestination, and his belief that God has no absolute will to save the whole of humankind. Whatever its merits, the congregation of Hippo had its full share of members who fell short of the ideals of the Gospel, as Augustine was all too well aware. God's judgments are inscrutable and His ways past finding out, but it would have been difficult for their pastor to believe that every member of his flock was destined to be a citizen of the

eternal Jerusalem. It was required of every intending communicant
that he should be free from open and grievous sin, but only God who
searches the heart and reins is aware of the secrets of the human
conscience.

It would therefore seem that Augustine's understanding of the
Church as a eucharistic community was based upon deeper and more
profound considerations than the day-to-day experience of episcopal
ministry, which often came close to what today are reckoned the
duties of a parish priest. It was based, in the first instance, on the
notion of Christ, the Mediator between God and man, that principle
upon which the Christian message rests. To that fundamental doctrine
was added the conception of Christ, the great High Priest, who offered
Himself as the one, true, perfect and sufficient sacrifice, oblation and
satisfaction on Calvary, and commanded that that sacrifice should be
continually shown forth in the worship of the Church which He
founded, until His coming again. The passage from Book 10 of *The
City of God* which illustrates this is so familiar, but it is so wholly
appropriate that I cannot forbear to cite it. It occurs in Chapter 20. In
the previous chapter Augustine had been denouncing those like the
Neoplatonist Porphyry, who thought that divine honors, which are due
to God alone, might be offered to angels, who are, in Augustine's
view, fallen angels, evil spirits who bar the way to God, appropriating
to themselves a false claim to divine status.

> For this reason the true Mediator, inasmuch as, taking *the form of
> a servant* (Phil. 2:17) He was made the Mediator *between God
> and man, the man Christ Jesus* (1 Tim. 2:5), although *in the form
> of God* (Phil. 2:6) He receives sacrifice with the Father, with
> whom He is one God, nevertheless, *in the form of a servant,* He
> preferred to *be* the sacrifice rather than to receive it, lest by His
> receiving it, anyone should suppose that sacrifice might be offered
> to something created. Therefore, He is a priest, both making the
> offering and being Himself what is offered. It was His will that
> the daily sacrifice of the Church should be the sacrament of His
> [supreme] sacrifice; and the Church, which is the Body of which
> He is the Head, learns to offer herself through Him. The earlier
> sacrifices of the saints were differing forms of this one true
> sacrifice, since this one sacrifice was prefigured by many, just as
> an object may be described by different words, so that a great
> deal may be expressed without boring the hearer. All the false

sacrifices of the past have been superseded by this supreme and true sacrifice.[45]

It is possible to learn a great deal from this passage—for example, that there was a daily celebration of the eucharist in the African Church in Augustine's day. However, the central message is the priesthood of Christ and the self-offering of the Church through Him which, as we have seen, is effected by the communion of the individual believer. Yet, as we have also seen, participation in the eucharist is not confined to the living communicant. The departed are commemorated as members of the Church,[46] and Augustine has no doubt that they may derive benefit from the eucharist for unrepented sins in the case of the elect, though the offering is of no avail for the unbaptized or for grievous sinners.

> Therefore, when sacrifices either of the altar or of any sort of almsgiving are offered for all the baptized departed, they are thanksgivings for the truly good, for the not very good they are propitiations, while as regards the very bad, they are some sort of consolation to the living, though they are no help to the dead.[47]

Augustine here seems to provide the theology justifying the later medieval establishment of chantries, but that is not to our purpose here. Rather, we can see how, for Augustine, the departed are involved in the offering of the eucharist. In this he was in harmony with African tradition, which went very much further than he did in understanding the character of that involvement, so that it was necessary for conciliar legislation to forbid the giving of communion to a dead body at the funeral celebration for, as the Fathers very reasonably observed: "The Lord has said, *Take and eat,* but corpses are unable to take or to eat."[48]

Accordingly, for Augustine, the participation of the departed in the eucharist must be of a different order from that of the living communicant. Although he does not discuss the matter, the same presumably holds true for the angels, whose relation to the liturgy must resemble that of the saints: they are partakers of the eternal light,[49] which is God, and they know themselves to be a sacrifice to God, no less than other members of the Church,[50] but being without human bodies, they do not partake, as living human beings may do, of the sacramental bread and wine. Nevertheless, they are fed, and fed by the Word, who is Himself the bread of the angels. "In order that man might eat the bread of angels, the Lord of the angels was made man."[51]

Perhaps, by a kind of paradox, one might say that, for Augustine, we are fed here on earth with the sacrament of the Body and Blood of Christ in order that hereafter, with the angels, we may feed upon the Word Himself forever.

There remains a paradox. In Book 20 of *The City of God* Augustine puts forward his view that the thousand-year reign of the saints with Christ described in Revelation 20:4 is even now taking place, since the Church Militant is the Kingdom of Christ and the Kingdom of Heaven. Yet, within this Church are to be found both good and bad, both the man who fails to do what he teaches, and the man who both teaches others to observe the commandments and observes them himself.[52] Both these live side by side in the communion of the Church, and so are members of the Kingdom of Heaven, but only one is a true member of that Kingdom and of the eucharistic fellowship of the Church. Augustine is aware of the problem raised by this mingling of good and bad. In a certain sense, he says, there is a difference between the Kingdom of God as it now is, and the Kingdom of God as it will be, when there will be no evil members.[53] Accordingly he urges the communicant, when he says "Amen" to the words: "The Body of Christ," to make the "Amen" a true one, that is, by living as befits a member of Christ's Body.[54] In the eucharist we have an anticipation of the Kingdom of Heaven, but because of the character of life in a fallen world it can only be a brief anticipation. Perhaps there is a parallel here to what Augustine says in his description of the Vision of Ostia, that ecstatic experience enjoyed with Monica shortly before her death. In their discourse, mother and son lift up their minds in contemplation from the created world to the Supreme Wisdom

> and while we were speaking of this and panting after it, we touched it slightly by a supreme effort of our heart. And we sighed and left behind, bound to it, *the first-fruits of the Spirit* (Rom. 8:23), and we returned to the sound of our own mouths, where a word both begins and ends.[55]

After this short ecstasy, Monica and Augustine reflect together on its significance and decide that, if the whole created world could fall silent, and God speak alone

> not by any tongue of flesh, nor by the voice of an angel, nor by the sound of thunder, nor by the darkness of a parable, and we could hear Himself, whom we love in all these things, without them—just as we had but now reached out and in a swift thought touched that eternal Wisdom abiding over all things; if this could be prolonged, and other visions of a far inferior kind taken away, and this one alone might ravish and absorb and hide the beholder in its most inward joys, so that eternal life might be such as was that one moment of understanding for which we had sighed—would this not be: *Enter thou into the joy of thy Lord* (Matt. 25:21)? And when shall this be? Shall it not be when *we shall all rise again, but we shall not all be changed* (1 Cor. 15:21)?[56]

A similar understanding, I suggest, might hold true of our experience of the Church as she shall be hereafter, enjoyed in this present life in the eucharist. The anticipations of eternity can only be of brief duration. We are *in via,* on the way, walking by faith and hoping to arrive in safety, but we do not walk alone, for we have Christ for our guide and the companionship of our fellow-Christians on the way to the eternal Jerusalem.

> There we shall be at rest and we shall see; we shall see and we shall love; we shall love and we shall praise. Behold what will be, in the end, without end. For what other end have we but to come to the Kingdom which has no end?[57]

Notes

(Translations by the author, except where otherwise stated)

1. On the pastoral aspect of Augustine's work, see F. Van der Meer, *Augustine the Bishop,* English tr. Brian Battershaw and G.R. Lamb (London and New York: Sheed & Ward, 1961). On his eucharistic theology, see especially Wilhelm Gessel, *Eucharistische Gemeinschaft bei Augustinus* (Cassiciacum Bd XXI) (Würzburg: Augustinus Verlag, 1966). On his angelology, see Émilien Lamirande, *L'Église céleste selon*

Saint Augustin (Paris: Études Augustiniennes, 1963) and Goulven Madec, art. "Angelus" in *Augustinus Lexikon,* vol. 1, fasc. 1/2 (Basel and Stuttgart: Schwabe & Co., 1986), cols. 303–315.

2. *Epist.* 21 (*CSEL* 34.1.49–54).

3. *Conf.* 5.8.15 (*CCSL* 27.65).

4. Ibid. 9.13.37: "Et inspira, domine meus, deus meus, inspira seruis tuis, fratribus meis, filiis tuis, dominis meis, quibus et corde et uoce et litteris seruio" (*CCSL* 27.154).

5. See Van der Meer, *op. cit.,* note 1 above, cap. 13: "A Sunday in Hippo," pp. 388–402; A.-G. Hamman, *La vie quotidienne en Afrique du Nord au temps de Saint Augustin* (Paris: Hachette, 1979); Bonner, "The Church and the Eucharist in the Theology of St Augustine," *Sobornost,* ser. 7, no. 6 (London, 1978), 448–461, repr. in *God's Decree and Man's Destiny: Studies on the Thought of Augustine of Hippo* (London: Variorum Reprints, 1987), no. VI.

6. *De utilitate credendi* 16.34: "haec autem seposita ratione, quam sinceram intellegere, ut saepe diximus, difficillimum stultis est, dupliciter nos mouet: partim miraculis, partim sequentium multitudine" (*CSEL* 25.1.43).

7. *C. epist. Parm.* 3.4.24 (*CSEL* 51.129–130); cf. *C. litt. Petil.* 2.97.224: "antiquior est unitas Christi quam pars Donati" (*CSEL* 52.143).

8. *De vera relig.* 3.5: " . . . Si haec per totum orbem iam populis leguntur et cum ueneratione libentissime audiuntur; si post tantum sanguinem, tantos ignes, tot cruces martyrum tanto fertilius et uberius usque ad barbaras nationes ecclesiae pullularunt; . . . si tam innumerabiles aggrediuntur hanc uiam, ut desertis diuitiis et honoribus huius mundi ex omni hominum genere uni deo summo totam uitam dicere uolentium desertae quondam insulae ac multarum terrarum solitudo compleatur; si denique per urbes atque oppida, castella, uicos, agros etiam uillasque priuatas in tantum aperte suadetur et appetitur a terrenis auersio et in unum deum uerumque conuersio, ut cottidie per uniuersum orbem humanum genus una paene uoce respondeat: "Sursum cor habere se ad dominum," quid adhuc oscitamus crapulam hesternam et in mortuis pecudibus diuina eloquia perscrutamur, si quando autem ad disputationem uenitur, Platonico nomine ora crepantia quam pectus uero

plenum magis habere gestimus?" (*CCSL* 32.191–192). English tr. John H.S. Burleigh, *Augustine: Earlier Writings*, Library of Christian Classics, vol. VI (London, 1953), 228–229.

9. Tertullian, *Apologeticum* 37.4: "Hesterni sumus, et orbem iam et uestra omnia impleuimus—urbes, insulas, castella, municipia, conciliabula, castra ipsa tribus decurias, palatium senatum forum. Sola uobis reliquimus templa" (*CCSL* 1.148).

10. *Conf.* 9.12.32 (*CSEL* 27.151).

11. Possidius, *Vita Augustini* 31.5 (*PL* 32.64).

12. *Enchiridion* 29.110: "Neque negandum est defunctorum animas pietate suorum uiuentium releuari, cum pro illis sacrificium mediatoris offertur uel eleemosynae in ecclesia fiunt" (*CCSL* 46.108).

13. *Civ. Dei* 20.9.2: "Neque enim piorum animae mortuorum separantur ab ecclesia, quae nunc etiam est regnum Christi. Alioquin nec ad altare Dei fieret eorum memoria in communicatione corporis Christi. . . . Cur enim fiunt ista, nisi quia fideles etiam defuncti membra sunt eius?" (*CCSL* 48.717).

14. *Conf.* 9.11.27. (*CCSL* 27.149).

15. *Enchiridion* 15.56; 16.61: "Quae tota hic accipienda est, non solum ex parte qua peregrinatur in terris, a solis ortu ad occasum laudans nomen domini, et post captiuitatem uetustatis cantans canticum nouum, uerum etiam ex illa quae in caelis semper ex quo condita est conhaesit deo, nec ullum malum sui casus experta est. . . . Haec ergo quae in sanctis angelis et uirtutibus dei est ecclesia, tunc nobis sicuti est, innotescet cum ei coniuncti fuerimus in finem ad simul habendam beatitudinem sempiternam" (*CCSL* 46.79; 82).

16. Ibid. 15.57: "Sed de illa quae in caelo est affirmare quid possumus nisi quod nullus in ea malus est, nec quisquam deinceps inde cecidit aut casurus est, ex quo deus *angelis peccantibus non pepercit,* sicut scribit apostolus Petrus, *sed carceribus caliginis inferi retrudens tradidit in iudicio puniendos seruari?*" (2 Pet. 2:4) (*CCSL* 46.80).

17. *Ep. ad Galatas Expositio* 24.5: "Mediator ergo inter deum et deum esse non posset, quia unus est deus: *mediator autem unius non est* (1 Tim. 2:5), quia inter aliquos medius est. Angeli porro, qui non lapsi sunt a

conspectu dei, mediatore non opus habent, per quam reconcilientur. (6) Item angeli, qui nullo suadente spontanea praeuaricatione sic lapsi sunt, per mediatorem non reconciliantur" (*CSEL* 84.86).

18.　*Civ. Dei* 20.9.1: "Alio modo igitur intellegendum est regnum caelorum, ubi ambo sunt, et ille scilicet qui soluit quod docet, et ille qui facit; sed ille minimus, ille magnus; alio modo autem regnum caelorum dicitur, quo non intrat nisi ille qui facit. Ac per hoc ubi utrumque genus est, ecclesia est, qualis nunc est; ubi autem illud solum est, ecclesia est, qualis tunc erit, quando malus in ea non erit. Ergo et nunc ecclesia regnum Christi est regnumque caelorum. Regnant itaque cum illo etiam nunc sancti eius, aliter quidem, quam tunc regnabunt; nec tamen cum illo regnant zizania, quamuis in ecclesia cum tritico crescant" (*CCSL* 48.716).

19.　See G. Bonner, "Augustine and Millenarianism," in *The Making of Orthodoxy: Essays in Honour of Henry Chadwick*, ed. Rowan Williams (Cambridge: Cambridge University Press, 1989), 235–254.

20.　*Serm.* 192.1: "Deos facturus qui homines erant, homo factus est qui Deus erat" (*PL* 38.1012).

21.　Athanasius, *De Incarnatione* 54.5: Αὐτὸς γὰρ ἐνηνθρώπησεν, ἵνα ἡμεῖς θεωποιηθῶμεν (*PG* 25.192 B).

22.　*Conf.* 7.17.23 (*CCSL* 27.107).

23.　Ibid. 7.18.24: "Et quaerebam uiam conparandi roboris, quod esset idoneum ad fruendum te, nec inueniebam, donec amplecterer *mediatorem dei et hominum, hominem Christum Iesum, qui est super omnia deus benedictus in saecula,* uocantem et dicentem: *Ego sum uia et ueritas et uita,* et cibum, cui capiendo inualidus eram, miscentem carni, quoniam *uerbum caro factum est,* ut infantiae nostrae lactesceret sapientia tua, per quam creasti omnia. Non enim tenebam deum meum Iesum humilis humilem nec cuius rei magistra esset eius infirmitas noueram. Verbum enim tuum, aeterna ueritas, superioribus creaturae tuae partibus supereminens subditos erigit ad se ipsam. . . ." (*CCSL* 27.108).

24.　*Civ. Dei* 10.24: "Porphyrius . . . noluit intellegere Dominum Christum esse principium, cuius incarnatione purgamur. Eum quippe in ipsa carne contempsit, quam propter sacrificium nostrae purgationis adsumpsit, magnum scilicet sacramentum ea superbia non intellegens, quam sua ille humilitate deiecit uerus benignus que Mediator, in ea se ostendens mortalitate mortalibus, quam maligni fallacesque mediatores non habendo se superbius extulerunt miserisque hominibus adiutorium deceptorium uelut inmortales mortalibus promiserunt" (*CCSL* 47.297).

25. *Enchiridion* 15.56: "Haec in sanctis angelis beata persistit, et suae parti peregrinanti sicut oportet opitulatur, quia utraque una erit consortio aeternitatis, et nunc una est uinculo caritatis, quae tota instituta est ad colendum unum deum" (*CCSL* 46.79). See Lamirande, *op. cit.*, note 1, pp. 39–40, 80–81, 134–135.

26. But see *Enchiridion* 15.58 (*CCSL* 46.80–81).

27. *Enchiridion* 15.56: ". . . Templum enim dei, hoc est totius summae trinitatis, sancta est ecclesia, scilicet uniuersa in caelo et in terra" (*CCSL* 46.80).

28. *Serm.* 272: "Recolite quia panis non fit de uno grano, sed de multis ... Grana multa pendent ad botrum, sed liquor granorum in unitate confunditur. Ita et Dominus Christus nos significauit, nos ad se pertinere uoluit, mysterium pacis et unitatis nostrae in sua mensa consecrauit" (*PL* 38.1247; 1248).

29. Ibid.: "Quod uidetur, speciem habet corporalem—quod intelligitur, fructum habet spiritualem. Corpus ergo Christi si uis intelligere, Apostolum audi dicentem fidelibus: *Vos autem estis corpus Christi et membra.* Si ergo *uos estis corpus Christi et membra,* mysterium uestrum in mensa Dominica positum est: mysterium uestrum accipitis. Ad id quod estis, Amen respondetis, et respondendo subscribitis. Audis enim: Corpus Christi; et respondes, Amen. Esto membrum corporis Christi, ut uerum sit Amen" (*PL* 38.1247).

30. See Gessel, *op. cit.*, note 1, pp. 196–198, 202–204.

31. *Serm.* 227: "Memor sum promissionis meae. Promiseram enim uobis, qui baptizati estis, sermonem quo exponerem mensae Dominicae Sacramentum, quod modo etiam uidetis, et cuius nocte praeterita participes facti estis. Debetis scire quid accepistis, quid accepturi estis, quid cottidie accipere debeatis. Panis ille quem uidetis in altari, sanctificatus per uerbum Dei, corpus est Christi. Calix ille, immo quod habet calix, sanctificatum per uerbum Dei, sanguis est Christi. Per ista uoluit Dominus Christus commendare corpus et sanguinem suum, quem pro nobis fudit in remissionem peccatorum. Si bene accepistis uos estis

quod accepistis. . . . Quod uides, transit; sed quod significatur inuisibile, non transit; sed permanet. Ecce accipitur, comeditur, consumitur. Numquid corpus Christi consumitur? numquid ecclesia Christi consumitur? numquid membra Christi consumuntur? Absit. Hic mundantur, ibi coronantur. Manebit ergo quod significatur, quamquam transire uideatur illud quod significat." *Sources Chrétiennes* 116.234; 242 (*PL* 38.1099; 1101).

32.　Irenaeus, *Adu. haereses* 3.17.2: ". . . Dominus pollicitus est mittere se Paracletum, qui nos aptaret Deo (Ioh. 16:7). Sicut enim de arido tritico massa una fieri non potest sine humore, neque unus panis: ita nec nos multi unum fieri in Christo Iesu poteramus, sine aqua quae de caelo est" (*PG* 7.930 A); Cyprian, *Epist.* 63.13: ". . . ut quemadmodum grana multa in unum collecta et commolita et conmixta panem unum faciunt, sic in Christo qui est panis caelestis unum sciamus esse corpus, cui coniunctus sit noster numerus et adunatus" (*CSEL* 3.2.712). Cf. *Epist.* 69.5: "nam quando Dominus corpus suum panem uocat de multorum granorum adunatione congestum, populum nostrum quem portabat indicat adunatum: et quando sanguinem suum uinum appellat de botruis adque acinis plurimis expressum adque in unum coactum, gregem item nostrum significat commixtione adunatae multitudinis copulatum" (*CSEL* 3.2.754). See Willy Rordorf et al., *The Eucharist of the Early Christians,* tr. Matthew J. O'Connell (New York: Pueblo Publishing Co., 1978), 167–174.

33.　Cyprian, *Epist.* 63.14.4: ". . . si Christus Iesus Dominus et Deus noster ipse est summus sacerdos Dei patris et sacrificium patri se ipsum optulit et hoc fieri in sui commemorationem praecepit, utique ille sacerdos uice Christi uere fungitur qui id quod Christus fecit imitatur et sacrificium uerum et plenum tunc offert in ecclesia Deo patri, si sic incipiat offerre secundum quod ipsum Christum uideat optulisse" (*CSEL* 3.2.713).

34.　*Civ. Dei* 10.1: "Sed quia ipsi [Platonici] quoque siue cedentes uanitati errorique populorum siue, ut ait apostolus, *euanescentes in cogitationibus suis* (Rom. 1:21), multos deos colendos ita putauerunt uel putari uoluerunt, ut quidam eorum etiam daemonibus diuinos honores sacrorum et sacrificiorum deferendos esse censerent" (*CCSL* 47.272).

35.　Ibid. 10.4: ". . . sacrificium certe nullus hominum est qui audeat dicere deberi nisi deo" (*CCSL* 47.276).

36.　*Enchiridion* 15.56: "Vnde nec tota nec ulla pars eius [sc. ecclesiae] uult se coli pro deo, nec cuiquam esse deus pertinenti ad templum dei quod aedificatur ex diis quos facit non factus deus" *(CCSL* 46.79–80). Note the reference to deification: "[dii] quos facit non factus deus."

37. *Civ. Dei* 10.5: "Quis autem ita despiat, ut existimet aliquibus usibus Dei esse necessaria, quae in sacrificiis offeruntur? Quod cum multis locis diuina scriptura testetur, ne longum faciamus, breue illud de psalmo commemorare suffecerit: *Dixi Domino, Dominus meus es tu, quoniam bonorum meorum non eges*" *(CCSL* 47.276).

38. Ibid. 10.6: "Proinde uerum sacrificium est omne opus, quo agitur, ut sancta societate inhaereamus Deo, relatum scilicet ad illum finem boni, quo ueraciter beati esse possimus" *(CCSL* 47.278).

39. Ibid.: "profecto efficitur, ut tota ipsa redempta ciuitas, hoc est congregatio societasque sanctorum, uniuersale sacrificium offeratur Deo per sacerdotem magnum, qui etiam se ipsum obtulit in passione pro nobis, ut tanti capitis corpus essemus, secundum formam serui. Hanc enim obtulit, in hac oblatus est, quia secundum hanc mediator est, in hac sacerdos, in hac sacrificium est. . . . Hoc est sacrificium Christianorum: *multi unum corpus in Christo.* Quod etiam sacramento altaris fidelibus noto frequentat ecclesia, ubi ei demonstratur, quod in ea re, quam offert, ipsa offeratur" *(CCSL* 47.279).

40. Ibid. 19.23.5: "Huius autem praeclarissimum atque optimum sacrificium nos ipsi sumus, hoc est ciuitas eius, cuius rei mysterium celebramus oblationibus nostris, quae fidelibus notae sunt, sicut in libris praecedentibus [e.g., in Book 10] disputauimus. Cessaturas enim uictimas, quas in umbra futuri offerebant Iudaei, et unum sacrificium gentes a solis ortu usque ad occasum, sicut iam fieri cernimus, oblaturas per prophetas Hebraeos oracula increpuere diuina" *(CCSL* 48.694–695).

41. *Enarr.* 128.8: "Mali mixti sunt bonis, non solum in saeculo, sedet in ipsa intus ecclesia mali mixti sunt bonis" *(CCSL* 40.1886).

42. *Serm.* 223.2: "Ecclesia enim huius temporis areae comparatur, habens mixta grana cum paleis, habens permixtos bonis malos; habitura post iudicium sine ullis malis omnes bonos" *(PL* 38.1092).

43. See above, notes 32 and 33.

44. *Russian Primary Chronicle*, s.a. A.D. 987. For the ascetic character of Augustine's liturgy, see Van der Meer, *op. cit.,* note 1, pp. 317–324.

45. *Civ. Dei* 10.20: "Vnde uerus ille mediator, in quantum *formam serui* accipiens *mediator* effectus est *Dei et hominum, homo Christus Iesu,* cum *in forma Dei* sacrificium cum Patre sumat, cum quo et unus Deus est, tamen *in forma serui* sacrificium maluit esse quam sumere, ne uel hac occasione quisquam existimaret cuilibet sacrificandum esse creaturae. Per hoc et sacerdos est, ipse offerens, ipse et oblatio. Cuius rei sacramentum cotidianum esse uoluit ecclesiae sacrificium, quae cum ipsius capitis corpus sit, se ipsam per ipsum discit offerre. Huius veri sacrificii multiplicia variaque signa erant sacrificia prisca sanctorum, cum hoc unum per multa figuraretur, tamquam uerbis multis res una diceretur, ut sine fastidio multum commendaretur. Huic summo ueroque sacrificio cuncta sacrificia falsa cesserunt" (*CCSL* 47.294); cf. *Enchiridion* 16.62: "Ac sic per illud singulare sacrificium in quo mediator est immolatus, quod unum multae in lege uictimae figurabant, pacificantur caelestia cum terrestribus et terrestria cum caelestibus" (*CCSL* 46.82).

46. *Civ. Dei* 20.9.2, quoted above, note 13.

47. *Enchiridion* 29.110: "Cum ergo sacrificia, siue altaris siue quarumcumque eleemosynarum, pro baptizatis defunctis omnibus offeruntur, pro ualde bonis gratiarum actiones sunt, pro non ualde bonis propitiationes sunt, pro ualde malis etiam si nulla sunt adiumenta mortuorum qualescumque uiuorum consolationes sunt" (*CCSL* 46.108–109).

48. *Breuarium Hipponense,* can. 4 a: "Vt corporibus defunctis eucharistia non detur; dictum est enim a Domino: *Accipite et edite*; cadauera autem nec accipere possunt nec edere" (*CCSL* 149.33–34).

49. *Civ. Dei* 11.9: "Cum enim dixit Deus: *Fiat lux,* et facta est lux, si recte in hac luce creatio intelligitur angelorum, profecto facti sunt participes lucis aeternae, quod est ipsa incommutabilis sapientia Dei, per quam facti sunt omnia, quem dicimus unigenitum Dei filium" (*CCSL* 48.329–330).

50. Ibid. 10.7: "nolunt [angeli] nos sibi sacrificari, sed ei, cuius et ipsi nobiscum sacrificium se esse nouerunt;" (25) "Haec est gloriosissima ciuitas Dei; haec unum Deum nouit et colit; hanc angeli sancti adnuntiauerunt, qui nos ad eius societatem inuitauerunt ciuesque suos in illa esse uoluerunt; quibus non placet ut eos colamus tamquam nostros deos, sed cum eis et illorum et nostrum Deum; nec eis

sacrificemus, sed cum ipsis sacrificium simus Deo" (*CCSL* 47.279; 300).

51. *Serm.* 126.5.6: "In sublimibus thronis, in partibus coelorum, in his quae supra coelos sunt, uidetur Verbum ab angelis, et gaudetur, et manducatur, et permanet. Sed ut panem angelorum manducaret homo, Dominus angelorum factus est homo. Haec est salus nostra: medicina infirmorum, cibus sanorum" (*PL* 38.701).

52. *Civ. Dei* 20.9.1, quoted above, note 18.

53. Ibid.

54. *Serm.* 272, quoted above, note 29; cf. *Serm.* 227: "Si bene accepistis, uos estis quod accepistis." Quoted above, note 31.

55. *Conf.* 9.10.24: "Et dum loquimur et inhiamus illi, attingimus eam modice toto ictu cordis; et suspirauimus et reliquimus ibi religatas *primitias spiritus* et remeauimus ad strepitum oris nostri, ubi uerbum et incipitur et finitur" (*CCSL* 27.147–148).

56. Ibid. 9.10.25: ". . . ut audiamus uerbum eius, non per linguam carnis neque per uocem angeli nec per sonitum nubis nec per aenigma similitudinis, sed ipsum, quem in his amamus, ipsum sine his audiamus, sicut nunc extendimus nos et rapida cogitatione attingimus aeternam sapientiam super omnia manentem, si continuetur hoc et subtrahantur aliae uisiones longe imparis generis et haec una rapiat et absorbeat et recondat in interiora gaudia spectatorem suum, ut talis sit sempiterna uita, quale fuit hoc momentum intellegentiae, cui suspirauimus, nonne hoc est: *intra in gaudium domini tui*? Et istud quando? An cum *omnes resurgimus, sed non omnes immutabimur*?" *(CCSL* 27.148).

57. *Civ. Dei* 22.30.5: "Ibi uacabimus et uidebimus, uidebimus et amabimus, amabimus et laudabimus. Ecce quod erit in fine sine fine. Nam quis alius noster est finis nisi peruenire ad regnum, cuius nullus est finis?" (*CCSL* 48.866).

PLATE 4. Saint Monica, in anguish over her son's departure for Italy, meditates before the altar. Alonso de Orozco (1500–1591), *Recopilación de todas las obras* (Valladolid: Sebastian Martinez, 1554).

Augustine on the Resurrection

Gerald O'Collins, S.J.

People who do not dare to believe in Christ's resurrection because they have been intellectually intimidated might be referred to passages by Saint Augustine on the Easter mystery. A passionate and articulate intellectual, Augustine repeatedly highlighted belief in Jesus' resurrection as the heart of Christian faith, a belief that sets Christians apart from Jews and adherents of other religions.

In his *Commentaries on the Psalms,* for example, Augustine defines the faith of Christians in terms of the resurrection. Commenting on Psalm 101, he says:

> The praise (*laus*) of the faith of Christians does not consist in their believing that Christ died but in believing that Christ is risen. Even the pagans believe that he died. . . . In what does your praise (*laus*) consist? It consists in believing that Christ is risen and in hoping that you will rise through Christ. This is the praise (*laus*) of faith (*Enarr.* 101.7).

Having said that, Augustine quotes Paul: "If you confess with your lips that Jesus is Lord and believe in your heart that God raised him from the dead, you will be saved" (Rom. 10:9).

When commenting on Psalm 120, Augustine says something very similar about belief in the resurrection defining Christian faith and identity:

> Through the passion the Lord passed from death to life; and for us who believe in his resurrection he opened the way by which we also should pass from death to life. It is no great thing to believe that Christ died; even the pagans, the Jews and all wicked people (*iniqui*) believe that. Everyone believes that he died. The faith of Christians is the resurrection of Christ. This carries great weight with us (*hoc pro magno habemus*)—that we believe that he rose.

Once again Augustine goes on to quote Romans 10:9 (*Enarr.* 120.6).

One could enlist further passages from Augustine to illustrate his conviction that belief in the resurrection forms and fashions the distinctive faith of Christians. Often he appeals to Romans 10:9 as a scriptural confirmation of this claim. At the beginning of an Easter sermon, for example, he declares: "In the resurrection of Christ our faith finds its stability (*constabilita est*). Even pagans, non-believers (*impii*) and Jews believe in the suffering of Christ, only Christians in his resurrection" (*Serm.* 233.1).

Against Faustus the Manichean, Augustine writes: "Even the pagans believe that Christ died: that Christ rose is the particular faith of Christians." Augustine goes straight on to quote Romans 10:9 in support of his claim (*C. Faustum* 16.29).[1]

For this essay I have chosen to sketch six major points in Augustine's reflections on Christ's resurrection. While a full-scale treatment of his understanding and interpretation of Easter would include much more material, these six points can serve to sample and illustrate what he has to say about the resurrection of the crucified Jesus. By comparing Augustine with other writers, we can discover and express the enduring value of his approach to the paschal mystery.

My first point concerns what I have just mentioned: resurrection faith identifies Christians for Augustine and is of fundamental importance to them. His Easter sermons, not to mention other writings, vividly witness to his conviction that faith in the resurrection sets Christians apart from others.

In the twentieth century one of the most interesting theological debates has been that between Karl Barth (1886–1968) and Rudolf Bultmann (1884–1976) over the resurrection. With his mildly critical review of Barth's 1924 book, *The Resurrection of the Dead,* Bultmann initiated this debate which lasted into the 1950s. Whatever their disagreements over the interpretation of the resurrection, Barth remained satisfied that he and Bultmann were in agreement on its central importance.

In his *Church Dogmatics* Barth wrote: "We must at least give him [Bultmann] credit for emphasizing the central and indispensable function of the event of Easter for all that is thought and said in the New Testament." Barth went on to compare Bultmann favorably with W.G. Kummel and Oscar Cullmann for not having neglected the resurrection as they did.[2] Barth's complaint could be directed against many other theologians and exegetes for failing to pay sufficient attention to the resurrection.

What is perhaps more serious has been the failure on the part of some Christian theologians to introduce the theme when interpreting their faith in Jesus to adherents of the great religions of Asia. In this inter-religious dialogue some Christians accentuate the incarnation, the Jesus of history and the cosmic Logos, but omit or practically omit the resurrection of the crucified Christ.[3] Augustine would find this astonishing. For him the resurrection is the central element, which distinguishes and identifies the faith of Christians.

Why hold this faith? What could explain and justify belief in Jesus' resurrection? These questions lead to my second and third points in this sampling of Augustine's Easter theology.

Although he confidently observes in *The City of God* (22.5) that practically "the whole world" now believes in Christ's resurrection, Augustine feels that some apologetic is in order. His first argument comes from the miracle of the world itself and from all the marvels we observe in it. "Why then," he asks, "cannot God make the bodies of the dead to rise again . . . seeing that he has filled heaven, earth, air and water so full of innumerable miracles, and that the world, which he made, is a greater miracle than any it contains?" (21.7). The innumerable wonders in the world (21.7–8) and the wonder that is the whole created world, "the most admirable work of all" (21.9), convinces Augustine that God can and will raise the dead. In short, the sheer wonder of God's creation lends credibility to our belief in the new creation of resurrection.

If nature makes the resurrection believable, so too does human history. Augustine argues from the visible effect which his audience could see for themselves (practically the whole Roman society by that time believing in the resurrection) to the only adequate cause for this historical phenomenon, Christ's victory over death. Given the fact that the apostolic witnesses were "of no social standing, the dregs of society, very few in number and unlearned," the success of this message about the resurrection cannot be explained through mere human resources. God must have been working in these people and attesting the truth of their message. Unless one accepts the resurrection, one cannot account for the "incredible" historical truth that "a handful of men, untrained in the liberal arts and thoroughly uneducated in philosophy, without any knowledge of literature, with no training in dialectics, without any high-sounding rhetoric, were sent by Christ as fishermen into the sea of this world with nets of faith only—and still more wonderful because rarer—(these fishermen) caught many fish of every kind, even in fact some philosophers" (22.5).

Martyrdom and associated miracles constitute Augustine's second argument, as further signs that confirm the truth of Christ's resurrection. There is a radical contrast between Roman heroes and the authentic heroism of the martyrs whom Christians honor (4.20.30; 5.14; 8.27). These martyrs are worlds apart from pagan vainglory, superstition, and magic. Their deaths have witnessed to the truth of God and Christ's resurrection (10.22; 13.5; 18.50) and to the way "the heat of love" keeps out "the cold of fear" (18.50).

Augustine refers to the miracles which continue to occur through the intercession of martyrs. Miracles show the power of the risen Christ in whom they believed and for whom they died: "For this faith they died, and now are able to obtain this power from him for whom they died. For this faith their endurance made the way for the power of these so powerful miracles to follow" (22.9; see 22.5.8).

Martyrdom and miracles that come through the intercession of martyrs count as signs lending credibility to belief in Christ's resurrection and our resurrection to come. At the same time, Augustine emphasizes that the "miracle as great as any of the rest" is that "the whole world" believed the Easter message given by a small band of poor, simple, unlearned men. This miracle cannot be explained unless Jesus truly rose from the dead (22.5).[4]

Before the time of Augustine others like Origen and Saint Athanasius had argued that the birth and subsequent history of Christianity could not be adequately explained unless they were caused by the resurrection of Jesus. This kind of argument from the observable effects in Christianity to the only adequate cause has continued to turn up right down to our own day: for example, in Hans Küng's apologetic for the resurrection as found in his *On Being a Christian.* Without clinching his case completely, Küng directs us toward an effective point that could be added to Augustine's Easter apologetic.[5] It is not simply that the human resources of the first disciples cannot explain the highly successful propagation of their message. The fate of Jesus himself created problems that were, humanly speaking, insurmountable. His crucifixion was seen as the death of a criminal who died banished from the divine presence, cursed by God, and in the place and company of irreligious men (Gal. 3:13; Heb. 13:12–13). To honor anyone who perished in that way was an awful and profound scandal (1 Cor. 1:23). Can one explain either how the disciples themselves came to proclaim such a person as their risen Lord or how their proclamation enjoyed such a striking success, unless Jesus truly rose from the dead?

In short, Augustine's argument from the observable effects in the history of Christianity to their only adequate cause (the resurrection) maintains its validity. But the argument can and should be strengthened.[6]

I have been reporting the *external* signs which Augustine recalls in support of the truth of Christ's resurrection. What he does not do in *The City of God* is appeal either to the appearances of the risen Jesus recorded in Scripture (for example, 1 Cor. 15:5–8; Luke 24:34) or to the discovery of the empty tomb (Mark 16:1–8; John 20:1–2) as evidence that the resurrection had happened. Instead, Augustine points to the signs of martyrdom and miracles—above all, the miracle of the universal spread of belief in the risen Christ—which remain inexplicable puzzles unless one accepts the truth of his resurrection.

When he spoke about the resurrection, Augustine was speaking from his own experience of the Easter mystery. He knew the importance of "evidence from the inside," that is to say, the way resurrection faith correlates existentially with our personal experience and expectations. Augustine appealed not only to objective evidence "out there," but also to the subjective concerns that make us all open to the Easter message and its promise.

In a sermon for Easter Monday, Augustine highlights our hunger for happiness. "You all wish to live happily," he observes. "But what brings human happiness?" He looks at various this-worldly stratagems for finding happiness and expects that his audience's experience will lead them to share his conviction: "No earthly thing will make you happy." He invites his people to look at the risen Christ:

> He shows you what you ought to know if you wish to be happy.
> . . . In this life you cannot be happy. No one can. You are looking
> for something good, but this earth is not the home of what you
> are looking for. What are you looking for? A happy life. But it is
> not here.

This sermon ends with Augustine putting into the mouth of the risen Christ the following promise:

> I invite you to my life, where no one dies, where life is truly happy, where the food does not decay. . . . See where I am inviting you: to the realm of the angels; to the friendship of the Father and Holy Spirit; to the eternal banquet; to my fraternal friendship; finally, to me myself. I invite you to my life.[7]

As a vivid, masterful preacher, Augustine appeals to our longing for happiness that can make us ready to accept Christ's resurrection and the promise it communicates to us.

In his own way Karl Rahner took a similar line in explaining and justifying Easter faith. The genesis of that faith involves not only the external historical witness coming from Christ's first disciples, but also our transcendental hope. A radical orientation toward a total and lasting fulfillment of our existence opens us up to the Easter message. Christ is risen and we will live with him.[8]

This third point may put some nerves on red alert, especially for those who recall Ludwig Feuerbach's view that belief in the resurrection is *simply* the projection of our hunger for eternal life.[9] Augustine and Rahner would deserve Feuerbach's suspicion if they merely justified Easter faith in terms of subjective orientation: our search for full and lasting happiness (Augustine) or our dynamic, transcendental hope (Rahner). But both Augustine and Rahner recognize the importance of external signs and evidence: the miraculous, public spread of Christianity (Augustine) and the historical witness of the apostles (Rahner). In their different ways both Augustine and Rahner maintain or at least imply that public evidence converges with personal experience and expectations in creating and sustaining Easter faith.

This faith means and brings life—my fourth point. In a sermon for Easter Monday, Augustine declares: "The resurrection of our Lord Jesus Christ is a new life for those who believe in Jesus."[10] Here, as elsewhere, Augustine recognizes how faith and life are but two sides of one coin for us. It is in believing that we live. Transposing the same conviction to the level of God's activity, we can say that revelation and redemption are but two sides of one coin. The revelation that invites our faith is ultimately the same as the redemption that offers us life.

We find a parallel in the way Rahner brings together the salvific and revelatory force of the resurrection. Through this event, he writes, God "communicates himself to the world in the Son whom the resurrection definitely identifies and acknowledges."[11] Revelation and redemptive grace form the two faces of the one process that Rahner likes to call the divine self-communication.

Like Saint Paul (for example, 2 Cor. 5:17; Eph. 4:24), Augustine highlights the *newness* of life that comes through faith in the risen Christ and reception of baptism. In a sermon on the Creed he promises his audience that "putting aside the old condition and putting on the new person, you become a new creature, singing a new song, and you will receive an eternal inheritance through the new covenant" (*Serm.* 212.1).[12] This theme of newness recurs in Augustine's Easter sermons. In an Easter Monday sermon quoted above, he says: "the resurrection of our Lord Jesus Christ is the new life for those who believe in Jesus" (*Serm.* 231.2). Citing Romans 4:25, he declares: "He was crucified to show on the cross the death of our old man, and he rose to show in his life the newness (*novitatem*) of our life." In brief, "his resurrection renews us" (ibid.).

This motif of the newness of Easter life has remained vividly present in our liturgies down to the present. It was the theme of a superb Easter meditation by Ronald Knox,[13] and of what was arguably the best Easter address by Pope Paul VI.[14]

My fifth theme from Augustine, the newness of Easter life, primarily concerns the change which the resurrection of Christ brings believers here and now. But what has it meant to Christ himself and what will it bring us? Augustine's lapidary answer is: "Christ's resurrection shows us the happiness of future life" (*Serm.* 233, 1).

In *The City of God* (e.g., 13.22; 20.20; 22, *passim*) and elsewhere (e.g., *Enchiridion* 1.89–91; *Serm.* 243.3–9), Augustine tries to say something about the transformed nature of the risen body and to meet objections to this hope (e.g., *Civ. Dei* 22.11–15). He sums up his hope as follows: "In the resurrection every man shall arise with the same body that he had, or would have had in his fullest growth, in all comeliness, and without deformity of even the least member" (22.20). Augustine is concerned about the resurrection of those who did not attain their "fullest growth," the limit cases being those of aborted fetuses and dead infants (22.12–14; *Enchiridion* 52.85, 87). What can he say about the resurrection of those who grew up physically handicapped or were unfortunate enough to be eaten by wild animals or even cannibals (*Civ. Dei* 22.12.20; *Enchiridion* 52.88)?

This brings me to my sixth point: Augustine's reflections on the nature of risen life, in particular our own resurrection.[15] Even if he affirms the new and spiritual state of the risen body (*Civ. Dei* 22.21), his vision of that state, when we will be perfected in quantity and quality (22.19–20), remains strongly material. The risen saints will be able to eat, even though there will be no need to do so (13.22). An Easter sermon, which takes its cue from the risen Christ's appearance to Mary Magdalene, discusses the function of our various organs before and after the resurrection (*Serm.* 243.3, 4, 6). It goes on to celebrate the beauty of the risen body and the eternal praise the saints will give God (*Serm.* 243.8, 9). Nevertheless, both in this sermon and elsewhere (for example, in the passages from *The City of God* just indicated), Augustine's attention to physical detail risks reducing our risen state to that of the kind of improved earthly bodies which people heaven in much Christian art. Readers of Augustine can decide that for themselves.[16]

I want to end by firmly endorsing Augustine's principle of rising with "the same body." Our personal identity is somehow bound up with bodily continuity. To be the same person we must be the same body. But in what sense must we or can we rise with the *same* body? What counts here as bodily "sameness" or identity? In a way that Augustine never dreamt of, modern biology has discovered the enormous and constant interchange of matter with our environment. That knowledge makes it difficult to speak of someone being the "same" body at six, sixteen, and sixty. It is problematic to say that we keep or that we are the "same" body within our earthly history. That alone may make us even more hesitant to maintain Augustine's principle of bodily continuity between this existence and our risen life.

But I think we should and can do so, by noting the connection between our body and our history. Through our bodiliness we freely create and develop a whole web of relationships with other people, the world, and God. Our history comes from our body being in relationship. As bodies we have our history—from conception right through to death. As human beings we enjoy a bodily or embodied history. Through resurrection our particular embodied history will be raised from death. That human, bodily history which makes up the story of each person will be brought to new life. In a transformed mysterious fashion their risen existence will express what embodied persons were and became in their earthly life.

We can develop Augustine's conviction about rising with the same body to make the following claim: "In the resurrection everyone shall rise with the same bodily history which they had." I realize that to some my proposal might sound like pure poetry—in the pejorative sense of "pure poetry." Nevertheless, if one asks "what has made me what I am?" it has surely been my embodied history and not the millions of molecules which in a passing parade have at different moments constituted my particular physical existence. So I propose expressing resurrection as God bringing to a new personal life the total embodied history of the dead individual. In that way we can and should maintain Augustine's proposition, but adapt it to read: "In the resurrection all will rise with the same embodied history."[17]

* * *

I have selected and highlighted these six points from Augustine's teaching on Christ's resurrection. Augustine repeatedly maintained that belief in the resurrection formed and fashioned the distinctive identity of Christians. Second, he developed a double apologetic for Easter faith, arguing that the wonder of the created world lends credibility to belief in the new creation, which is resurrection from the dead. Along with this argument from creation, Augustine points to the "incredible" spread of the Church, her martyrs and their miracles as visible, historical effects for which there is only one adequate cause, the actual resurrection of Jesus. Third, Augustine appealed to our hunger for full and lasting happiness as the subjective condition which makes us open to Easter faith. Fourth, he holds together Easter faith and Easter life—or, in other terms, the redemption and revelation that reached their climax with the paschal mystery. Fifth, in elucidating the redemption effected by the resurrection, Augustine beautifully expresses the newness of Easter life. Finally, Augustine's principle of continuity between our earthly and our risen body should be maintained, at least in the sense of the resurrection of our embodied history.

Of course, there is much more to be said about Augustine's understanding and interpretation of the Easter mystery. At the very least, however, we can value Augustine for the firmness of his resurrection faith and his refusal to be intimidated from joining with Saint Paul in confessing that God raised Jesus from the dead (Rom. 10:9).

Notes

1. See further *Serm.* 234.3; *Trin.* 22, 17, 29; *Enarr.* 138.8; *Epist.* 55.2.

2. Karl Barth, *Church Dogmatics,* vol. 3, part 2, ed. George W. Bromiley and Thomas F. Torrance, tr. Harold Knight et al. (Edinburgh: T. & T. Clark, 1960), p. 443. For further details, see Gerald O'Collins, *Jesus Risen* (London: Darton, Longman, and Todd, 1987), 51–57.

3. See, for example, Paul F. Knitter, *No Other Name? A Critical Survey of Christian Attitudes Toward the World Religions* (London: SCM Press, 1985). This survey of Christian attitudes toward world religions has very little to say about Christ's resurrection (pp. 197–200; see also pp. 161–162, 177, 179, and 264). Among other things, this brief treatment misrepresents Rahner's understanding of the Easter mystery.

4. On the themes of resurrection, miracles, and martyrs according to *The City of God,* see Marthinus Versfeld, *A Guide to The City of God* (New York: Sheed & Ward, 1958).

5. Hans Küng, *On Being a Christian,* tr. Edward Quinn (London: Collins, 1977), 343–345.

6. For further details, see O'Collins, *Jesus Risen,* pp. 89–90 and 99.

7. *Augustin d'Hippone, Sermons pour la Pâque,* ed. and tr. Susanne Poque, *Sources Chrétiennes* 116 (Paris, 1966), 252, 254, 256, 258 (= *Serm.* 231.4.5).

8. Karl Rahner, *Foundations of Christian Faith: An Introduction to the Idea of Christianity,* tr. William V. Dych (New York: Crossroad, 1978), 268–278.

9. Ludwig Feuerbach, *The Essence of Christianity,* tr. George Eliot, Harper Torchbooks (New York, Evanston, and London: Harper & Row, 1957), 135–136; 170–184.

10.   S. Poque, *Sermons pour la Pâque*, p. 246 (= *Serm.* 231.2).

11.   K. Rahner, "Resurrection," *Sacramentum Mundi* 5, p. 331 (= *Encyclopedia of Theology: A Concise Sacramentum Mundi*, p. 1440).

12.   See *Sermons pour la Pâque*, p. 181, n. 2.

13.   See "The Risen Christ," *The Pastoral Sermons of Ronald A. Knox*, ed. Philip Caraman (London: Burns & Oates, 1960), 392–395.

14.   At Easter 1977, Paul VI said Christ "is risen, opening a new, boundless horizon for life. . . . A new world is founded; a new mode of existence is inaugurated." Death is "the dream which precedes a new day without sunset." On what Christ's victory means to us the Pope added: "[The risen Lord] makes us share in his resurrection. He gives us his Spirit and fashions in us a new heart which ought to renew our life and our love and which will contribute to the transformation of the earth" (*Osservatore Romano*, 12–13 April 1977, p. 1). See also Jürgen Moltmann, *Religion, Revolution and the Future*, tr. Douglas Meeks (New York: Scribner, 1969), 3–18, 42–62.

15.   On the quality and identity of the risen body, see M. Alfeche, "The Rising of the Dead in the Works of Augustine (1 Cor. 15:35–57)," *Augustiniana* 39 (1989), 54–98.

16.   In the case of Christ, Augustine linked the ascension with the resurrection as a further stage of transformation and glorification; see *Civ. Dei* 22.5.9; William H. Marrevee, *The Ascension of Christ in the Works of St. Augustine* (Ottawa: University of Ottawa Press, 1967).

17.   For Augustine's understanding of human bodiliness, see George Lawless, "Augustine and Human Embodiment," *Collectanea Augustiniana: Mélanges T.J. van Bavel*, ed. B. Bruning et al. (Louvain: University Press, 1990), 167–186, especially pp. 182–184. Augustine's high regard for the human body and its future, transformed destiny leads him to name the resurrection of the body as one of the key motives for Christ's incarnation (*Trac. Joh.* 23.6), along with the human fall into sin and the divine love (*Serm.* 174.2).

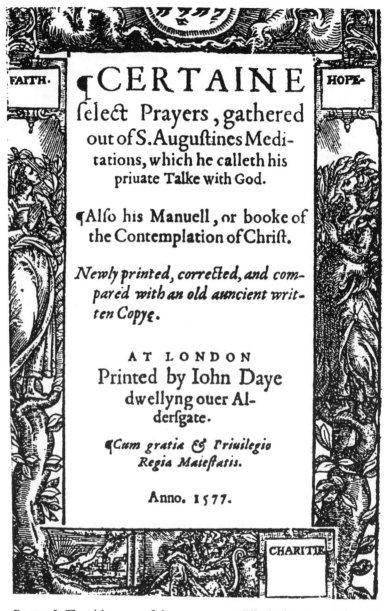

FAITH.

HOPE.

¶**CERTAINE**
ſelect Prayers, gathered
out of S. Auguſtines Medi-
tations, which he calleth his
priuate Talke with God.

¶Alſo his Manuell, or booke of
the Contemplation of Chriſt.

Newly printed, corrected, and com-
pared with an old auncient writ-
ten Copye.

AT LONDON
Printed by Iohn Daye
dwellyng ouer Al-
derſgate.

¶*Cum gratia & Priuilegio*
Regia Maieſtatis.

Anno. 1577.

CHARITIE

PLATE 5. The title page of the anonymous Elizabethan translation of the *Soliloquies* and the *Manual* published by the zealous reformer John Day (1522–1584). Pseudo-Augustine (13th century), *Certaine Select Prayers . . . Also his Manuell* (London: John Day, 1577).

Augustine on Nature and Human Nature

Elaine Hiesey Pagels

The enormous transformation in Christian perspectives on freedom and the power of the will which occurred as the situation of Christians changed from that of persecuted sectarians to that of the emperor's coreligionists, is accompanied by another element of Augustine's theology: the holistic view of nature that came to dominate Christian thought, and whose first principle is that human beings wield—or once did, through Adam—great power over nature (an apparent paradox, given Augustine's conviction that human beings, whose common ancestor had the power to transform nature, now are powerless to evade the consequences of that transformation).

For millennia, Jews and Christians have attempted to explain the mystery of human suffering as moral judgment—the price of Adam and Eve's sin. The creation story of Genesis, addressing the question Why do we suffer and why do we die?, makes the empirically absurd claim that death does not constitute the natural end of all lives but intruded upon our species solely because Adam and Eve made the wrong choice. According to Genesis, God said to the woman,

> "I will greatly multiply your pain in childbearing; in pain you shall bring forth children, yet your desire shall be for your husband, and he shall rule over you." And to Adam he said, "Because you have listened to the voice of your wife, and have eaten of the tree of which I commanded you, 'You shall not eat of it,' cursed is the ground because of you; in toil you shall eat of it all the days of your life; thorns and thistles it shall bring forth to you; . . . In the sweat of your face you shall eat bread till you

---

> return to the ground, for out of it you were taken; you are dust,
> and to dust you shall return." (Gen. 3:16–19)

Thus pain, oppression, labor, and death are punishments that we (or our ultimate ancestors) *brought upon ourselves.* "In the beginning" the willful choice of the first man and woman changed the nature of nature itself, and all humankind thereafter suffered and died.

Perhaps part of the power of this archaic story, from which Christians have inferred a moral system, lies in its blatant contradiction of everyday experience, its attribution of supernatural power to certain human beings. What Adam's supernatural power once effected, Paul declares, only Christ's supernatural power can undo: *"For as by a man came death, by a man has come also the resurrection of the dead.* For as in Adam all die, so also in Christ shall all be made alive" (1 Cor. 15:21–22). The gospels claim that Jesus' merest word could not only still a thunderstorm and heal diseases but call the dead back to life. In the Sermon on the Mount Jesus himself demanded that his followers control their own natures by taking moral responsibility for their acts, and mastering such instinctual responses as anger and sexual desire (Matt. 5:21–22, 27–28).

Zealous Christians of the first few centuries tested the extreme limits of human virtue (Latin *virtus,* literally "strength") by demonstrating their power over their own sexuality. Many early Christians also believed that they could triumph even over death, not only in the future resurrection but here and now, if they could break the power of natural impulses—above all, sexual desire.[1] According to the Gospel of Luke Jesus himself had said:

> *"The children of this age marry, and are given in marriage; but those who are accounted worthy of the age to come and the resurrection from the dead neither marry nor are given in marriage, nor can they die any more; for they are equal to the angels in heaven, and, being children of God, are children of the resurrection."* (Luke 20:34–36)

Inspired by such words, many Christians pursued that unnatural—or, as they would say, supernatural—life.

Yet stories of heroic ascetics, including the story of Jerome's protégée the young widow Blaesilla, who died in her attempted asceticism, raised obvious questions among Christians, as well as among their critics. What is the extent—and what are the limits—of human choice? What can we control, and what is beyond us? Can we actually govern sexual desire, suffering, and death, or do these conditions belong to the structure of nature? Are they "acts of God" and thus beyond our power—or is this power a matter of degree? Is death, in particular, *natural*? Or is it *unnatural,* an enemy, as Paul said (1 Cor. 15:26), intruding on human life because of Adam's sin?

During the formative period of Christian tradition, many thoughtful Christians struggled to understand not only the nature of the universe but human nature in particular. During the fourth and fifth centuries, certain Christians—including Pelagius, a devout Catholic ascetic from Britain—influenced by Greek science and philosophy, argued in his later teaching that human desires and human will, in themselves, have no effect on natural events—that humanity neither brought death upon itself nor could it, by an act of will, overcome death: death was in the nature of things, despite the clear statement to the contrary in Genesis. But Pelagius's contemporary Augustine vehemently rejected this view of nature, and the majority of Christians for more than a thousand years thereafter followed his example.

During his later years Augustine argued against those who agreed with John Chrysostom,[2] and then against followers of Pelagius, both of whom insisted that Christians, through their baptism, are free to make moral choices; that, although our will cannot affect the course of nature, it can—and must—effect our moral decisions. By 417, the city of Rome was so divided between the supporters and the opponents of Pelagius that partisans of both sides had actually rioted in the streets. Two years earlier, two councils of bishops in Palestine had declared Pelagius orthodox; but two opposing councils of African bishops, led by Augustine and his colleagues, condemned him and persuaded Pope Innocent, bishop of Rome, to take their side. When Innocent died, his successor, Pope Zosimus, at first declared Pelagius's teaching orthodox; but after receiving vehement protests from Augustine and other African bishops, he reversed himself and excommunicated Pelagius.[3]

By this time, too, Christian bishops had learned to use for their own purposes not only ecclesiastical censure but also imperial power.[4] During the battle against Pelagius and his advocates, many of them influential Romans,[5] Augustine and his colleagues openly courted the emperor's support. Augustine's friend and fellow African bishop Alypius brought eighty Numidian stallions as bribes to the imperial court and successfully lobbied there against Pelagius. The result gratified Augustine: in April 418, not only did the pope excommunicate Pelagius, but the emperor Honorius condemned the newly declared heretic and ordered him fined, expelled from office, and exiled along with his intransigent supporters.

The exiled Pelagius died soon afterward; but the most energetic of his followers refused to yield. Julian of Eclanum, an articulate and intellectual young Italian bishop, took up Pelagius's views and extended them. Julian even dared challenge the powerful Augustine, the most famous theologian of his day, and engaged the aging bishop in a battle that obsessed Augustine during the last twelve years of his life.

Augustine, summoning all his eloquence and fury, argued for a view of nature utterly antithetical to scientific naturalism. It was human choice—Adam's sin—that brought mortality and sexual desire upon the human race and, in the process, deprived Adam's progeny of the freedom to choose not to sin. Augustine amplified his argument in the six volumes of his *Opus imperfectum contra Julianum* ("Unfinished Work Against Julian").

Augustine's views prevailed, but the question is why? Why did the eloquent, passionate, and politically able Augustine finally succeed, after more than a decade of struggle, in having Pelagius's powerful supporters and friends, many of whom were monks, priests, bishops, and lay Christian persons, condemned as heretics, exiled, and deposed? How did Augustine persuade the majority of Christians that sexual desire and death are essentially "unnatural" experiences, the result of human sin?[6]

Certainly neither Pelagius nor Augustine set out to be "scientific" in anything like our sense of the word; neither, I suspect, would have regarded the term as a compliment. Instead, both began their reflections upon the natural universe with a common religious perspective, beginning with Genesis 1–4, from which each drew very different conclusions.

Pelagius, who shared the common Christian conviction that nature was good, as God created it, and that humankind was morally free, made in God's image, was dismayed when he first read Augustine's *Confessions.* For years Pelagius had respected Augustine's work, especially *On Free Will,* the treatise praising human freedom that Augustine had written as a young man. But when Augustine wrote his *Confessions* in his mature years, he declared that he had overestimated the power of human freedom. Now, he said, he realized that human beings are not free, as Adam was, to resist sin. We have no power to choose not to sin, and we cannot even control our sexual impulses. What is worse, "fleshly desire"—*concupiscentia carnis*—involves far more than its surface manifestations, which are only a symptom of deeper impulses that baffle, confound, and defeat our best attempts to control them.[7] Yet since everyone is conceived, as Augustine argued, through sexual desire, and since sexual desire is transmitted to everyone through the very semen involved in conception, he concludes, as we have seen, that all humankind is tainted with sin "from the mother's womb."

Augustine's theory was a radical departure from previous Christian doctrine, and many Christians found it pernicious. Many traditional Christians believed that this theory of "original sin"—the idea that Adam's sin is directly transmitted to his progeny—repudiated the twin foundations of the Christian faith: the goodness of God's creation; and the freedom of the human will. Most Christians agreed, at any rate, that even if before baptism we are stained by sin—Adam's sin and our own—baptism cleanses the believer from *all* sin, so that, in the words of the Egyptian teacher Didymus the Blind, "now we are found once more such as we were when we were first made: sinless and masters of ourselves."[8] In their argument with Augustine, Pelagius and his followers could claim the support of the revered fathers of the church, from Justin, Irenaeus, Tertullian, and Clement of Alexandria in the second century through John Chrysostom in the fourth.

According to his biographer Georges de Plinval, Pelagius himself had once agreed with the majority of his Jewish and Christian contemporaries—and with Augustine himself, for that matter—that

death came upon the human race to punish Adam's sin. Yet as
Augustine developed his view into a theory of human depravity,
Pelagius's followers came to argue the opposite.[9] Universal mortality
cannot be the result of Adam's punishment, since God, being just,
would not have punished anyone but Adam for what Adam alone had
done; certainly he would not condemn the whole human race for one
man's transgression. Mortality, therefore, must belong to the structure
of nature: mortality, which human beings share with every other
species, is not, nor ever was, within the power of any human being to
choose or reject.

Julian of Eclanum, the son of one of Augustine's fellow bishops,
and himself the bishop of a provincial town in southern Italy, saw the
controversy between Pelagius and Augustine engage Christians from
Rome to Africa.[10] Julian, who once shared the nearly universal
admiration for Augustine's learning and teaching, became convinced
that on the question of nature, the aging bishop was simply wrong. He
charged, too, that Pelagius's opponents had engineered his
condemnation through personal influence at court, bribery, and false
accusations. He himself intended to defend Pelagius's views through
the serious theological debate he believed they deserved. Thus Julian
championed and extended the ideas earlier expressed by John
Chrysostom and other Christian teachers in order to reduce to
absurdity Augustine's idea of original sin.

Augustine's enormous error, Julian believed, was to regard the
present state of nature as punishment. For Augustine went further than
those Jews and Christians who agreed that Adam's sin brought death
upon the human race: he insisted that Adam's sin *also* brought upon
us universal moral corruption. Julian replied to this that "natural sin"
does not exist:[11] no physically transmitted, hereditary condition infects
human nature, much less nature in general. To understand the human
condition, Julian says, we must begin by distinguishing what is
natural from what is *voluntary*.[12] Which conditions belong to the
structure of nature, and so to "acts of God" beyond our power, and
which depend upon human choice? What is natural, and therefore
beyond our will, and what is voluntary?

Such questions led both Julian and Augustine back to Genesis,
and each claimed its authority. Julian insisted that neither death nor

sexual desire troubled Adam and Eve in Paradise, for both death and desire were, "from the beginning," natural:

> God made bodies, distinguished the sexes, made genitalia, bestowed affection through which bodies would be joined, gave power to the semen, and operates in the secret nature of the semen—and God made nothing evil.[13]

What about death? Doesn't Genesis teach that death is punishment for sin? Certainly, Julian responds, but not *physical* death. He insists that the death one suffers as punishment for Adam's sin is different from the universal mortality natural to all living species. Although the Genesis account says that God warned Adam that "on the day" of his transgression, "you shall surely die," Adam did not die *physically*. Instead, Julian says, Adam began to die morally and spiritually from the day he chose to sin. Adam's progeny confronts the same choice that Adam faced. For God gives to every human being what he gave to Adam—the power to choose one's own moral destiny, the power to choose the spiritual way of life or spiritual self-destruction. As for original sin, "the *merit of one single person is not such that it could change the structure of the universe itself.*"[14]

But Augustine insists that through an act of will Adam and Eve *did* change the structure of the universe; that their single, willful act permanently corrupted human nature as well as nature in general. Augustine's position is paradoxical in that he attributes virtually unlimited power to the human will but confines that power to an irretrievable past—to a lost paradise. According to Augustine, human power alone reduced us to our present state, one in which we have wholly lost that power. In our present state of moral corruption, what we need *spiritually* is divine grace, and what we need *practically* is external authority and guidance from both church and state.

Augustine, in his debate with Julian, contrasts actual human experience with an imaginative reconstruction of our lost Paradise—human life as he believes it "ought to be," a condition in which women experience painless childbearing and enjoy marriage without oppression or coercion.[15] But now Eve is under punishment, for God had said to her, "I will greatly multiply your pains in childbearing; in pain you shall bring forth children, yet your desire shall be for your husband, and he shall rule over you" (Gen. 3:16). As a result, Augustine says, women suffer the nausea, illness, and pains of pregnancy as well as the painful contractions of parturition that accompany normal labor. Many women experience the greater agonies of miscarriage, or "tortures inflicted by doctors, or the shock and loss of giving birth to an infant stillborn or moribund."[16] According to Augustine, these sufferings are not *natural,* but prove that nature itself, as we now experience it, is diseased:

> *Nature, which the first human being harmed, is miserable.* . . .
> What passed to women was not the burden of Eve's fertility, but of her transgression. Now fertility operates under this burden, having fallen away from God's blessing.[17]

As woman's fertility brings involuntary suffering, so also does sexual desire: the blight of male domination has fallen upon the whole structure of sexual relationships.[18] In their dealings with men, as in the pains they suffer with their children, women experience the consequences of the fall. Augustine catalogues these sufferings like a man who has felt and witnessed them: some babies, he says, are born blind, deaf, deformed, or without the use of their limbs; and others are born into such other forms of human suffering as demonic insanity or chronic and fatal disease. Even the fortunate ones, the children born normal and healthy, Augustine says, evince the terrifying vulnerability that pervades nature: every infant is born ignorant, wholly subject to passions and sensations, bereft of reason or articulate speech, entirely helpless.[19]

As Eve's sin brought suffering upon women, Adam's sin brought suffering upon men, according to Genesis 3:17–19:

> Cursed is the ground because of you; in toil you shall eat of it all the days of your life; thorns and thistles it shall bring forth to you; and you shall eat the plants of the field. In the sweat of your face you shall eat bread till you return to the ground, for out of it you were taken; you are dust, and to dust you shall return.

As God had first created it, the earth was free of thorns and thistles, bringing forth a marvelous abundance of food, according to Augustine. Then Adam sinned, and "all nature was changed for the worse";[20] thorns and thistles suddenly sprang up from the once fertile land. God had placed man in Eden "to till it and to cultivate it," and before he sinned, Adam worked "not only without laboring, but, indeed, with pleasure for the soul."[21] But now, Augustine says, every man experiences pain, frustration, and hardship in his labor, as every woman does in hers: the miseries of human nature now beset both sexes "from infancy to the grave."[22]

Worst of all is what awaits us at the end—"the last enemy, death." In the beginning, God granted "the power to live, not any necessity of dying."[23] Death was in no sense *natural* but arose only after Adam chose to sin, bringing upon himself and all his progeny this dreadful agony, along with "the innumerable forms of illness that bring people to death."[24] Adam's single arbitrary act of will rendered all subsequent acts of human will inoperative. Humankind, once harmonious, perfect, and free, now, through Adam's choice, is ravaged by mortality and desire, while all suffering, from crop failure, miscarriage, fever, and insanity to paralysis and cancer, is evidence of the moral and spiritual deterioration that Eve and Adam introduced. Ever since Augustine, the hereditary transmission of original sin has been the official doctrine of the Catholic church.

Augustine thus denies the existence of nature *per se*—of nature as natural scientists have taught us to perceive it—for he cannot think of the natural world except as a reflection of human desire and will. Where there is suffering, there must have been evil and guilt, for, Augustine insists, God would not allow suffering where there was no prior fault. How, Augustine challenges Julian, could a just and all-powerful God allow infants to suffer

> the evils that nearly all infants suffer in this transitory life, if nothing calling for punishment were contracted from parents? Without a glance you bypass those evils which . . . all of us see them suffer. You say, "Human nature, at the beginning of life, is adorned with the gift of innocence." We agree, in regard to personal sins, but not about original sin. . . . You must explain why such great innocence is sometimes born blind or deaf. If nothing deserving punishment passes from parents to infants, who could bear to see the image of God sometimes born retarded, since this afflicts the soul itself? Consider the plain facts; consider why some infants suffer from a demon.[25]

In reply, Julian cites the New Testament Gospel of John, in which Jesus is asked whether a certain man was born blind because he had sinned or because his parents had sinned. Jesus answers, "Neither, but so that the glory of God might be revealed in him" (John 9:3), and proceeds to heal the man, restoring his sight. For Augustine, this story is irrelevant; what Jesus says about one man he healed cannot apply to people in general:

> These words cannot be applied to the innumerable infants born with such a wide variety of physical and mental handicaps. For many, indeed, are never healed, but die, disabled by their disabilities . . . even in infancy. Some infants retain the disabilities with which they were born, while others are afflicted with even more.[26]

Suffering *proves* that sin is transmitted from parents to children: "If there were no sin, then infants, bound by no evil, would suffer nothing harmful in body or soul under the great power of the just God."[27] To say that infants are innocent but suffer nonetheless, Augustine believes, is to abandon faith in divine justice. Augustine taunts Julian, "You see your whole heresy shipwrecked upon the misery of infants!"[28]

For Augustine, natural and moral evils collapse into one another. But Julian objects that "what is natural cannot be called evil," to which Augustine answers, "To say nothing of many other natural defects that afflict the body, we could regard natural deafness as an evil."[29] Such a perception of evil necessarily implicates everyone, for such infirmities as deafness are part of everyone's experience. What we now call *nature* we have come to know only in a state of chronic disease.

Julian predictably opposes this view and says that Augustine, like the Manichaeans, "defends natural evil . . . against the truth of the Catholic faith."[30] Christian faith, as Julian sees it, rests upon what he calls the five praises: the praise of creations; the praise of marriage; the praise of the law; the praise of the saints; the praise of the will. He rejects Augustine's equation of suffering with evil and guilt, and insists that nature is good—although, he admits, its "good" includes physical suffering.

Julian answers Augustine's reading of Genesis 3 point for point, claiming to have

> explained these things from the sound testimonies of the Scriptures, so that nothing remains of all Augustine's arguments and propositions that has not been refuted. . . . I proved that many things in his invention are false, many foolish, and many are sacrilegious.[31]

As for Augustine's claim that Eve's punishment has fallen upon all women, "This indeed is insane that the pains of parturition came into being because of sin."[32] Labor pains, which form part of "the condition of the sexes," have nothing to do with sin.[33] Innocent animals, including cattle, sheep, and cats, experience similar contractions to expel foetuses from the womb. If labor pains indicate sin, why do baptized women, released from sin, experience them as other women do? Furthermore, Julian continues, the severity of labor pains varies considerably. Arguing that extreme pain in childbirth cannot be regarded simply as a universal "given," Julian observes that

> certain barbarian women and nomads, accustomed to endure physical exertion, give birth in the course of their travels with such facility that, without stopping, they go out to gather food for their young, and continue on their way, transferring the burden of their womb to their shoulders; and, in general, village women do not require physicians for childbirth. . . . in fact, where luxury and softness increase, more women die in childbirth.[34]

But why does God say to Eve, "I will greatly multiply your pain in childbearing; in pain you shall bring forth children; yet your desire shall be for your husband, and he shall rule over you" (Gen. 3:16)? Julian insists that the passage means exactly what it says. The painful contractions that women, like animals, suffer are a natural part of the birth process (*naturaliter instituta*).[35] But the suffering involved in that natural process was increased and amplified in Eve's case to punish her disobedience. Man's rule over woman, Julian adds, forms part of the order of nature, "an institution of nature, not a punishment for sin."[36] Both Julian and Chrysostom concede, however, that male domination, like labor pain, while originating in God's "good" creation, may become, through sin, both painful and oppressive.

What about the man? Julian recalls the language of Genesis 3:17–19, emphasizing the words that refer to Adam's *experience* of nature:

> Cursed is the ground *in your works;* in sorrow *you shall eat from it all the days of your life;* thorns and thistles it shall bring forth *for you,* and you shall eat the produce of the field, in the sweat of your face you shall eat bread, until you return to the earth, for you were taken from it; for you are earth, and you shall return to earth.

Although the passage gives no hint that thorns, thistles, and sweat already existed on earth before sin, Julian asks, did these, then, as Augustine claims, spring up only after Adam's transgression, to punish Adam and his progeny?

Even before sin, Julian points out, Adam's task was to cultivate the garden (Gen. 2:15), as Eve's work was to bear children (Gen. 1:28). As contractions already formed a natural part of a woman's labor, Julian says, so sweating, exertion, and physical pain formed part of the man's. "Sweat is a natural help in physical exertion,"[37] not an innovation introduced to punish sin. Furthermore, Julian continues, just as in the case of women, the extent to which a man suffers in his work varies according to his physical condition, social position, and cultural situation. Not all men sweat in the fields; the rich do not labor, and not all who work sweat: "Some work with hard labor; others, with responsibilities." Some accomplish their work by thinking and writing, or engage in philosophy and learning; others choose, as their only "exercise" (*askesis*), an ascetic vocation.

What actually changed, then, after sin? For Julian the Genesis passage does not indicate a universal and permanent change in nature, or even in human nature, nor does the passage intend to express objective fact. Would God curse and blight the innocent earth because of human sin? Are we to believe Augustine that thornbushes and thistles—species previously nonexistent—suddenly sprang up on earth to torment us? No, Julian argues; instead, the passage expresses the subjective experience of one who sins. Calling the earth "'cursed in [Adam's] works'" expresses the viewpoint of a person who is spiritually dying," the emptiness of one who, having "failed to cultivate his own possibilities," projects onto the world his own sense of loss. Such a person foolishly sees the earth itself—indeed, all of nature—as cursed and afflicted. Yet, Julian adds—perhaps referring to the pessimistic Augustine himself—"this lie cannot injure nature, nor the earth, in this curse, but only his own person, and his own will."

The person who is spiritually dying, then, experiences nature as resistant, hostile, the source of nearly intolerable frustrations and disasters. So Cain and Abel, who shared the same human nature but differed in their exercise of will, experienced nature in entirely different ways. Abel successfully cultivated the fields and praised God for his abundant harvest. He experienced no evil at the hands of nature herself, but only at this brother's hands: "That first death clearly showed that it was not a bad thing to die, for the righteous one was the first one to die." But when Cain, on the contrary, chose to sin, polluting the ground with his brother's blood, his own act set him into an antagonistic relationship with the earth, "as if by a curse from the earth, as it is written: 'cursed are you from the earth'" (Gen. 4:11).[38]

For Julian, such sufferings are more than merely a projection onto the world of one's own anger, grief, and terror. Cain's story suggests to Julian that sin actually has the power to transform the experience of the sinner. One who first chooses to sin, and then becomes enmeshed in sin, actually experiences life as unremitting misery. As Julian sees it, Augustine is just such a person: one whose view of "vitiated nature" reflects back to him his own obstinate sinfulness. Such a person would see bodily death, too, as Augustine characterizes it, as the final and worst affliction of all, as a kind of punishment. To this Augustine angrily replies, How *else* could anyone envision our "last enemy"?

Julian answers that the sentence concerning death ("until you return to the earth from which you came; for you are earth, and you shall return to earth") shows God's mercy, not his wrath: "Through the promise of an end to suffering he consoles humankind." Everyone, "through the natural senses," remains vulnerable to pain, but God promises that every suffering known to humankind "is moderated by the specific span of time, as though God were to say, 'Truly, you shall not suffer this forever,' but only 'until you return to earth:'"

Our mortality is not the result of sin, but of nature! Why does Genesis not say, "because you sinned and transgressed my precepts"? This should have been said, if bodily dissolution were connected with a crime. But recall, what does it say? "because you are earth." Surely this is the reason why one returns to earth, "because you were taken out of it." If this, then, is the reason God gives, that one was from earth, I think it can be assumed that one cannot blame sin. Without doubt it is not because of sin, but because of our mortal nature . . . that the body dissolves back into the elements.[39]

That death forms a natural and necessary condition of human existence Christ himself confirms; for, Julian says, he teaches that God created and blessed human fertility, even before sin, to "replenish the earth" that was to be depleted by mortality.

Physical death merely offers us the necessary transition to eternal life, "so that in the corruptible bodies of the holy ones, eternal glory shall prevail, 'for this corruptible must put on incorruption, and this mortal must put on immortality'" (1 Cor. 15:53). Julian continues to quote Saint Paul:

"Death, where is your victory? Grave, where is your sting? The sting of death is sin . . ." That is, you, eternal death, who bear the sting of sin, wounding those who have abandoned justice, if you were not armed with this sting—that is, voluntary sin—you would not harm anyone![40]

Those who allow themselves to be wounded by sin and who live, consequently, in guilt, anger, terror, and despair, may experience, through their own fault, with unspeakable agony, the "sting of death." Yet, Julian adds,

you see this sin and this sting shattered by people of faith, who resist sin through God, "who gives us the victory." Such persons pass from corruptible life on earth to eternal life with God.

Julian says that "God created fully innocent natures, capable of virtue according to their will,"[41] not only in Paradise, but now as well. Human nature—mortal, sexual, and vulnerable as it is—participates in the wholeness and goodness of the original creation.

Augustine, when he looks at nature, sees the opposite. For Augustine, the truth of his own experience (and so, he believes, of everyone's) involves, above all, human helplessness. Three primary experiences—infancy, sexuality, and mortality—offer, he believes, irrefutable evidence of such helplessness. Julian, however, answers that "human nature in infants is whole and sound, and, in adults, capable of choosing [good or evil]."

But since Augustine believes that suffering comes from prior guilt, he rejects the moral innocence of infants and insists upon their helplessness, their incapacity to survive by themselves, much less to speak or reason. For Augustine finds the rage, weeping, and jealousy of which infants are capable proof of original sin, and he recalls his own infancy for confirmation. Augustine chides these "foolish new heretics," and especially their spokesman Julian ("O abominable and damnable voice!"), for saying that, even apart from sin, the natural human condition includes not only mortality but all its accompanying forms of disease and deformity. "Behold, then," Augustine mocks, "the Paradise of the Pelagians":

> Let us place there, then, men and women dedicated to chastity, struggling against sexual desire; pregnant women, nauseated, pale, unable to tolerate nourishment; others in labor, pouring forth immature foetuses in miscarriage; others, groaning and screaming in labor; and those that are born, all wailing, or laughing at one moment, then talking and babbling, later brought into school, that they might be taught to read, under the threat of whips, crying like girls because of an ingenious variety of punishments; and above all, innumerable diseases; incursions of demons, and attacks with various blows, some by which they are tormented, others by which they are consumed; and those, indeed, those who are healthy, are nurtured through difficult times of suffering through their parents' solicitude, for there are bereavements and mourning everywhere. . . .
>
> But the task is a long one, to relate how many evils abound in this life.[42]

In his later life, Augustine had only contempt for those who regarded sexual desire as a natural energy which every person may express or sublimate—who held that one's sexual impulses, in other words, are subject to one's will. For Augustine, these assumptions were facile and contrary to his own experience. What he believed instead was that we are helpless to control sexual desire; that "this diabolical excitement of the genitals"[43] arises in everyone, hideously out of control. Even in marriage he finds "boundless sloughs of lust and damnable craving."[44] If not for the restraints imposed by Christian marriage, "people would have intercourse indiscriminately, like dogs." Julian calls sexual desire "vital fire"; but Augustine admonishes us:

> Behold the "vital fire" *which does not obey the soul's decision, but, for the most part, rises up against the soul's desire* in disorderly and ugly movements.[45]

Julian believes that Augustine confuses sexual excess with desire itself; we must, he says, choose how we express that desire. Augustine replies in anger:

> Who can control this when its appetite is aroused? No one! In the very movement of this appetite, then, it has no "mode" that responds to the decisions of the will. . . . What married man *chooses* that the appetite be aroused, except when needed? What honest celibate *chooses* that the appetite *ever* be aroused? Yet what he wishes he cannot accomplish. . . . In the very movement of the appetite, *it has no mode corresponding to the decision of the will.*[46]

Bitterly, Augustine adds:

> You say, "In the married, it is exercised honestly; in the chaste, it is restrained by virtue." *Is this your experience of it?* . . . Indeed, since it is very pleasant, let the married effusively and impulsively seek each other whenever it titillates. . . . Let the union of bodies be legitimate wherever this, your "*natural good,*" spontaneously arises![47]

Julian was evidently restrained in sexual matters, and probably had little experience of the passions Augustine describes. Yet Augustine's question came from the heart, for the celibate Augustine was, by his own admission, insatiable, a man who never married and whose experience of sexual pleasure was illicit and guilt-provoking. Augustine assumes that frustrated desire is universal, infinite, and all-consuming. Julian, who had once—and probably briefly—been married to the daughter of a bishop, in a ceremony celebrated by a family friend as renewing the innocence of Adam and Eve, obviously wrote from a different kind of experience. For Julian, sexual desire is innocent, divinely blessed, and, once satisfied, entirely finite. Sexual desire, as Julian sees it, offers us the opportunity to exercise our capacity for moral choice.

Augustine concludes that not only are we helpless in infancy, and defenseless against sexual passion, but we are equally helpless in the face of death. We die; *therefore* we must be guilty of sin. For if we are not all sinners, then God is unjust to let us all die alike, even infants prematurely born, who have had no opportunity to sin.

If we are helpless before physical death, we are also helpless before spiritual death. This is a paradox; for spiritual death, Augustine says, comes from choosing evil; but even in our "free will" we are incapable of avoiding evil. *We choose evil involuntarily,* even "against our better judgment." Even when we want to do good, we cannot. "Is one driven, then," Julian asks, "by a captive will?" Yes, replies Augustine. "If a person is aware of the 'law of the [bodily] members,' and cries out with Paul, 'I cannot do what is good,' should you not say that the person is driven to evil by a captive will?"[48] So, Augustine concludes, physical death and spiritual death collapse into one: both rule over a lost humankind.

But according to Julian, here, too, Augustine confuses physiology with morality. Death is not a punishment for sin but a natural process, like sexual arousal and labor pains, natural, necessary, and universal for all living species. Such processes have nothing to do with human choice—and nothing to do with sin:

> Whatever is *natural* is shown not to be *voluntary.* If [death] is *natural,* it is not *voluntary.* If *voluntary,* it is not *natural.* These two, by definition, are opposites, like necessity and will. . . . The two cannot exist simultaneously; they cancel each other out.[49]

Although we are helpless before physical death, Julian says, *spiritual* death is a matter of choice. Here we are not mere animals but can exercise the free choice that God bestowed upon humankind in creation. Our free will engages us in the sphere of the *voluntary*—and the multiple possibilities available to individual choice: "Naturalia ergo necessaria sunt; possibilia autem voluntaria" ("Natural things, therefore, are necessary; possible things are voluntary").[50]

Although death is necessary and universal, each of us has the means—indeed, the responsibility—to choose the response we take to our mortal condition. Rather than resisting death as a mortal enemy, Julian says, the sinner may welcome death or even seek it as a relief from the sufferings induced by sin, while the saint may receive death as a spiritual victory. No one, saint or sinner, escapes suffering, which remains unavoidable in nature. Yet each of us holds in our hands our spiritual destiny, which depends upon the choices we make.

For more than twelve years Augustine and Julian debated, shouting back and forth their respective views, until Augustine died. After considerable controversy, the church of the fifth century accepted his view of the matter and rejected Julian's, having concluded that Augustine, the future saint, read Scripture more accurately than the heretic Julian. Recently, however, several scholars have pointed out that Augustine often interprets scriptural passages by ignoring fine points—or even grammar—in the texts. Augustine attempts to rest his case concerning original sin, for example, upon the evidence of one prepositional phrase in Romans 5:12, insisting that Paul said that death came upon all humanity because of Adam, "*in whom* all sinned." But Augustine misreads and mistranslates this phrase (which others translate "in that [i.e., because] all sinned") and then proceeds to defend his errors *ad infinitum,* presumably because his own version makes intuitive sense of his own experience.[51]

When Julian accused him of having invented this view of original sin, Augustine indignantly replied that he was only repeating what Paul had said before him. Had not the "great apostle" confessed that even he was incapable of doing what he willed?

> *I do not do what I will, but I do the very thing I hate. . . . So then it is no longer I that do it, but sin which dwells in me. For I know that nothing good dwells in me, that is, in my flesh. I can will what is good, but I cannot do it.* (Rom. 7:15–18)

Augustine's argument has persuaded the majority of Western Catholic and Protestant theologians to agree with him; and many Western Christians have taken his interpretation of this passage for granted.

But, as Peter Gorday has shown,[52] when we actually compare Augustine's interpretation with those of theologians as diverse as Origen, John Chrysostom, and Pelagius, we can see that Augustine found in Romans 7 what others had not seen there—a sexualized interpretation of sin and a revulsion from "the flesh" based on his own idiosyncratic belief that we contract the disease of sin through the process of conception. Other theologians assumed that Paul used these words to dramatize the situation of one who, still unbaptized and unredeemed, lacks hope; for Paul goes on to praise God for his own freedom, found in Christ:

> *Thanks be to God, through Jesus Christ our Lord. . . . For the law of the spirit of life in Christ Jesus has set me free.* (Rom. 7:25; 8:2)

Augustine alone applied the despairing expressions of the previous passage to the baptized Christian; other readers assumed that the triumphant and joyful note of the rest of the chapter expressed Paul's experience of his life in Christ.

Julian often attends more carefully than Augustine to the wording and context, but he, too, reads his own experience—experience very different from Augustine's—into the biblical texts. The controversy between Augustine and Julian, as the German scholar Bruckner says, comes down to a clash between "two different worldviews." Bruckner happens to side with Augustine, claiming that "the strength of Augustine's view must be in his 'deeper experience of life'" (which depths Bruckner does not elaborate).[53] Augustine's argument may be arbitrary, but Bruckner contends that his "*deeper religious experience* . . . more adequately interprets the contents of the Holy Scriptures than the *superficial rationalism* of Julian."[54] The British scholar John Ferguson disagrees and sides instead with his fellow Briton Pelagius. What Bruckner takes as evidence of Augustine's "deeper religious experience" Ferguson sees as his stubborn refusal to acknowledge the data of ordinary experience:

> There is another side to our experience, of equal validity, and that is our knowledge of our own free will. It is there that Augustine lapses alike from logic and from common human experience.[55]

And so, after 1600 years, the argument goes on.

If Julian's argument looks simple—merely common sense—that simplicity is deceptive. In fact, it presupposes a Copernican revolution in religious perspective. That we suffer and die does not mean that we participate in guilt—neither Adam's guilt nor our own. That we suffer and die shows only that we are, by nature (and indeed, Julian would add, by divine intent), mortal beings, simply one living species among others. Arguing against the penal interpretation of death, Julian says, "If you say it is a matter of *will,* it does not belong to *nature;* if it is a matter of nature, it has nothing to do with *guilt.*"[56]

Like Copernicus's revolution, Julian's threatens to dislodge humanity, psychologically and spiritually, from the center of the universe, reducing it to one natural species among others. He rejects Augustine's primary assumption that Adam's sin transformed nature. To claim that a single human will ever possessed such power reflects a presumption of supernatural human importance. When Augustine claims that a single act of Adam's will "changed the structure of the universe itself," he denies that we confront in our mortality a natural order beyond human power.[57] For Augustine insists that we became susceptible to death solely through an act of will: "Death comes to us by *will,* not by *necessity.*"[58]

Why did Catholic Christianity adopt Augustine's paradoxical—some would say preposterous—views? Some historians suggest that such beliefs validate the church's authority, for if the human condition is a disease, Catholic Christianity, acting as the Good Physician, offers the spiritual medication and the discipline that alone can cure it. No doubt Augustine's views did serve the interests of the emerging imperial church and the Christian state.

For what Augustine says, in simplest terms, is this: human beings cannot be trusted to govern themselves, because our very nature—indeed, *all* nature—has become corrupt as the result of Adam's sin. In the late fourth century and the fifth century, Christianity was no longer a suspect and persecuted movement; now it was the religion of emperors obligated to govern a vast and diffuse population. Under these circumstances Augustine's theory of human depravity—and, correspondingly, the political means to control it—replaced the previous ideology of human freedom.

Yet the requirements of an authoritarian state alone cannot account for the durability of such teaching throughout the centuries. We can see, too, that such interpretations of suffering as the result of sin are by no means limited to Christianity, much less to Catholicism. Jewish tradition has interpreted personal tragedy similarly, attributing, for example, the sudden death of an infant to the demon Lilith, to whose malevolence the child's parents had made themselves susceptible either through the husband's infidelity or the wife's insubordination. Some rabbis of ancient times would explain, too, to a young widow that she herself caused her husband's sudden heart attack by neglecting ritual regulations concerning the timing of intercourse.[59] Religions far from both Judaism and Christianity often express similar assumptions. A Hopi child is bitten by a poisonous spider while playing near its hole. As the boy hovers between life and death, the medicine man learns that the boy's father has neglected to prepare ritual ornaments for Spider Woman, the tribe's protector, which, he proclaims, has brought on his son's illness.[60]

The British anthropologist Evans-Pritchard tells the story of a sorcery investigation that followed the death of several Azande tribespeople who were resting in the shade of a granary that suddenly collapsed, killing them. The Azande fully recognized what we would call "natural causes": that the wood had begun to rot and crumble, that the nails had given way, that the supports were weakened by weeks of rain. The question was not why the granary collapsed, but why it collapsed at the very moment when these particular people could be trapped and crushed beneath it.[61] The Azande expected to find—and claimed to find—the cause of this disaster in human evil. But Jesus of Nazareth, referring to a remarkably similar disaster, challenged a similar assumption among his fellow Jews by asking, "Those eighteen upon whom the tower in Siloam fell and killed them, do you think that they were worse than any of the people who lived in Jerusalem?" and answering, "I tell you, No . . .".[62] But Jesus' dissent was an anomaly. The overwhelming weight of traditional Jewish and Christian teaching—and perhaps a human tendency to accept personal blame for suffering—implies that suffering and death are the wages of sin.

If Augustinian theology, or that of the rabbis or shamans who have also attributed suffering to sin, served only as a means of social control, why would people accept such sophistry? Why do people *outside* religious communities often ask themselves, as if spontaneously, the same questions, and give similar answers, blaming themselves for events beyond their power as if they had caused—or deserved—their own suffering?

The "social control" explanations assume a manipulative religious élite that *invents* guilt in order to dupe a gullible majority into accepting an otherwise abhorrent discipline. But the human tendency to accept blame for misfortunes is as observable among today's agnostics as among the Hopi or the ancient Jews and Christians, independent of—even prior to—religious belief. For quite apart from political circumstances, many people need to find reasons for their sufferings. Had Augustine's theory not met such a need—were it not that people often *would rather feel guilty than helpless*—I suspect that the idea of original sin would not have survived the fifth century, much less become the basis of Christian doctrine for 1600 years. I am not speaking, now, of cases in which guilt may be appropriate—cases in which people have chosen to take certain risks, or to inflict pain upon themselves or others, with predictable results. Instead I am speaking of those cases in which guilt seems to be an inexplicable, irrational, inappropriate response to suffering. But why would anyone *choose* to feel guilty?

One may know perfectly well the statistical possibilities concerning natural disasters, freak accidents, and life-threatening diseases and regard these—theoretically, at least—as fully natural phenomena. But when such events suddenly threaten (or spare) one's own life, questions occur, so to speak, in the first person. Like the Azande, one asks not what *caused* the earthquake, fire, or disease (for this may be obvious enough) but "Why did this happen now, in this way, to this person?"

What are we to make, I wonder, of this peculiar preference for guilt? Augustine would, I suspect, take it as evidence that human nature itself is "diseased," or, in contemporary terms, neurotic. I would suggest, instead, that such guilt, however painful, offers reassurance that such events do not occur at random but follow specific laws of causation; and that their causes, or a significant part of them, lie in the moral sphere, and so within human control. Augustine, like the Hebrew author of Genesis 2–3, gives religious expression to the conviction that humankind does not suffer and die randomly, but for specific reasons. Asserting one's own guilt for suffering may also encourage one to make specific, perhaps long overdue, changes. Guilt invites the sufferer to review past choices, to amend behavior, redress negligence, and perhaps by such means improve his or her life.

Psychologically simple and compelling, Augustine's view accords with responses that, for many people, arise as if instinctively in the face of suffering: Why has this happened? And why me? Augustine's answer simultaneously acknowledges and denies human helplessness; in this paradox, I suspect, its power lies.

To the sufferer, Augustine says, in effect, "You *personally* are not to blame for what has come upon you; the blame goes back to our father, Adam, and our mother, Eve." Augustine assures the sufferer that pain is unnatural, death an enemy, alien intruders upon normal human existence, and thus he addresses the deep human longing to be free of pain. But he also assures us that suffering is neither without meaning nor without specific cause. Both the cause and the meaning of suffering, as he sees it, lie in the sphere of *moral choice,* not *nature.* If guilt is the price to be paid for the illusion of control over nature—if such control is, as Julian argued, in fact, an illusion—many people have seemed willing to pay it.

By contrast, Julian offers a much reduced sense of power over nature. Our human ancestors no longer are the mythical, semimagic beings celebrated in Jewish legend—for instance, Adam,

> the ball of whose foot shone more glorious than the sun, whose radiant presence filled the universe with light . . . whose body spanned the continents, and whose shining face filled the angels with envy and awe.[63]

The Protestant Christian painter and engraver Dürer depicted the awesome power of Adam and Eve, as tradition had taught him, in vivid form. While they stand ready to take the fateful bite of that forbidden fruit, a cat waits at their feet, posed to pounce upon the unsuspecting mouse. Her capacity for murderous violence—and that of all living creatures—is about to be unleashed by human sin.[64]

Julian denies that the human will has this power over nature: "All that a person has from nature . . . he has from necessity" . . . since everything in nature depends upon an "immutable order."[65] Free will is not impotent, as Augustine argues, but it enables us "either to *consent* to wrongdoing, or to *refrain* from it." Free will provides the possibility of moral action. Julian might agree with the gnostic or Buddhist precept that "all life is suffering," yet he does not take this as an indictment of human existence, as if ordinary life were an illusion or the result of a "fall," or a form of spiritual death. Instead, Julian stands upon the Jewish and Christian tradition that affirms the essential goodness of the created world: "What is natural cannot be qualified by evil."[66]

Yet if suffering is necessary and normal, misery is optional. Misery, which Augustine equates with suffering, involves, as Julian sees it, human choice: it involves specific—and specifically *sinful*—ways one chooses to deal with natural conditions. One person accepts a terminal disease with patience, faith, and love, taking it as the occasion for spiritual growth; another rages against God and nature and weeps with self-pity and terror, turning inevitable suffering into nearly intolerable misery. So, Julian explains, although every one of us will die, "death is not always an evil; since, to the martyrs, for instance, it is for the sake of glory."[67] Julian would agree with the Buddhist teacher who pointedly rejects the usual Christian view of death as, in Paul's words, the "last enemy." For those who are on the path to enlightenment, "death is not . . . an enemy to defeat, but a compassionate friend." But those who choose to indulge in anger, envy, pride, and the consuming fears that suffocate faith, Julian says, experience the physical vulnerabilities common to our species with their pain "greatly increased" through their own fault.

Augustine's holistic, antinaturalistic view of nature—one in which Adam's will directly affected natural events, and in which suffering occurs solely because of human fault—appeals, then, to the human need to imagine ourselves in control, even at the cost of guilt. Julian's alternative, although more consonant with a scientific view of nature, is not in itself scientific but religious—a view that rests upon the ancient affirmation that the world, as originally created, is good, and that each person bears responsibility for moral choice.

Augustine's theology resembles the moralizing views of suffering that arise in many cultures, but with a difference. For unlike all other views, the Augustinian theory of original sin claims that our moral capacity has been so fatally infected that human nature as we know it cannot be trusted. Consequently, Augustine does not urge people to remedy their situation, as the Hopi shaman might, nor, like a rabbi, does he call them to moral reform; for humanity's moral disease is not only universal but also, apart from divine grace, incurable. Throughout Western history this extreme version of the doctrine of original sin, when taken as the basis for political structures, has tended to appeal to those who, for whatever reason, suspect human motives and the human capacity for self-government. The counterpoint to the idea of original sin expressed in the hope of humanity's capacity for moral transformation, whether articulated in utopian and romantic versions or in the sober prose of Thomas Jefferson, has appealed, conversely, to more optimistic temperaments.

Yet, Christians during the first centuries would not have imagined that their vision of a society characterized by liberty and justice could be the basis for a political agenda. Instead, most Christians, like many Jews, saw such freedom, and the elevation of the oppressed, as blessings to be anticipated in the Kingdom of God (as Luke says Jesus did). Among the Jews, the Essenes attempted to live out this egalitarian idea in their monastic community as a model of that coming kingdom; and certain Christians, too, like the author of the New Testament book of Acts, projected a similar ideal back onto the early Christian movement during the "golden age" of the apostolic church. Centuries, even millennia, would pass before such visions began to inform actual political aspirations and institutions; and only the most optimistic among us may still hope that such visions will one day achieve political reality.

Meanwhile, Christian practices and perceptions concerning sexuality, politics, and human nature changed from the first century through the fourth. After Jesus had called people to prepare for the coming Kingdom of God, and Paul proclaimed both its imminence and its radical demands, some intensely ascetic Christians in subsequent generations tried to put their teachings into radical practice, while others attempted to accommodate Christian teaching to existing social and political structures.

When state persecution pressed Christians to revere the emperors and the gods, the boldest among them, like Perpetua and her companions, defied government officials in the name of liberty and maintained their loyalty to Jesus, crucified for treason against Rome, as their "divine King," and others, like Justin, denounced the emperors and all their gods as the panoply of devils. These embattled Christians forged a vision of what Tertullian called the new "Christian society," which he boasted was marked by freedom from compulsion, voluntary contributions for the welfare of all members, mutual love, and common faith.

As the Christian movement grew, despite persecution, and increasingly developed its own internal organization, its leaders expelled nonconformists from their ranks, including gnostic Christians. They insisted that only orthodox Christians preached the true gospel of Christ—the message of moral freedom, given in creation and restored in baptism.

Some of the most intense Christians, who refused any compromise with "the world," sought to realize that liberty through the ascetic life, rejecting familial, social, and political obligations in order to recover the original glory of humankind, created in the "image and likeness of God." After the persecutions ended, asceticism offered a new path for uncompromising "witness"—a new form of self-chosen martyrdom.

Finally, just as Christian views of freedom changed when Christianity, no longer a persecuted movement, became the religion of the emperors, Augustine not only read into the message of Jesus and Paul his own aversion to "the flesh," but also claimed to find in Genesis his theory of original sin. In his final battle against the Pelagians, Augustine succeeded in persuading many bishops and several Christian emperors to help drive out of the churches as "heretics" those who held to earlier traditions of Christian freedom. From the fifth century on, Augustine's pessimistic views of sexuality, politics, and human nature would become the dominant influence on Western Christianity, both Catholic and Protestant, and color all Western culture, Christian or not, ever since. Thus Adam, Eve, and the serpent—our ancestral story—would continue, often in some version of its Augustinian form, to affect our lives to the present day.

Notes

1. Ton H.C. Van Eijk, "Marriage and Virginity, Death and Immortality," *Épektasis: Mélanges patristiques offerts au cardinal Jean Danielou*, ed. Jacques Fontaine and Charles Kannengiesser (Paris: Beauchesne, 1972), 209–235.

2. For a different perspective on John Chrysostom and Augustine in the Pelagian controversy, see F.J. Thonnard, "Saint Jean Chrysostome et Saint Augustin dans la Controverse Pélagienne," *Mélanges Venance Grumel* (Paris: Institut Français d'Études Byzantines, 1966), 189–218. Thonnard concludes that Augustine's view of original sin "ne manque ni de valeur scientifique ni de vraisemblance historique" (217).

3. For a detailed discussion, see Georges de Plinval, *Pélage: ses écrits, sa vie et sa réforme. Étude d'histoire littéraire et religieuse* (Lausanne: Payot, 1943); also the more recent study of Otto Wermelinger, *Rom und Pelagius, die theologische Position der römischen Bischöfe im pelagianischen Streit in den Jahren 411–432* (Stuttgart: A. Hiersemann, 1975).

4. Cf. Noel Quinton King, *The Emperor Theodosius and the Establishment of Christianity* (Philadelphia: Westminster Press, 1960). Constantine himself, the first Christian emperor, had deferred to the clergy as to his spiritual superiors; some sixty years later, Augustine's revered teacher Ambrose, the powerful bishop of Milan, literally brought the emperor to his knees. Ambrose had denounced Theodosius the Great for ordering a massacre of people in Thessalonica, and refused to allow the emperor to participate in communion until he had publicly repented.

5. See Peter Brown, "Pelagius and His Supporters: Aims and Environment," *Journal of Theological Studies*, n.s., 19, 1 (1968), 93–114; and "The Patrons of Pelagius: The Roman Aristocracy Between East and West," *Journal of Theological Studies*, n.s., 21, 1 (1970), 56–72.

6. For discussion of the social and historical events of Pelagius's condemnation, see the sources cited above, especially the studies of Plinval, Wermelinger, and Brown.

7. See the excellent discussions by Gerald I. Bonner, "*Libido* and *Concupiscentia* in St. Augustine," *Studia Patristica* 6 (Berlin: Akademie

Verlag, 1962), 303–314, and Peter Brown, "Sexuality and Society in the Fifth Century A.D.: Augustine and Julian of Eclanum," *Tria corda: scritti in onore di Arnaldo Momigliano,* ed. E. Gabba (Como: Edizioni New Press, 1983), 49–70; also Elizabeth A. Clark, "Vitiated Seeds and Holy Vessels: Augustine's Manichaean Past," in Elizabeth A. Clark, *Ascetic Piety and Women's Faith: Essays on Late Ancient Christianity* (Lewiston, N.Y.: E. Mellen Press, 1986), 291–352.

8. Didymus the Blind, *De Trinitate* 2.12.

9. de Plinval, *Pélage,* 344.

10. On Julian, see Albert Emil Bruckner, *Julian von Eclanum: sein Leben und seine Lehre. Ein Beitrag zur Geschichte des Pelagianismus,* Texte und Untersuchungen zur Geschichte der altchristlichen Literatur, 15, 3 (Leipzig: J.C. Hinrichs, 1897).

11. Augustine, *Opus imperfectum contra Julianum* 4.91. Hereafter cited as *Opus imperfectum.*

12. Ibid. 4.92–93: "Quidquid enim naturale est, voluntarium non esse manifestum est. . . . Istae duae definitiones tam contrariae sibi sunt, quam contrarium est necessitas et voluntas, quarum confirmatio ex mutua negatione generatur. Nam sicut nihil est aliud voluntarium, quam non coactum; ita nihil est aliud coactum, quam non voluntarium." Unlike Bonner, who agrees with de Plinval (*Pélage,* 360) that Julian concerns himself primarily with *libido,* I agree with François Refoulé, O.P., whose excellent article "Julien d'Éclane, théologien et philosophe" (in *Recherches de science religieuse* 52 [Paris, 1964], 42–84) shows that Julian concerns himself above all with the question of *nature* and *will.* Refoulé states clearly and accurately that "C'est . . . par sa notion de nature que Julien d'Éclane sépare fondamentalement d'Augustin. Toute sa polémique contre l'interprétation d'Augustin du péché originel se fonde sur une distinction rigoureuse entre *nature* et *volunté,* étrangère à Augustin" (67).

13. *Opus imperfectum* 4.40.

14. Ibid. 6.30: Non est enim tanti unius meritum, ut universa quae naturaliter sunt instituta perturbet. Emphasis added.

15. Ibid. 6.26.

16. Ibid. 4.114.

17. Ibid. 6.25. Emphasis added.

18. Ibid. 6.26.

19. Augustine often returns to this theme, as Peter Brown notes in *Augustine of Hippo: A Biography* (Berkeley: University of California Press, 1969), 397; for a few references, see *C. Julianum* 3.3–6; 9; *Opus imperfectum* 3.159; 198.

20. *Opus imperfectum* 6.27.

21. Ibid.

22. Ibid.

23. Ibid. 6.30, ". . . potestas vivendi, nec nulla moriendi necessitas."

24. Ibid. 6.27.

25. *C. Julianum* 3.3–5.

26. Ibid. 3.6.

27. *Opus imperfectum* 6.23.5.

28. Ibid. 3.109. For a fine discussion of Augustine's view of divine justice as it relates to original sin, see Yves de Montcheuil, S.J., "La Polémique de Saint Augustin contre Julien d'Éclane d'après l'*Opus imperfectum*," *Recherches de science religieuse* 44, 2 (Paris, 1956), 193–218.

29. *Opus imperfectum* 5.22.

30. Ibid. 1.1–2.

31. Ibid. 1.14.

32. Ibid. 6.26.

33. Ibid.

34. Ibid. 6.29.

35. Ibid. 6.26; for Julian's reply, 6.26–29.

36. For a fine and nuanced discussion of Chrysostom's position, see Elizabeth A. Clark, "The Virginal *Politeia* and Plato's *Republic:* John Chrysostom on Women and the Sexual Relation," in Elizabeth A. Clark, *Jerome, Chrysostom, and Friends: Essays and Translation* (New York: E. Mellen, 1979), 1–34.

37. *Opus imperfectum* 6.27.

38. Ibid.

39. Ibid.

40. Ibid. 6.40.

41. Ibid. 3.82.

42. Ibid. 3.154.

43. Ibid. 2.33.

44. *C. Julianum* 3.14.

45. Ibid. 3.13. Emphasis added.

46. Ibid. Emphasis added.

47. Ibid. 3.14. Emphasis added.

48. *Opus imperfectum* 3.109.

49. Ibid. 4.92. Emphasis added.

50. Ibid. 5.45.

51. For some discussion of the exegetical issues, see Gerald Bonner, "Augustine on Romans 5, 12," *Studia Evangelica* 2 (Berlin, 1968), 242–247; S. Lyonnet, S.J., "Le péché originel et l'exégèse de *Rom.* 5, 12–14," *Recherches de science religieuse* 44, 1 (Paris, 1956), 63–84;

also by Lyonnet, "Le sens de ἐφ'ᾧ en Rom. 5, 12 et l'exégèse des pères grecs," *Biblica* 36 (Rome, 1955), 436–456; A. d'Alès, "Julien d'Éclane, Exégète," *Recherches de science religieuse* 6 (Paris, 1916), 311–324; Harry A. Wolfson, "Philosophical Implications of the Pelagian Controversy," *Proceedings of the American Philosophical Society* 103 (Philadelphia, 1959), 554–562; A. Bruckner, *Julian von Eclanum,* pp. 114–123.

52. Peter Gorday, *Principles of Patristic Exegesis: Romans 9–11 in Origen, John Chrysostom, and Augustine* (New York: E. Mellen, 1983), 1–135.

53. A. Bruckner, *Julian von Eclanum,* p. 100.

54. Ibid., pp. 123–127. Emphasis added.

55. John Ferguson, *Pelagius: A Historical and Theological Study* (Cambridge: W. Heffer, 1956).

56. *Opus imperfectum* 6.35. Emphasis added.

57. Ibid. 6.30. "Man had it in his power not to die, had he not sinned."

58. Ibid. 6.35. Emphasis added.

59. *Midrash Rabbah,* Numbers 9, 4–10.

60. *Sun Chief: The Autobiography of a Hopi Indian,* ed. Leo W. Simmons (New Haven: Yale University Press, 1942), chap. 1.

61. E.E. Evans-Pritchard, "The Notion of Witchcraft Explains Unfortunate Events," *Witchcraft, Oracles, and Magic Among the Azande* (Oxford: Clarendon Press, 1976), 18–32.

62. Luke 13:4–5.

63. *Midrash Rabbah,* Gen. 12:6; 21:3; 24:2, *passim*; Louis Ginzberg, *The Legends of the Jews,* tr. Henrietta Szold (Philadelphia: The Jewish Publication Society of America, 1925), 1:49–101; 5:63–142.

64. I am grateful to Dr. Zephirah Gitay for sharing with me her research on Dürer's depictions of the Paradise story.

65. *Opus imperfectum* 5.49; cf. 3.103.

66. Ibid. 3.109. For further references and discussion, see Refoulé, "Julien d'Éclane," pp. 66–72.

67. *Opus imperfectum* 6.40.

Augustine on History, the Church, and the Flesh[1]

Paula Fredriksen

Augustine, as a late Latin Christian intellectual, inherited two opposing strategies for constructing reality. I will call these, crudely, the cosmic, intellectualist tradition (i.e., "Greek"), in the one instance, and the biblical historical tradition (i.e., "Jewish"), in the other. Christianity in all its varieties represents a multitude of sustained negotiations between these essentially different ways of looking at the world. I propose to lay them out briefly in this essay to show what is valued in each, and how each contributes to the formation of Christian tradition. I would then like to examine the situation in late Latin Christianity, so as to give a sense of the possibilities and problems facing Augustine as he addressed issues that, in his lifetime and for his community, had reached something of a crisis.

The Greek intellectualist tradition viewed material existence as a somewhat awkward fact: in light of its definition of God, the material world, or cosmos, should not really exist. Sallustius, a pagan author and near contemporary of Augustine's, remarked: "As the gods are incorporeal, the world ought to be incorporeal too."[2] This system defined its High God as transcendent, spiritual, radically perfect and thus unchanging. Yet, he (or it) stood as the ultimate source of a cosmos that was bounded by time, change, matter, and evil. It was an uneasy relationship.

The imagined nature of man repeated in miniature the stresses of this system: the fleshly body "fitted" the soul as poorly as the material cosmos "fitted" God. "Enchainment of past and future/ Woven in the weakness of the changing body"—the insulting mutability of the flesh pronounced its kinship with the material realm. But something marked man out, distinguishing him from other animals: Man had mind. The soul, the seat of the mind, expressed what was timeless and ordered and spiritual in man: it was, thus, that part of man most truly definitive of his self. The body, not quite real in the way the soul was thought to be, was only tenuously attached to who man really was. According to Plotinus, a third-century pagan philosopher, the body was more like a shadow cast by the soul—just, indeed, as the cosmos was a sort of shadow cast by the divine. Flesh served merely as the soul's inconvenient vehicle as it sojourned in the realm below the moon.

That, of course, is the question: What is a soul doing in such a gross material environment—the fleshly body, most immediately, but also the earth itself? To fully appreciate the question, we must consider the ancient cosmos as antiquity imagined it. Its architecture encoded a consistent hierarchy of order and of value: what was good was "up"; the less good, indeed the bad, was "down". Organized as a series of concentric spheres, the heavens themselves revealed the nature of the good. The outer- and upper-most sphere was the realm of the fixed stars; further downward and inward, motion: the spheres of the five planets known in antiquity, the sun, and the moon. Below the moon, in contrast to the harmony and increasing perfection of the upper spheres, matter grew thick, sinister, maddeningly mutable; hostile forces congested the sublunar atmosphere. Below this, finally, at the absolute center where the drossest matter had sunk, stood earth. And on earth stood the great human anomaly, the lonely sublunar outpost of spirit: Man.[3]

Man's mind provided the key to his liberation. His true self, the soul, if properly trained, would be drawn to reason, virtue, and the (literally) higher realities. While visions, ecstasies or dreams could provide man's spirit with a temporary liberation from its earthly bonds, the final great hope lay in death. With the body shed, the soul might progress up through the cosmos, back to its "true" home in the heavens. Man's final spiritual destiny was thus in principle, according to this system, non-terrestrial, non-corporeal, and individual: it lay in ascent to (or back to) the divine realm of the upper world. This redemption is also non-historical: time and cosmos do not alter. Man moves through them. The cosmos is thus a medium for redemption, but its locus and focus is the individual soul.[4]

Some version of these views on redemption stands behind Paul's pronouncements on this matter in his letters: the Kingdom is a heavenly commonwealth, not earthly (Phil. 3:20); believers join the returning Christ in "the upper air" (1 Thes. 4:16); 'flesh and blood cannot inherit the kingdom' (1 Cor. 15:51). Some version of it, too, stands behind Augustine's renunciation of Manichaeism in Milan, when Ambrose and various Neoplatonists enabled him, finally, to imagine a reality that was purely spiritual (*Conf.* 7, *passim*). And heaven has long been a familiar spiritual suburb.

Biblical historical tradition presents a different map of reality, a different view of God, a different concept of salvation, and, concomitantly, a different view of man. The paradigm is Jewish, its template Jewish history. The Jewish Bible begins with a God who wills to create the universe, who creates male and female in his own image, and who remains concerned throughout for the justice of human social relations. It ends (unlike the Christian Old Testament) with 2 Chronicles, the liberation from exile and a call to make aliyah: "Thus says Cyrus king of Persia: The Lord, the God of Heaven . . . has charged me to build him a house in Jerusalem. . . . Whoever is among you of all his people, may the Lord his God be with him. Let him go up" (36:23).

These two narrative poles of the Bible establish the typological field of later eschatology. The apocalyptic imagination projected Israel's redemption from Babylon onto the whole world and all peoples. When final redemption comes, it will come as a renovation of creation. Renewed human society will dwell on a renewed earth. God will intervene in history to end the exile of Israel both living and dead. At this point and by the revelation of the Lord, all the nations will have been redeemed, finally, from the error of idolatry. They too will gather at the new Jerusalem and together with Israel worship God in his new or renewed Temple.[5]

It is within this particular, and peculiarly Jewish, idea of historical redemption that we must place the hope of *tehiat hamatim*, the resurrection of the dead. In the late Second Temple period—the period that saw the mission of Jesus and the beginnings of Christianity—this belief was most associated with the Pharisees, though it is probably more accurate to say that (almost) everyone but the Saduccees so believed. Physical resurrection represents and affirms a particular theodicy, proclaiming that God is just and will thus vindicate the righteous, who through tyranny have suffered persecution in this life. "Person" is not primarily soul, but soul and body taken together. And the scriptural insistence on terrestrial redemption, the insistence that the *quality* of physical existence would be changed, but not the fundamental fact of physical existence itself, serves to affirm Creation.

Further, while individuals rise and are judged individually, the root metaphors of restoration theology are social: eating together, worshipping together, living in peace with one another.[6] And, finally, given the idiom of the Babylonian Captivity in which much of this construct is expressed, this historical redemption, implicitly and often explicitly, is political. The image of eschatological society serves as a counterpoint to and commentary on the unrighteous kingdoms that will be displaced by the Kingdom of God.

Christianity, even once its ethnic and cultural base had moved well beyond its original Jewish context, inherits fully this biblical, historical model of redemption. The ultimate literary shape of its foundational document, the Christian Bible, expresses its main refinement of the Jewish paradigm. For Christians, the record of God's relation to humans opens with Genesis and culminates with Apocalypse, or Book of Revelation. The Kingdom of God, for Christians, would be signalled by the *second* coming of Christ, whose Parousia would mark as well the resurrection of the dead. Indeed, according to Revelation, there would be not one, but two resurrections: the first, lasting for a thousand years, would involve only the saints (that is, martyrs); the second, after Satan's final defeat, would see a general resurrection and final judgment (Rev. 20:1-4). Thus, for all his "hellenistic dualism," the mid-second-century philosopher and apologist Justin Martyr fully expected a reign of the saints on earth, centered on a renewed Jerusalem in the land of Israel (*Dialogue with Trypho* 81). So did Tertullian, Irenaeus, and before them, Papias, who preserved Jesus' prophecy that, when the Kingdom came, the land would yield so many grapes and so effortlessly that each would compete to be first to jump into the mouths of the saints.[7]

Throughout the generations, many Christians continued to proclaim that Christ would return soon. But how could they know, precisely, when? One way was to study prophetic and evangelical catalogues of apocalyptic disasters and their cryptic descriptions of kings, armies, and empires, and see whether these matched the times. Particularly in periods of persecution, the features of the Whore of Babylon could swim suddenly into sharp focus. The author of Revelation, whose Babylon had straddled seven hills, clearly intended Rome (17:9). Irenaeus interpreted the beasts named in Daniel and

Revelation as "the empire currently in power"; 666, the number of the beast, encoded the name LATINUS. The persecution of the saints—God's New Israel—by this new Babylon clearly indicated that the end was at hand.[8]

Other Christians so inclined sought a less episodic way to know what time it was on history's clock. Liberating millenarian expectation from the tyranny of current events, they evolved a scientific method to calculate the time of the End. Psalm 90:4, quoted in 2 Peter 3:8, provided one building block of this tradition: "With the Lord, one day is as a thousand years, and a thousand years as one day." Another came from Revelation 20, the expectation of the thousand-year reign of the saints on earth with Christ. Genesis 1, with its sketch of the days of creation, provided another. Together, these gave scriptural foundation to a key Christian eschatological concept: the cosmic week, or the ages of the world. As God had created the world in six days, and rested on the seventh, and as a day in his sight is as a thousand years, so too would the world endure for six ages, or "days," of a thousand years each. Then at the end of the sixth age, six thousand years since the Creation, Christ would return in glory to establish his millenarian sabbath-rest with his saints (Rev. 20), in the first resurrection. To know the time of the End, one merely had to calculate the age of the world.[9]

This tradition, too, might strike one as bizarre, exotic, unfamiliar, and odd. In the formative period of Christianity, from the second to fourth century, it was anything but. In an age before a universal chronology (*anno domini* is a medieval convention—one that nearly cost Bede his reputation), it shaped Christian identity and, thus, the Christian sense of history in two important ways. First, it integrated the particulars of (recent) Christian revelation with the broad sweep and prestigious antiquity of Biblical history. And second, by imposing a plot on time, millenarian chronography supported the churches' image of their community as the pinnacle of God's efforts, the institution toward which all history led.

Its appeal was not universal. Great intellectuals such as Origen and his lesser disciples preferred to allegorize these biblical passages rather than integrate them into human time.[10] But sober chronographers applied themselves to the task of working out the age of the world. When Hippolytus and Julius Africanus, writing in the third century, calculated that the year 6000 since creation would fall in the year 500 by our dating system, they were not only pin-pointing the Parousia: They were also telling contemporaries to relax. Lactantius repeated the calculation in the early fourth century; and, in 397, Augustine's exact contemporary, the African bishop Hilarianus, reiterated that the year 6000 was a scant century off.[11] I would expect that Hilarianus's audience would be rather less relaxed than Hippolytus's.

This tradition, in any case, was fated not to age gracefully. After 312, with Constantine's sudden support of the Catholic church, its intrinsic anti-imperialism grew suddenly awkward. And as the long-traditional target date of 6000 since the Creation / 500 C.E. inched ever closer, we can detect a certain nervousness in ecclesiastical reports of plagues, battles, eclipses, and military campaigns. The collapse in 410 of the city of Rome, ironically, now signalled a Christian disaster. Augustine sarcastically parroted the millenarians' response. "Behold," he repeats, "behold from Adam all the years have passed, and behold, the 6000 years are completed, . . . and now comes the Day of Judgment!" (*Serm.* 113.8). Others, spurred by earthquake and drought, or, conversely, by the very success of the Christian mission since the conferral of imperial patronage, divined likewise that the times had been fulfilled.[12] Donatists, still hounded by the Empire (now in its Catholic guise), could point to the fact of this persecution to confirm both their own identity as the true church of the martyrs and the approach of the End. The ambivalence about nearing the end of the age, in other words, was just that: simultaneous attraction and repulsion. Dread could co-exist with eager anticipation of the reign of the saints on earth, and this was nowhere more true than in the bible belt of Latin antiquity, Roman North Africa.

We can discern the strength and ubiquity of this millenarian hope in the popular celebration of the cult of the saint. Catholic and Donatist alike, repairing, on the saints' day, to the tomb of the saint, would anticipate their coming earthly reign at the Parousia by feasting, dancing, and copious drink. The martyrs' relics would work cures—the restoration of bodily integrity, a kind of fleshly resurrection in microcosm. The reading of the martyr's *passio* would also inspire the faithful. Augustine loathed these *laetitiae,* or "jolly-ups," and condemned their enthusiasm as unseemly, their excess as sordid and carnal. His effort to reform his congregation's observances in Hippo very nearly cost him his job.[13] But as these Christians rejoiced around the martyrs' mensa, they likewise anticipated, and even affirmed through enactment, the Church's ancient hope that when the Kingdom came it would come on earth, and that once it did, labors would cease, social distinctions dissolve, life would be joy, food and drink would be abundant and got without effort.

So we come, finally, to Augustine. To his one side flourished energetic millenarianism, both popular and élite. As Christians feasted at martyrs' gravesites, the years ticked off in traditional chronographies bringing the year 6000 ever closer. And as the Catholic persecution of Donatists, in which he was so instrumental, gathered force, so did the Donatist identification with the tradition of the martyrs: the persecuted Church was the true Church. To his other side stood Manichean dualism, with its emphasis on the soul's escape from this universe as the measure of its redemption. Less exotic, and thus to Augustine more insidious, was the Pelagians' construction of person. Their insistence that the will was free and man therefore morally perfectable, that the sexual drive was morally neutral and certainly, through the free exercise of the will, controllable, and that flesh alone was inherited from Adam, tended too strongly toward that assumption, common to Manichees and pagan philosophers alike, that what was most truly human was the soul.[14] And behind him, finally, lay the ruins of Origen's reputation. Unlike the great Alexandrian theologian, Augustine was no longer free to allegorize prophetic texts radically or to present apocalyptic thought as a mere *façon de parler.*

Augustine argued tirelessly, in countless treatises, sermons, and letters, against these various opponents. We find his clearest statement against them all in the books of *The City of God.* It is there that his various arguments—hermeneutical, anthropological, philosophical, eschatological—come together in a coherent and audacious theology.

To the millenarians Augustine argued that the signs of the times cannot be read. Against inferring from the fall of Rome, or any other disaster, that the End was at hand, he observed that things had been worse and could always get worse: contemporary historical events are opaque and cannot be read in light of ancient oracles. And those evangelical prophecies bespeaking the *second* coming of the Son of Man in glory—commonly taken to refer to the Parousia—Augustine held to have *already* been fulfilled, in the coming of the Son of Man's glorious body, the Catholic Church. The thousand-year reign of the saints, spoken of in Apocalypse 20, during which the Devil's power is bridled, had again already been fulfilled. The saints reign in their power, which is particularly manifest in their healing miracles at their gravesites, now, in the Church.[15]

And they will reign, indeed, for 1000 years. This may seem to leave open the possibility for another, albeit extended, millenarian calculation, where the Parousia might be thought to come in the thousandth year since the foundation of the Church (in A.D. 1000 or 1033). But Augustine, a man who takes a long view, is quick to refute this interpretation. One thousand, he points out, is actually 10x10x10. A cubed number stands for perfection or fullness. Therefore "1000" is a symbol, not a quantity: it cannot stand as the base of something so crude as an empirical calculation.[16]

Through a hermeneutical tour de force, Augustine systematically dissolved the eschatological import of traditionally eschatological prophecies, and turned them instead into veiled metaphors for the current life of the Church. And he did the reverse. He took passages long thought to describe the "true Church" as perfect—"without spot or wrinkle"—and aimed carefully at the perfectionist Donatists, arguing that *these* verses are eschatological. The perfect Church can appear only at the end of time, which in principle we cannot know.

By so re-reading Scripture, by advocating so thorough-going a historical agnosticism, Augustine effectively recast the chronology of the world. If the thousand-year reign of the saints has already begun, not with Christ's Parousia, but with his first post-resurrection advent in his glorious body, the Church, then this millennium is domesticated; it is part of normal history. Time, literally, has lost its edge.

Against the Pelagians, a more subtle opponent, Augustine constructed a more complicated argument. In the Pelagian view, while the flesh was compromised by the sin of Adam, the soul was sinless, fresh in every child. Augustine, holding that soul and body must be taken together as definitive of human nature, must further hold that soul as well as body are inherited from Adam, and both by him were blighted. The body is now afflicted with the punishment of mortality; but the soul itself, Augustine urges, is afflicted as well by a wounded will, the expression of the original sin. The Fall caused a double disjuncture: within the soul, will and affect diverge: man can effectively will neither to love nor not to love; while the soul and body, though created to embrace one another as true marriage-partners, are inevitably wrenched apart, unwilling and unhappy, at death.[17] At the End, then, whenever that may be, more than just body and soul will be reintegrated. Soul, at that point, will be reintegrated with itself: God will have healed the human heart. And flesh, no longer balky and insubordinate, will be under that calm and complete control of the newly whole soul: it will have become, as Paul proclaimed in 1 Corinthians 15, "spiritual flesh."

It is in his definition of the spiritual body that Augustine both scores his major blow against the cosmic intellectualist tradition and, oddly, lets it in the back door. The fleshly body, he insists with Paul, will be raised spiritual (1 Cor. 15), but "spiritual," Augustine insists, refers to the body's moral orientation, not its substance. The risen flesh will have corporeal substance.[18] It will even have gender: women, too, shall as women be raised. Amputees will have their limbs restored; people fat in this life will not be fat in the Kingdom; all will be roughly that age that Christ was when God raised him.[19]

But this raised perfected corporeal body will not dwell on a transformed earth. Defying the scientific thinking of his day, Augustine asserted that these raised corporeal bodies would dwell in the heavens: the Kingdom of God would not come on earth. Apocalyptic traditions of social harmony and agricultural fecundity thus drop out of Augustine's picture: no food, no sex, and no social relations in the Kingdom. His saved individuals in their perfect bodies of thirty-three-year olds, will stand in comradely contemplation of the beatific vision of God.[20]

* * *

How persuasive, and ultimately successful, was Augustine on these issues? In what sense did he win?

Apocalyptic eschatology—the foundation of Christianity—is a deeply unfashionable subject, adumbrated more frequently in popular evangelical pamphlets than in thoughtful systematic theologies. Eschatology itself fares little better, usually hanging on at the very end of systematic theologies, squeezed in just before the index. Theologians exert much time and energy on explanations of the Trinity, or on arguments for global ecumenicalism, on egalitarian language, Jewish-Christian relations, metaphysical ruminations on Creation, or evil. Very few speak excitedly about conceptions of heaven. The intellectual action is elsewhere. We cannot attribute current theological fashion to Augustine, although we might note that the deepest implications of his own work inadvertently anticipated the modern mood.

Against the Pelagians, Augustine scored a technical political victory: banning their texts, anathematizing their views, driving them from their sees. But the Western Church and Western culture generally, on such issues as sexuality, marital relations, and the nature of human will, continued in their semi-Pelagian way for many centuries after Augustine's lifetime.

The longest-lived legacy of Augustine's controversy with Pelagius lies elsewhere, in two utterly unrelated modern disciplines: New Testament criticism, on the one hand and psychoanalysis, on the other. New Testament critics continue to reconstruct the apostle Paul's call to preach Jesus to the Gentiles as a conversion, that is, a move from one religion (Judaism) to another (a Christianity already supposedly formed within a few years of Jesus' execution). Unhappy with one religious system, spiritually hungry, this Paul is drawn with Augustine's palette, based on his autobiographical interpretation of the Epistles and Acts. Paul the anguished, introspective convert, tormented by his own sinfulness even after the reception of grace—the reading of Romans 7 so prominent in Augustine's anti-Pelagian arsenal[21]—has passed through Luther to his modern counterparts, whose reconstructed apostle more often resembles not the first-century Jew, but the fifth-century bishop (whom, usually, they have never even read).[22]

And the divided self, the hero of the *Confessions* and Augustine's ultimate weapon against Pelagian constructs of human freedom, has found a lasting home in modern psychology. The sad themes of this anthropology—sexuality as a premier occasion of human loneliness and self-alienation, moral paralysis as the uncontrolled divergence of will and affect—continue to resonate in modern psychoanalytic discussion. The classic atheism of the latter system provides more comfort, perhaps, than Augustine's: divine nonexistence excuses God from a causal—indeed, punitive—role in such occurrences of mental anguish.

Augustine's clearest victory lies in the fight he most clearly lost, the Christian calculation of the End of the World. Just as he had argued, the world did not end in the year 500. And the simple passage of time has vindicated the essence of his argument: there seems to be no sure way to tell when the end will come.[23]

Yet, Christian millenarianism has never gone out of fashion. In every generation people see the signs of the End; millenarian predictions are constantly proven wrong but never lastingly discredited. Such an obsession with the global date is inevitable in light of Christian proclamation itself, with its twin poles of the Now/Not Yet, its already-arrived messiah and its messianic age that is yet to be. We shall see a particular crest in the wave now: the enhanced gravitational pull of the approaching end of the century and of the millennium has created a kind of lunar high tide in popular apocalyptic. But Augustine has been right so far: The world still has not ended. I would wager that it will continue not to end—at least, not through divine initiative—well past the year 2000. But the calculations will continue.

How should I conclude this examination of Augustine's views on history, the Church, and the flesh? I shall note two things. First, I am struck by the stoney integrity of Augustine's position. In the face of Christian triumphalism, he insisted that the present Church could never be perfect, and that history—biblical revelation notwith-standing—would always remain opaque. And in the face of Christian ascetic perfectionism, he pressed two uncomfortable points. Human love, he insisted, could never be well directed through human will, but only by divine grace. And human flesh, he equally insisted, will ever remain—even in heaven—the true love and partner of the human soul, created to be such by the good God.

And I am struck, finally, by the continuing force of his presence. Augustine's various solutions to different religious questions are very much the products of his own time and place, the fifth-century Latin West. Few of us live in a universe where saints' relics thwart demons (cf. the closing chapters of *The City of God*), where compulsive appetite is viewed as divinely mandated punishment. Yet, though Augustine's answers remain his, his questions—Why do men choose evil? Why can't will direct love?—remain ours. His passion and insight still speak to us, an unintended audience, across the gap of sixteen centuries. This too, though unintended, is no less his accomplishment.

Notes

1. Portions of this essay have appeared in previous articles: "Beyond the Body/Soul Dichotomy: Augustine on Paul Against the Manichees and the Pelagians," *Recherches augustiniennes* 23 (1988), 87–114; "Apocalypse and Redemption in Early Christianity: From John of Patmos to Augustine of Hippo," *Vigiliae Christianae* 45, 2 (1991), 151–183; and "Vile Bodies: Paul and Augustine on the Resurrection of the Flesh," *Biblical Hermeneutics in Historical Perspective: Studies in Honor of Karlfried Froehlich on His Sixtieth Birthday,* ed. Mark S. Burrows and Paul Rorem (Grand Rapids: Eerdmans, 1991), 75–87. I thank my editors for their permission to republish here.

2. Sallustius, *On the Gods and the World* 13.

3. This cosmic architecture was confirmed through scientific observation and celestial tours, ecstatic visions and dreams. It represents a paradigm at once religious and scientific. On Hellenistic astronomy and the theory of the spheres, e.g., Aristotle, *De caelo* 5; *Metaphysics* 11.8; good introductions to this literature are provided by J.L.E. Dreyer, *A History of Astronomy from Thales to Kepler* (New York: Dover Publications, 1953), 9–206; and Pierre Duhem, *Le Système du Monde: histoire des doctrines cosmologiques de Platon à Copernic,* vols. 1 and 2 (Paris: A. Hermann, 1954–1959, orig. pub. 1908). On the religious and, thus, anthropological and social implications of this cosmology, see Eric Robertson Dodds, *Pagan and Christian in an Age of Anxiety: Some Aspects of Religious Experience from Marcus Aurelius to Constantine* (New York: Norton, 1970), especially chap. 1. Star maps and zodiacs turn up everywhere, from the tauroctonies of the Mithraea to the floor of Galilaean synagogues to the outer curtain of the Temple in Jerusalem, which "portrayed a panorama of the heavens" (Josephus, *Jewish War* 5.212). This imagined architecture of the universe, in brief, was apparently ubiquitous and, in a sense, theologically ecumenical. It could accommodate the various mythologies of antiquity—pagan, Jewish, and eventually Christian.

4. Sallustius, *Gods* 4, on the Milky Way as the zone at which body subject to Passion begins; Porphyry explains that souls descend to earth at Cancer, the northeast point of the zodiac, and ascend at Capricorn, *On the Cave of the Nymphs,* 22–28. See also Alan Segal, "Heavenly Ascent in Hellenistic Judaism, Early Christianity, and Their Environment," *Aufstieg und Niedergang der römischen Welt* 2.23.2 (1980), 1334–1394.

5. On Jewish restoration theology, see E.P. Sanders, *Jesus and Judaism* (Philadelphia: Fortress Press, 1985), 77–119, 22–41; earlier, Joachim Jeremias, *Jesus' Promise to the Nations,* tr. S.H. Hooke (Naperville: A.R. Allenson, 1958), 55–72; more recently, Paula Fredriksen, "Judaism, the Circumcision of Gentiles, and Apocalyptic Hope: Another Look at Galatians 1 and 2," *Journal of Theological Studies* 42 (1991), 532–564, especially pp. 544–548; for a systematic presentation, with copious references to primary material, Emil Schürer, *The History of the Jewish People in the Age of Jesus Christ,* rev. ed., tr. T.A. Burkill, Geza Vermes, and Fergus Millar (Edinburgh: Clark, 1979), 2, 488–544, which treats as well speculations about a further, non-terrestrial redemption after the age of the messiah, the *olam ha-ba,* the World or Age to Come.

6. The evangelists' portraits of a Jesus concerned with questions about precedence (Mark 10:37), meals (14:25) and marriages (12:18–27) in the Kingdom, as well as their insistence on his physical resurrection (especially Matt. 28:9; Luke 24:36–43; John 20:24–29), attest to the roots of the Christian movement in this Jewish apocalyptic tradition.

7. Papias *apud* Irenaeus, *Against Heresy* 5.33.3; Jesus' putative prophecy is also found verbatim in the Jewish *Apocalypse of Baruch* 29:5. For a fuller discussion of patristic millenarianism, see my essay "Apocalypse and Redemption in Early Christianity" (note 1 above).

8. *Against Heresy* 5.26.1; 30.3; cf. Victorinus of Pettau (ca. 300) who awaited "the destruction of Babylon, that is, the city of Rome" (*On the Apocalypse* 8.2; also 9.4).

9. On these traditions of Christian chronography, see especially Richard Landes, "Lest the Millennium be Fulfilled: Apocalyptic Expectations and the Pattern of Western Chronography 100–800 CE," *The Use and Abuse of Eschatology in the Middle Ages,* ed. Werner Verbeke, Daniel Verhelst, and Andries Welkenhuysen (Leuven: Leuven University Press, 1988), 137–211.

10. E.g., Origen, *On First Principles* 2.10.3; 11.2–3. Origen's disciple Bishop Dionysis of Alexandria wrote a pointed refutation of millenarianism, *On the Promises.* See Eusebius's interpretation of these arguments in his *Ecclesiastical History,* Book 7.

11. Hippolytus, *Commentary on Daniel* 4.23–24; cf. 4:18–19; Julius Africanus, *Chronography* (fragments), ed. and tr. in the *Ante-Nicene*

Fathers 6.130–138; Hippolytus, *De cursu temporum* in *Chronica minora,* ed. C. Frick (Leipzig: Teubner, 1892), 1, 155–174; discussion in Robin Lane Fox, *Pagans and Christians* (New York: Knopf, 1986), 265–267.

12. See especially Augustine's correspondence with the bishop Hesychius, *Epist.* 197–199.

13. *Epist.* 29.11; cf. *Civ. Dei* 20.7.1; and the vivid discussion in F. Van der Meer, *Augustine the Bishop: Religion and Society at the Dawn of the Middle Ages,* tr. Brian Battershaw and G.R. Lamb (New York: Sheed & Ward, 1961), 471–526.

14. Good introductions to these issues and controversies may be found in Peter Brown, *Augustine of Hippo* (Berkeley: University of California Press, 1967), Gerald Bonner, *St. Augustine of Hippo: Life and Controversies* (London: SCM Press, 1963), and Eugene TeSelle, *Augustine the Theologian* (New York: Herder and Herder, 1970). On the Donatists, see especially Robert Austin Markus, *Saeculum: History and Society in the Theology of S. Augustine* (Cambridge: Cambridge University Press, 1970; rev. ed. 1988); on the Pelagians, see my essay "Beyond the Body/Soul Dichotomy" (note 1 above).

15. *Civ. Dei* 20. Many of Augustine's arguments draw on the work of his fellow African, the Donatist Tyconius. See, for more detailed discussion, my essay "Apocalypse and Redemption," pp. 157–166 and notes.

16. *Civ. Dei* 20.6.2–3.

17. Augustine's ideas on the divided will crystallize in the late 390s, especially in his comments on Romans 9 in *Answers to Simplicianus,* Book 1, and the masterwork that followed, the *Confessions.* His concept of the organic, intimate and enduring relation between soul and body begins to emerge in Book 10 of his *De genesi ad litteram,* written c. 412.

18. *De genesi ad litteram* 7.7.18; cf. 35.68; *Civ. Dei* 22.2. I very much doubt that Paul would have agreed with him; see my essay, "Vile Bodies: Paul and Augustine on the Resurrection of the Flesh," pp. 80ff. (note 1 above).

19. *Civ. Dei* 22.15–17.

20. Against scientific arguments on the weight of the elements telling against physical bodies in heaven, see *Civ. Dei* 22.4 and 11; on the physical perfection of those raised, see 22.15.

21. On Augustine's construction of Paul, and the way it reinforces his view of his own conversion, see "Body/Soul Dichotomy," p. 102f.; before that, "Paul and Augustine: Conversion Narratives, Orthodox Traditions, and the Retrospective Self," *Journal of Theological Studies* 37 (1986), 3–34.

22. Krister Stendahl's seminal essay, "Paul and the Introspective Conscience of the West," in *Paul Among Jews and Gentiles, and Other Essays* (Philadelphia: Fortress Press, 1976; orig. pub. 1963), dealt a solid blow against such interpretations. Yet, modern critics continue to see in Romans 7 some sort of "autobiographical" statement of anguish on Paul's part; "Paul and Augustine," *art. cit.,* reviews the literature and this historiographical problem.

23. His contemporaries were in less of a position to appreciate this, because for them, with the waves of Germanic tribes that broke over the Western Empire from the 430s on, the world very nearly did "end" on time. The Donatist chronicler of the year 452 had no trouble divining, beneath the name of the Vandal Genseric, King of Carthage, the number of the beast, 666. Augustine's own protégé Quodvultdeus interpreted current events through the lens of John's Apocalypse. See Fredriksen, "Apocalypse and Redemption," especially p. 167 and notes.

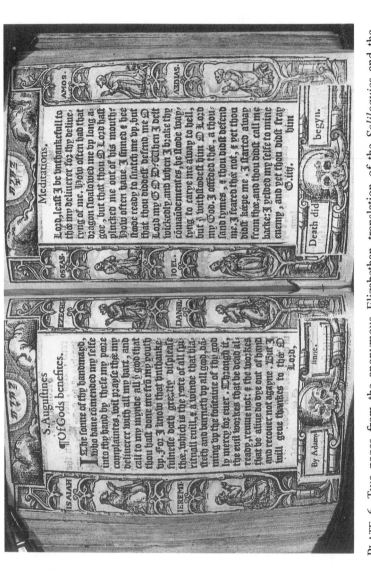

PLATE 6. Two pages from the anonymous Elizabethan translation of the *Soliloquies* and the *Manual* published by the zealous reformer John Day (1522–1584). Pseudo-Augustine (13th century). *Certaine Select Prayers . . . Also his Manuell* (London: John Day, 1577).

Art, Wisdom and Bliss:
Their Interplay in Saint Augustine

Robert J. O'Connell, S.J.

One of the finest Jesuit Superiors I ever knew was Fr. John McMahon. He was *the* Provincial who was most responsible for the wave of New York Province Jesuits of my generation, who were sent to the leading universities of the world for advanced degrees. His visits to the houses of studies, in fact, regularly provoked a whispering campaign among the younger element, *us*. We were certain he would ask the question we translated as: "What do you want to do when you grow up." Such is the mindless irreverence of youth!

One of the young scholastics he questioned was, to safeguard the innocent, someone we will call Jack. "Would you be interested in studying mathematics?" asked Fr. Provincial. Then, as if to sugarcoat the pill, "St. Augustine was very interested in figures, you know." For a long moment, Jack regarded him with a look of ingenuous innocence. Then, matter-of-factly, he asked, "Was that before or after his conversion?" Years later, dear old Fr. McMahon still wondered if he had been had.

The fact is, however, that Augustine's esthetics does center on figures, and in both senses of that ambiguous term. That really comes down to saying that Augustine had, not one, but two distinct—and even opposed—esthetic theories, and never quite succeeded in bringing them into harmony.

The first of those theories focused on "figures" in the mathematical sense. It supposed, as the Neo-Pythagoreans did in those days, that beauty in the sensible world of sights and sounds was the effect of mathematical relationships: of equality, balance, and proportion. Leonardo Da Vinci's famous drawing of the human body as illustrating the "golden section" is one familiar embodiment of this insight. What Augustine added to it, inspired by his readings in the Neoplatonists, was this. Every time we espy an instance of such equality or proportion—what Augustine called "measure"—we could be confident that it was merely an imperfect reflection, in the world of sense-realities, of some archetypal model in a resplendent higher world, beyond the reach of sense. This world of pure and perfect numerical and geometrical relationships was the transcendent pattern, the *Logos* after which the Creator fashioned the sense-world. [1]

"Euclid alone has looked on beauty bare," Edna St. Vincent Millay assures us, implying that in one "blinding hour . . . [one] holy, terrible day" a shaft of vision transfixed his soul, a vision of pure forms, "light anatomized," "intricately drawn" in the mind's own "luminous air." [2] And we are told that the great physicist, Charles Steinmetz, dissolved in tears when first he beheld how splendidly the Brooklyn Bridge translated those abstract figures of the mathematical universe into a feast for the percipient eye. [3]

It is of some consequence to notice that the original point of this esthetic theory was to stimulate the mind to strip away and leave behind the husks of matter which clothed those pure forms, and in clothing them, defiled them. In so doing, the mind could equally leave behind its own dependence on deceptive sense perceptions and imaginative images, until, like Euclid, it mounted high enough to gaze on that transcendent world of "beauty bare."

The assumption presiding over all this is, of course, the Platonic and Neoplatonic conviction that purely spiritual reality is superior in every way to material reality, as well as to any amalgam of spirit and matter. So it is that that same insight encourages the way Augustine thinks of all the symbolic materials we use in the creation of artworks—shapes and colors in painting and sculpture, sounds and words and meter in poetry and music, the rhythmic movements of the human body in dance, and so forth. Augustine regards all of these, precisely insofar as they are material, as so much vesture, clothing we wrap about the spiritual import which gives meaning to every work of art. The result is that we gain only an indirect and mediated vision of that spiritual import, which the artistic vesture half-reveals and half-conceals, the way a loose-fitting gown betrays the figure of the person wearing it. Moreover, the process of clothing the spiritual with matter necessarily results in a deterioration of the spiritual: the artistic creation, since it is an amalgam of spirit and matter, is for that very reason inferior to the original purely spiritual import.[4]

There is an element of mercy involved in the artist's doing that. Augustine thinks that our sinful fallenness has so weakened our spiritual vision that most of us could no more gaze mentally on a purely spiritual reality than we could stare directly with our bodily eyes at the noonday sun, blazing down from a cloudless sky. We need to have our exposure to spiritual beauty "wrapped up," so to say, in some material envelope; that envelope acts as a kind of sunscreen which cuts down the blinding brightness so that we can behold it. What the artist does, therefore, is to make the higher spiritual world accessible to us; he "brings it down" to us, so to speak. But he does so, Augustine is convinced, by reducing spiritual reality to the inferior status of an ingredient in an amalgam of spirit and matter. This the artist does in order to accommodate spiritual beauty to our level of being, for as fallen humans we are similar amalgams of spiritual soul and corruptible matter.

However, Augustine goes on to warn us, we are not meant to remain in a lifelong dependence on such artworks and their power to provide us entry into the world of spirit. Again like Plato, and like his Neoplatonic disciples, Augustine believes that our power of seeing spiritual reality can grow stronger, precisely in the measure in which we ourselves become more and more spiritual—precisely in the measure, that is, in which our growth in Christian spirituality succeeds in repairing the ravages of our sinful fallenness. He is convinced that spiritual progress will bring us beyond and above all dependence on the mediating works of artistic creation.[5]

This is the background against which, almost exactly 1600 years ago, in his treatise *On True Religion,* Augustine issued that uncompromising condemnation of all the workings of imagination:

> Give me some one who can see without having to imagine any corporeal reality. . . . Give me some one who resists the fleshly senses, and the wounds they inflict upon the soul. . . . [Give me some one] who does not delight in vain, exterior things, . . . who can tell himself that if only one Rome exists . . . that Rome is false which I create in my thinking of it . . . and if I have but one friend, that friend is false which I create in my thinking of him. . . . Such things are all so many illusory realities, and no one can make illusions into objects of understanding . . . [for] what I truly

contemplate with the eye of understanding must be genuine
realities (64).

Augustine was convinced, therefore, that after the soul has
reached a certain level of progress, the realities conjured up by the
creative imagination would only distract the mind, sidetrack it from
its ascending quest for that higher world which we can genuinely
"know," with the kind of knowledge which Augustine labels
"science," *scientia.* That is why, according to *this* theory, all of the
liberal *artes* are like "music," in that they achieve their perfect form
when they become *scientiae,* "sciences." For they all lead the mind
upward to the direct, unmediated contemplation of that higher world
of pure essences, where neither matter nor sense nor imagination can
have any further role to play.

If taken seriously and pursued logically, of course, this theory
could be transformed into policy, and that policy would amount to a
death warrant for the creative arts. Yet, notice that the theory
underlying it also has its inebriating side. No less a genius than Plato
has passed this way, piping his enchanting melodies about another,
higher, purer realm of being; and the human heart still leaps to the
sound of his flute. There is some incurable yearning in the human
heart which makes us thrill to the prospect of being transformed into
angels. Yet, there are dangers in such moments of angelic nostalgia;
and, when it comes to the angelistic esthetic we have been describing,
no one has targeted its limitations in more trenchant terms than Henri-
Irénée Marrou:

> I am well aware that there is an esthetic, a theory of artistic
> beauty in the works of Saint Augustine . . . but it is necessary to
> see the role it plays: its function is not to ground the esthetic
> experience by reason, not to justify it: on the contrary its function
> is to transcend [that experience] . . . to pass from art to science;
> [Augustine's esthetic] annihilates to the soul's gaze the fallacious
> magic of sensation by reducing it to its rational elements.[6]

Marrou is writing here as though Augustine had only one esthetic; he
is largely correct in that assumption, since the theory we have just
sketched—call it Augustine's "ascensional" theory—is the one which
eventually succeeds in almost entirely eclipsing its rival. We shall

examine that rival theory after looking at this ascensional theory more closely.

First, it answers the question which Augustine always claimed lay at the very center of philosophical concern: How are human beings to achieve happiness? From that early dialogue, *On Happiness*—which was the first to reach completion after his conversion—to the monumental *The City of God,* which has rightly been called the *On Happiness* of his later years, Augustine never wavers on that conviction. We all yearn for happiness. And so, Augustine thinks, we are all compelled to wonder why human life as we know it is so obstinately unhappy, why it is, as Job pronounced it, one unremitting *temptatio,* one long, protracted trial. It was that problem of evil which once made a Manichee of the young Augustine. But we must never forget that even after leaving Manichaeism, he understood both Catholics and Manichees as teaching that to attain happiness we were required to mount upward in order to escape from "this" visible, corporeal world of our sense-experience, to the other, higher world which was our soul's native air.

This, then, was the reason why the esthetic we have been examining ultimately buried the rival theory which makes its sporadic appearance in Augustine's early writings: the ascensional theory fitted so neatly with the theory of happiness which formed the very backbone of his thought, that it virtually merged into identity with it. For the human being, accordingly, "wisdom" consisted in realizing that the bliss we all ache for is the happiness of blissful contemplation—the direct beholding of the Eternal Wisdom, stripped of every garment which might obstruct our vision. And that Eternal Wisdom was identical with the Divine "Beauty, ever ancient, ever new."

Augustine's ascensional esthetic, then, is the furthest thing from some tiny pocket of philosophical theory, of no more than secondary importance for understanding the man's thought and influence. It is much more a life program, a program for ordering our loves, establishing priorities among all our values. That program brings us right to the mainspring of Augustine's ethical theory: to the principle that there is only one thing truly "necessary" for any of us, only one thing we must absolutely strive to attain and possess and—in his favorite term for it—to "enjoy," *frui.* That is the vision of the God Who is absolute Beauty. Everything else in the universe, from food to friends, from material prosperity to maternal fidelity, is there to be "used" in our single-minded pursuit of that vision.[7]

Those familiar with the *Spiritual Exercises* of Saint Ignatius will recognize, of course, the Augustinian forebear of Ignatius's famous "Principle and Foundation." Others will be reminded of those countless liturgical prayers begging for the grace to despise the things of earth, material things, the things of time, so that our souls may rise to the love of their opposites—heavenly, spiritual, eternal goods. So too, the standard works on Christian asceticism almost uniformly depict the soul's progress as mounting the contemplative ladder from purgative through the "illuminative" to the so-called "unitive" way: thereby, Augustine's esthetic has been transmuted into a spirituality. But is this a spirituality, one wonders, for angels or for humans, for Christians or for Neoplatonists? In any event, it is a spirituality which aims to catapult us, quite literally, "out of this world."

A perfectly analogous relationship holds between Augustine's esthetic and the value he attributes to human sexuality. Peter Brown rightly refers to the "ascetical paradigm" which dictated his view of sexuality.[8] But I would be happier if he shifted the stress somewhat and spoke of the ascetical-*mystical* paradigm. What grounded Augustine's asceticism, what fueled his upward flight, was not so much rejection of this world, or of the body, or of sex, as his ardent longing for the enrapturing beauty of that other, higher world, the longing for a vision which he regularly portrays as a passionate embrace, a total possession.

In his *Soliloquies,* without the slightest embarrassment, he pictures his love for Divine Wisdom after the fashion of a man's love for a beautiful woman, whom he longs to "behold and embrace, stripped of every intervening garment" (1.22). Would not that supernal Wisdom, he goes on to ask, be entitled to a single-hearted fidelity which precluded all competing love affairs? Once asked, the question, of course, answers itself.

Similarly, in the *Confessions,* he asks, "What do I love, when I love my God?" and answers in a series of images, several of them unmistakably suggesting the sexual union between man and woman (10.8). Freudians would talk of sublimation here, and such talk, if correctly understood, would not be entirely out of place. Augustine, though, might just as appropriately reply, "What's wrong with sublimation?"

Anders Nygren might repeat his charge that Augustine's model for loving is pagan *Eros* rather than Christian *Agape*. Defenders of Augustine could again reply that it is the Judeo-Christian God Himself, Who is revealed to us as both *fascinosum* and *tremendum,* paralyzingly awesome but at the same time infinitely attractive. He was the one who implanted this erotic longing for Him in the restless human heart.[9]

What I am suggesting is that there was nothing wrong in Augustine's allowing his esthetic insights to broaden out until his esthetic virtually swallowed up his entire thought-world. Given a good esthetic theory, I would argue that such a process of self-expansion is entirely legitimate. Or, to be more exact, there was nothing wrong in principle. If there was anything wrong, it was this. Of the rival theories discernible in his early writings, I am persuaded that Augustine chose, albeit only half-deliberately, the wrong theory for this process of self-expansion.

Augustine's other esthetic rivals his other-worldly, ascensional theory. By the very nature of the case, this second theory never assumed the fully articulated form its victorious rival did; history is always written by the winners! But we have fragmentary clues enough to complete the edifice which Augustine's scattered remarks suggest to the imagination.

The ascensional theory we have been examining looks upon Beauty as a kind of magnet, attracting us, sending its cupid's arrows of desire into our hearts and drawing us to Itself—or, as Augustine imagines it, to Herself. Augustine tells us that the first essay ever to come from his pen, the lost youthful work *On the Beautiful and the Fitting,* began with the rhetorical question, "What else do we love, if it be not beauty?"—and typically, the love he speaks of is evidently the erotic love of desire.[10]

Yet, even from his fragmentary description of that early essay, it appears that he stumbled half-unwittingly on quite another notion of beauty. That was the notion that beauty does not minister to our desires, to our pleasure or comfort. Those are the functions, not of beauty itself, but of beauty's counterpart, or perhaps one should say its counterfeit. Pleasure, comfort—in a word, "agreeableness"—are the reasons we like a shoe that fits our foot, a dog who makes a good hunting companion, and more generally, a world whose climate and inhabitants are what Augustine calls "fitting"—*aptum,* in Latin—

meaning that they "agree with" us, are good to us and for us, but always good, *relative to us.* They bring us pleasure and comfort, rather than the reverse.

The youthful Augustine saw, however, that Beauty need not bespeak any such relation to human desires for pleasure or comfort. Beauty is beautiful in and of itself, for its own sake; beauty is measured on a scale which is entirely independent of our self-concerned preferences and likings. Hence, beauty does not "draw" or "attract" us; it does not cater to our desires so much as it *arrests* us, stops us in our tracks, as it were, and commands us to *pay attention.*

In the terms alluded to above, which are borrowed from Rudolf Otto's study of *The Holy,* beauty has much more to do with the *tremendum* than with the *fascinosum,* much more to do with creation as the flickering mirror of God's awesomeness than of his attractiveness.[11] Christ provides an instance of what I am trying to express: it was his mysterious attractiveness which persuaded those first apostles to ask, almost to plead, "Rabbi, where dwellest thou?" "Come, and see," he replies (John 1:38–39). And they find the invitation so irresistible that they still remember, years afterwards, exactly what time of day it was when they first met him. But Peter, after that miraculous draught of fishes, responds to another side of Christ entirely. He has caught a glimpse of a moral and spiritual beauty so pure, so blindingly awesome, that instead of pleading to be with Him, he cries out, "Depart from me, O Lord, for I am a sinful man!" (Luke 5:8). When Augustine wrote that first book ever to come from his pen, accordingly, he came to the insight, at least momentarily, that the appropriate response to beauty is not desire, but a silent kind of reverence. Beauty does not invite us to chase after it; it reduces us, rather, to a hushed stillness. It insists that we not merely look at it, but keep looking at it, that we not hurry by, but take time out in order genuinely to see it, as though for the first, and perhaps for the last time. Beauty commands that we literally behold it, that we become, as it were, nothing but a wondering pair of eyes, that we see it—not as serving ourselves, our pleasure, or even our happiness, but as Dag Hammarskjöld once wrote, that we see it—"in its sacred independence."[12]

Beauty, in sum, does not prompt the question, "What's in this for me?"—rather, it dismisses all such self-regarding, all such self-interested questions—yes, even the question of happiness. They are so secondary as to be irrelevant. Beauty demands that we be self-effacing, or at least that we strive to become so. Yet, Beauty also promises that the more singly we concentrate on her, and less on ourselves and what we care for, the more she will lull us into forgetting ourselves and our petty concerns, so that we become more and more deeply lost in devotion to her.

I have given Augustine words here, provided him with ways of expressing the fundamental insight of his work *On the Beautiful and the Fitting,* which no one in his century could have elaborated in exactly that way. But we are encouraged to do just that. Writer after writer in succeeding centuries has come to basically the same insight and provided us with their own embroidery of it. I could illustrate that claim by citing Immanuel Kant's view that beauty requires that we surrender ourselves to a kind of disinterested contemplation, or Roger Fry's theory of art as embodying significant form, or Edward Bullough's stress on "Psychical Distance" as essential to properly esthetic experience.

Why did Augustine consider this disinterested notion of beauty an important one? For he does consider it important—so much so that he never entirely abandons it, despite the fact that it is profoundly at odds with the "ascensional" notion of beauty examined above.

That "ascensional" notion of beauty harmonized with and confirmed his central conviction: that human beings were other-worldly creatures who desired a happiness which they could never attain except by rising above and beyond *this* sensible, corporeal world. It was an esthetics of "escape," therefore, in which beauty responded to the deepest human desire for happiness, and so, suspiciously came to resemble its competitor, the "fitting."

This alternate esthetic, however, starts boldly by contrasting beauty against the fitting. Its very first step, therefore, legislates that both beauty and esthetic philosophy be contemplated in clean independence from any theory of human happiness. This immediately threatens to compromise Augustine's entire emphasis: that both Beauty and happiness could be found not in this world, but only "there," in that other, higher world of contemplative delights to which transcendent Beauty summons us. The way Beauty summons us, of course, is by leaving reflected traces of Herself in the sensible world. And so the question now becomes, What message should we read from those traces?

The ascensional esthetic would answer that we must permit each limited sensible trace of supernal Beauty to arouse our impatience to rise upward to the supernal Beauty it recalls to us. The esthetic of the beautiful as contrasted with the fitting, on the other hand, would counsel almost exactly the opposite. "Stop," it cries to us, "don't be in such an all-fired rush. Have a bit more reverence for how the God of beauty has fashioned His creation. Look, keep looking—behold!"

"Don't just sit there, *do* something!" the mentors of my generation used to tell us. And their advice seemed to make sense. We were Americans, after all, the "can-do-ers," the "up-and-at-'em kids," the achievers, the accomplishers. Then along came the flower children of the sixties and seventies. They brashly reversed the saying, "Don't do something," they countered, "just sit there." Sit there and behold what's all around you. Take it in, soak it up. Don't hurry on to wherever it is you want to get to—take time out to look at the flowers!

Don't miss the flowers! It is an insult to God to run so fast that you never "behold the lilies of the field," so carefully, so exquisitely crafted that "not even Solomon in all his glory was arrayed" as one of them. Oh, I know you have places to get to and things to do, but don't tell me you have to be in all that much of a hurry! And above all, don't tell me that God designed this sensible universe as a kind of barren desert, meaning for us to race across it, allowing ourselves to be as little distracted by its charms as we possibly can manage. If that were so, why would He have expended so much artistic attention on the architecture of the humble mosquito—to say nothing of its poor relation, the lowly flea?

I have deliberately chosen two of Augustine's own favorite examples—the mosquito and the flea. (He can also go a trifle ga-ga about the elegance of the earthworm.) The way he regularly applies this insight to the distinction between what is fitting relative to us, and what is beautiful in and of itself, shows that he is hunting much larger game. He is challenging his readers, as he repeatedly challenged his hearers in the church of Hippo Regius, to alter their more accustomed way of contemplating the entire universe about them. He is asking them to neutralize their feelings of self-interest and self-concern and replace them with a selfless gaze of pure objectivity.

Few people needed that insight more keenly than Augustine himself, in order to maintain some measure of spiritual balance. No one was more sensitive than he to the thorns and thistles which can so often make human existence such a vale of tears. When he invites our imagination to dwell on the *peregrinatio* that human life represents for him, meaning life's "wayfaring" character, we are sorely tempted to think that this lugubrious theme inspires him to rise to quite unwarranted flights of eloquence. How movingly he can embroider the tapestry of pain and illness, of dangers and treachery, of loss and disappointment and unfulfilled hopes with which each of us is all too familiar. Indeed, he sometimes seems happiest when regaling us with the abundant reasons we have for being sad.

It is not difficult to understand why a youth of Augustine's temperament proved so vulnerable to the Manichees' emphasis on the evils of this world and to their mythic explanation of how human existence came to be so accursedly miserable. Nor is it surprising that, once he had abandoned Manichaeism, he felt obliged repeatedly to refute the Manichee view of this bodily world as the product of an evil anti-God. And in that task of refutation, which came down in fact to nothing less than vindicating the Judeo-Christian "creator of things both visible and invisible," Augustine regularly returns to this distinction between the beautiful and the fitting. The Manichees, he contends, have allowed their view of the sensible universe to narrow down. They ask only whether things in the sensible universe—like scorpions and fleas and mosquitoes—are fitting, agree with them, enhance their peace and comfort. They never ask the question which Augustine himself eventually learned to ask—whether the entire sensible universe, and the variegated array of realities composing it, was beautiful!

That was the larger game Augustine was hunting when inviting his readers to pause and dwell on, genuinely behold, the beauty of the mosquito and the flea. He is prodding them to be less small-minded, to stop their belly-aching for a moment and broaden their regard until it takes in the full expanse of this wide, wide world. He is bent on getting them to see for themselves that God was wise and right and good in creating, not only those shimmering angelic majesties, the Cherubim and Seraphim, Thrones and Dominations, but even the least and humblest denizens of this sensible world.

I often find myself wishing that Augustine had more fully exploited this way of looking at beauty—more fully and more consistently. In its positive acceptance and valuation of the bodily and sensible world, the rival esthetic theory does seem to harmonize more comfortably than his ascensional esthetic does, with the Christian's faith in the mysteries of Creation, Incarnation, and Resurrection. And it is a fact that those mysteries came to mean more and more to him as time went on.

Despite that, however, when it came to announcing the message he heard created beauty speaking to his heart, Augustine regularly echoes to the very end that ardent cry from his *Confessions:* he is frightened at the thought that we might dawdle and slow our impatient journeying to that higher world, by gazing with enjoyment at the blossoms along the roadsides of this world. No, Christ Himself did not tarry, *non tardavit, sed cuccurrit.* Like that exultant giant the psalmist prophesied (Ps. 18:6), He ran, ran shouting to the rest of us, and Augustine shouts with Him, *Rape, rape tecum ad Deum,* "snatch them up," those beauties you see strewn all about you, and "bear them away to [God]" (*Conf.* 4.19). Here Augustine is thinking of the "violent" of Saint Matthew's gospel, who violently "bear the kingdom away" (*rapiunt;* Matt. 11:12). "Act, Lord, do!" he later repeats, "awaken us and call us back, enflame us and bear us away" (*rape*), "let us love, let us run" (*amemus, curramus; Conf.* 8:9). He does not spontaneously think of "this world" as offering us occasions for slowing down, for taking time out, for simply beholding.

Augustine himself confesses to an everyday incident which may serve to sum up my argument. He pictures himself passing through a field (*Conf.* 10.57), his eye caught by a hare fleeing from a pursuing hound. The artist's eye that was naturally his comes immediately to the alert. He is tempted to stand there "vacant-minded," as he tells it, his eye following the movements of the chase—movements which, he admits, come from the "wondrous creator and orderer of all things." We are almost led to expect Augustine to leave us with a gem-like vignette of this small, frightened creature, leaping, turning, darting toward some haven of survival, in its lightsome swift grace, describing timeless figures of the body's resurrection. Instead, he is resolved to "rise up from the sight by some reflection [on God], or to spurn the whole incident and pass it by." For myself, and here I may be speaking only for myself, I sometimes muse on the difference it might have made for Western theology and spirituality, if in moments like these Augustine had not been in such a precipitous hurry.

Notes

1. For background on the "sources" in the esthetics of the ancient world which Augustine exploited, Karel Svoboda's *L'Esthétique de Saint Augustin et ses sources* (Paris-Brno, 1933) still remains valuable.

2. "Euclid Alone Saw Beauty Bare," in *Collected Poems* (New York: Harper & Row, 1962).

3. *Loki: The Life of Charles Proteus Steinmetz*, by Jonathan Norton Leonard (Garden City: Doubleday, Doran, 1929).

4. For more thorough treatment of this topic, see my *Art and the Christian Intelligence in Saint Augustine* (henceforth: *Art*) (Cambridge, Mass.: Harvard University Press, 1978), 96–101, 108–110, 146–164, along with references.

5. Compare the passages cited in note 2 above with the analogous approach taken to scriptural imagery, by Tarcisius Van Bavel in his "L'Humanité du Christ comme *lac parvulorum* dans la spiritualité de saint Augustin," *Augustiniana* 7 (1957), 245–281.

6. See Henri-Irénée Marrou, *Saint Augustin et la fin de la culture antique* (Paris: E. de Boccard, 1938), 184, note 1.

7. See *Art,* pp. 67, 137–138.

8. See especially "Augustine and Sexuality," in *Colloquy* 46 (1983), 1–13, for development of this paradigm.

9. This is the essence of Oliver O'Donovan's reply to the charges in Anders Nygren's famous *Agape and Eros*; see *The Problem of Self-Love in St. Augustine* (New Haven: Yale University Press, 1980), 137–159. I am inclined to think, for my part, that God put more into the human heart than that: see, insofar as this touches on Christian esthetics, the closing chapter of *Art,* pp. 143–172.

10. Augustine recounts his memories of writing this book in his *Confessions* 4.20–27.

11. *The Idea of the Holy,* tr. John W. Harvey (London: Oxford University Press, 1931).

12. *Markings,* tr. Leif Sjöberg and W.H. Auden (New York: Knopf, 1964),
     174.

On Re-reading the *Confessions*

Henry Chadwick

In this notable conference we commemorate a momentous event in the life of Augustine, his ordination to the presbyterate, for which at the time he felt no enthusiasm. Augustine wanted to be a monk, not an urban priest or diocesan bishop, and during his years as a layman he made a systematic point of not visiting churches which were looking for a suitable bishop.[1] The coercion of Valerius's little congregation at Hippo was not unusual at that time and place as a route to the priesthood. Augustine himself tells us that most clergy in North Africa had been ordained *violentia populorum.*[2] In his *Questions on the Heptateuch* he has occasion to observe that ordination is a call of the Church which cannot be refused without forfeiting the respect of the community.[3] To refuse would be to declare oneself the man entrusted with a single talent who selfishly buried it in the earth.[4] Nevertheless, candor requires note of the facts that the clergy of the North African churches were far fewer than the pastoral needs of the people demanded,[5] that it appears frequently to have been the case that the plebs, whose voice in an election could be considerable, were more inclined to look for a bishop to answer their temporal concerns than for one whose ministry might so make them weep for their sins as to get them to heaven,[6] and that Augustine utters misgivings at the practice of seizing laity to be priests and bishops against their will.[7] The method did not always produce ideal results.

In the Western Church we have become influenced by a pietist expectation that the initiative in offering for ordination will lie with the postulant, who decides to be a candidate because his heart has been strangely warmed, because he, or indeed she, feels a sense of inward calling by an incommunicable divine monition, which the overt and public act of prayer and laying on of hands by a bishop in Catholic communion hardly does more than acknowledge as an almost inherent right. In the Eastern Orthodox churches there is perhaps a more obvious belief that the initiative lies with the Church: the individual receives the divine call by and through the community, which may use some pressure on an apparently qualified but reluctant candidate who is morally obliged to submit and may be dragged before the bishop by large men resembling wrestlers.

The classic ancient instance in the Greek world is the contemporary narrative of the ordination to the priesthood of the stylite saint Daniel, whose pillar stood on the European shore of the Bosporus (by Rumeli-Hisar) during the reign of the emperor Leo, twenty-five years after Augustine's death. At the emperor's order the ecumenical patriarch solemnly proceeded to the foot of the column; but the holy man refused leave for the ladder to be placed so that the patriarch might ascend for spiritual conversation. The day became hotter. After several hours the exhausted patriarch raised his hands and ordained Daniel from a distance and in defiance of his reluctance. Daniel bowed in submission, allowed the patriarch to ascend, and concelebrated with him at the top of the column.[8] (Pillar saints had a flat platform on top of their column, but two celebrants may well have been a little precarious.)

Reluctance to be ordained was not universal. Constantine the Great had worries about keen candidates whose main motive in seeking ordination was to be free of curial duties.[9] As Church resources grew, the social rather than the pastoral and sacramental duties of a bishop made the position attractive. The office of bishop or even of presbyter was held in honor; unlike the deacon, the presbyter had a seat in the apse and acted as assessor in the bishop's court.[10] The bishop naturally had a prestige which a presbyter did not, and at Hippo there were those who misread Augustine's tears at the moment of his ordination to mean that his ambitions to be a bishop *per saltum* were being disappointed.[11] A bishop had an apostolic commission: he was the source of order, and thereby embodied visibly and tangibly the continuity, universality, and legitimacy of the community and of the sacraments entrusted to him. It was distinctly unusual for a presbyter to do much preaching, if he were attached to the cathedral where the bishop was the normal teacher,[12] just as he was also the regular minister of baptism and president of the eucharistic synaxis. Presbyters who baptized and celebrated were likely to be assigned to rural congregations, or to the suburbs of large cities.

Bishops enjoyed some perquisites of office. One of Cyprian's letters (65.3) speaks of ambitious men wanting to be bishops "for the fees and presents and profits, the grand dinners and banquets," and an alarming chapter of his *De lapsis* (6) describes some bishops as principally using the office to feather their own nests. Augustine once wrote to warn a newly elected Donatist bishop to beware of the silk coverings on his throne and the choir of nuns singing him into his seat: *Transit gloria mundi.*[13]

Augustine the ascetic was speaking in that letter. At heart he was always, after July 386, a monk on his guard against the pleasures of the senses, the hollow crowns of honor and wealth, the insidiousness of flattery. His biography might be summarized as that of a bookish but highly sexed man who painfully brought himself to renounce marriage and a secular career to become a contemplative ascetic, but who was then dragged from his quiet quasi-monastic life to serve a troubled and turbulent church which needed him as a pastor and defender of the faith. The *Confessions* tell the first stage in some detail, and explain how the young man, who took to his bed a low-class but Catholic girlfriend at Carthage,[14] nevertheless joined the sect of the Manichees for whom procreation was a forbidden act, and who thought of sexual intercourse as a diabolical invention.[15] They go on to tell how he lost confidence in Manichee mythology, became drawn toward Neoplatonic mystical quests for which, once more, sexual acts were not thought to be desirable,[16] and finally returned to the Catholic faith and practice of his mother having made the surprising discovery that the Catholica had room for lay ascetic communities. The *Confessions* do not directly record anything of his reaction to the ordination of 391, six or seven years before the composition of the book. Yet the book reveals obliquely a number of things about his understanding of ordination, and in this paper I hope to submit evidence to support that proposition.

In the first place, we may remind ourselves that the work popularly thought of as a candid catalogue of moral transgressions, publicly coming clean about a too colorful past, is in effect an essay in self-defense rather than in self-accusation. The double sense of the Latin *confessio,* meaning both admission of fault and praise, helped Augustine here. He can praise his Maker not only for the redeeming grace which has rescued him from a life alienated from God, but also for the splendid personal endowments of a good memory, facility in the use of the Latin language, and a rare gift for friendship.[17]

As all students know, the autobiographical sections are not quite a simple record. Important theological theses are being illustrated by the autobiographical matter: the theme that the soul here is a pilgrim which has wandered from its true home in God and is, by grace, finding its way back again—and in this regard is a microcosm of the entire created order; the grinding theme that the only thing wholly his own which sinful man can contribute to salvation is sin.[18] At one point he even states this last point in the surely exaggerated form that sin is all that he imparted to his clever natural son Adeodatus.[19]

At the same time, there is a continual awareness of critics who thought a poor training for pastoral ministry a past life of sexual irregularity,[20] Manichee heresy, skeptical philosophy, and highly secular employment—teaching pagan literature soaked in idolatry and fornication, and purveying to the young the meretricious arts of rhetoric for a remunerative career in the law courts.[21]

When he became a presbyter, Augustine asked Bishop Valerius for time off to study the Bible, of which he felt too ignorant.[22] The study of Holy Scripture, so repellent to him at the age of eighteen, now had an extraordinary effect once he had assimilated Ambrose's principle of spiritual interpretation.[23] His excellent memory was an ideal tool for bringing together texts from very remote parts of the Bible and from different contexts. How deep an effect ordination brought to his mind is writ large in his writings. When he himself drew up his own reckoning of his published works in the *Retractationes,* he not only recorded no comment on anything written before his conversion (such as the study of aesthetic theory, *De pulchro et apto*), but also divided the reappraisal into two sections. The point of division comes at his ordination as a bishop. Ordination, first as presbyter then as bishop, came to mark watersheds in his life as a Christian.

His letters give a vivid portrait of the endless distractions to which the life of an urban priest and bishop was vulnerable. Augustine never resented the provision of help for orphans, foundlings, those whose names were on the church list for receiving financial support. (The *matricula pauperum* is a phrase which Augustine first attests.)[24] In his preaching, the duty of almsgiving is a prominent theme.[25] In *The City of God* we find the observation born of experience that the problem of poverty was too great to be solved by private charity and could be met only by state action and some measure of redistributive taxation.[26] So the fostering of works of mercy was part of the vocation of the clergy, never to be grumbled at. The more secular aspect of the calling, however, was less congenial. The writing of recommendations to get good jobs for supportive members of the congregation was faintly distasteful, though it was the accepted system.[27] (He liked to quote a wise man's saying: "I have too much regard for my own reputation to vouch for that of my friends.")[28] The worst part of a bishop's task, to which the presbyters acted as assessors, was the Monday morning court for arbitrations between quarrelling members of the flock.[29]

The duty of episcopal arbitrations arose from the apostle's stern precept that the Corinthians must never take their disagreements before the secular magistrates, whose authority "counts for nothing in the Church" (1 Cor. 4:6). If the dispute was between rich and poor, there was especially high tension. God, cries Augustine in the *Confessions* (12.34), is the very life of the poor. A bishop was expected to be a voice for the powerless, voiceless, landless, oppressed, destitute, whose perpetual temptation was to solve the problem of their hunger by stealing.[30] Admittedly Augustine would note that the number of truly destitute were few, but relative poverty was a considerable social factor,[31] and the clergy were expected to exercise bias in favor of this category. Yet, the rich man in the bishop's court could be entirely in the right in terms of the law of private property, and to decide against him was sure to incur anger and resentment against the arbitrating bishop. "Mercy to the poor is not justice."[32] In the sermons on Saint John he recalled a painful case between father and son where he had decided for the son.[33] Ambrose found the experience of arbitrating between disputing members of the same family particularly awful, and in his work *On Duties* he advised bishops to decline money disputes.[34]

There were also delicate issues when property was bequeathed to the church and aggrieved heirs wanted to dispute the legacy.[35] Augustine as bishop found himself the object of obloquy in his congregation because of his reluctance to accept for the church chest legacies which left the children short of resources.[36] In the church at Hippo he found himself surrounded by detractors,[37] though there were certainly impassioned admirers, too, for whom no sermon by their bishop could go on too long.[38]

Politically delicate situations could arise when asylum was sought at the church by slaves on the run from cruel punishments or by pathetic debtors being hunted by the authorities. Augustine did not defend inviolable asylum for known criminals and perjurers, but otherwise he thought it socially justifiable.[39] For those who experience secular society as violent and unjust, sanctuary is a lifeline. In the *Confessions* he writes of the obligation to "rescue a person suffering injustice from the hands of the powerful and provide the shelter of protection by the mighty force of just judgment" (13.21). A bishop was expected to be the advocate if one of his flock was in trouble with the magistrate or the taxman. As we should expect, civil governors could be deeply irritated by episcopal interventions. Both Basil and Augustine record how ineffective their intercessions often were.[40] In one famous sermon Augustine rather bitterly reminds his congregation how long he was kept waiting at the governor's office before he was coldly granted a hearing for an intercession on their behalf.[41] "No one who has not been a bishop would ever believe what people expect us to do."[42]

The high profile of the bishop of Hippo was enhanced by the acclaim accorded to his writings, at least after the publication of the *Confessions,* which rapidly became a best-seller, though the book had some severe critics. The lead which he took in organizing the rebuttal of the Donatist majority in Numidia and his repute as a preacher and disputant brought him constant demands to visit other churches, to be the "keynote" speaker or visiting preacher,[43] e.g., if a wealthy benefactor had provided a new basilica,[44] or if a disagreement had to be settled in an episcopal election where the congregation wanted the son of their former bishop translated from a nearby see and where the consecrating provincial bishops thought this choice strikingly inappropriate.[45] The time-consuming and exasperating affair of Antoninus of Fussala brought him to threaten resignation if the Roman see were to support this criminous clerk whose diocese found his rule insufferable.[46] Truly, ordination brought him a heavy burden of duty far beyond that of pastoral and sacramental ministry, the *sarcina episcopi.*[47]

"By this book I am confessing to you who I now am, not what I once was" (10.4), and how "you brought me to preach your word and dispense your sacrament" (11.1). The *Confessions* answer accusations. At the time when the elderly primate of Numidia Proconsularis, Megalius of Calama, was asked by Valerius of Hippo to consecrate Augustine to be his coadjutor bishop, Megalius initially wrote a letter expressing consternation at the proposal.[48] The African churches too well remembered Augustine's combative Manicheism, humiliating half-educated bishops with his criticisms of the Old Testament.[49] His activities encouraging the founding of monastic communities in Africa aroused widespread alarm: were they Manichee cells in disguise? The ascetic movement, with which Augustine was fully identified, was under severe criticism in the 380s and 390s from Christians who thought it Manichee infiltration. Augustine claimed to have been baptized by Ambrose at Milan. Custom prescribed that a bishop should write to the home church from which a candidate for baptism came, inquiring into his good character and conduct. Had Ambrose written to Thagaste or to Carthage? An unpleasant report said that, to a distressed lady who had become part of a "triangle" and whose marriage was in trouble, Augustine had responded by giving some blessed bread which had been interpreted as a love-charm to foster her adulterous desires.[50]

So in the *Confessions* Augustine will describe how he came to be enrolled for baptism, together with Alypius and his natural son Adeodatus. Characteristically, the *Confessions* do not specifically mention Ambrose as the baptizer, though that was certainly so.[51] He will describe how his liaison with his son's mother had been one of mutual fidelity, ended because of her inappropriateness as consort for an aspirant to be governor of a minor province and because, in a world where all public offices were for sale, his ambition could be realized only with the dowry of a rich wife. So he will use his autobiographical record to show how, in astonishing ways of which at the time he was unaware, long before his conversion and baptism at Milan, God was preparing him to be a dispenser of the word and sacraments to the people of God.

It follows that the *Confessions* are being misinterpreted if we start complaining about episodes that Augustine may have omitted.[52] The episodes recorded are there to illustrate one or other of his central themes, and above all aim to justify himself against those critics who judged him unsuitable for the episcopate. He saw a mysterious hidden providence in the succession of events which brought him to Ambrose at Milan. He left Thagaste because every street corner vividly recalled the memory of the dead young friend to whom he had been deeply attached (4.12). He left Carthage because the students were turbulent (3.6; 5.14). He found Rome uncomfortable because the students there were not honest about paying him their proper fees (a dishonesty precisely paralleled for the pagan Palladas at Alexandria at the same time).[53] He got the post at Milan because influential Manichee friends put his name to the militantly pagan city prefect Symmachus. Symmachus gave him an audition and no doubt satisfied himself that Augustine was no Catholic Christian and could safely be recommended for the appointment in close contact with the imperial court of Valentinian II. The moves which he had made were not in the least motivated by a desire to serve God and his Church. Yet that was how it had fallen out. "At Milan I came to Ambrose the bishop . . ." (5.23).

Repeatedly in the *Confessions* Augustine stresses that what is to our human minds mere chance is not fortuitous at all. In retrospect a wise providence is discernibly at work. By chance in a lecture at Carthage attended by Alypius, Augustine (at that period still a Manichee Hearer) happened to include a scornful aside about people addicted to the low pleasure of the circus; the words felt like an arrow in the mind of Alypius. How providential, too, that when Alypius was falsely accused of attempted theft by the Carthaginian silversmiths, he had the luck to be seen by an influential friend, the city architect, who had often met him at a senator's soirées, and then to run into the slave-boy of the real thief. "The future dispenser of God's word and examiner of many arbitrations in God's Church went away with increased experience and wisdom" (6.15).

Just as the adolescent Augustine was carried off by the other boys at Thagaste to steal pears, an act which "alone he could never have done," so, too, Alypius would learn the power of the gang and the intoxication of an excited crowd when he was captivated by the blood-lust of the amphitheater. "He was not now the person who had come in but merely one of the crowd." That was eventually to teach him that without God's help the human will can be swept into irrationality and surrender to inebriating pleasures that diminish one's humanity (6.13).

Because the one and only source of real goodness is grace, if someone is reformed in character, the reformation does not result from the clever rhetoric of the preacher but from a hidden divine power (9.18). Human life apart from this saving grace is an experience of incoherent mess, of a chaotic sequence of events where the best laid plans can be suddenly overthrown, where storms of meaningless events tear one's thoughts to pieces. Augustine the bishop knew in what bewildering times he was living; inward security and unity would come only at that final day when "purified and molten by the fire of God's love, I flow in a single stream which merges into God himself" (11.39, cf. 10.39).

Augustine understood his mastery of Latin rhetoric and his facility in expressing himself as a gift of natural endowment, not implanted or even much fostered by the rotten teachers he encountered at Thagaste, Madauros, or even Carthage. From this perhaps comes his skepticism as to whether skill in public speaking was something capable of being imparted to somebody not possessing the innate gift for it (8.13). This secular school of oratory and literature was assuredly corrupt, a meretricious business of selling the arts of flattery and deception. All the emphasis was on a well turned elegance of style indifferent to moral content: *integritas verborum* mattered far more than *veritas rerum* (*Trin.* 14.11.14). It was therefore understandable that some Christians are put on their guard if polish and high style are employed to present truth; insofar as a fine style does not make anything true, they are right (*Conf.* 5.10). Yet provided one is deploying verbal skill on the side of truth, not in opposition to it, that is good (*C. Faustum* 14.9).

Accordingly, the story of Marius Victorinus's conversion, which fills some pages of Book 8 of the *Confessions,* is more than a model for the conversion of a leading intellectual like Augustine himself, and no doubt like some of the readers he hoped to address. The paradoxical welcome given by Rome's outstanding teacher of rhetoric and logic to the emperor Julian's prohibition of Christians from teaching literature and oratory showed Victorinus's complete dedication of his skills to a higher and sacred end, the communication of divine truth (8.7).

The extent to which Augustine thought of his preaching task as an extension of a pedagogic vocation may be illustrated by remarks in a letter he wrote to his friend in the government service, Marcellinus (*Epist.* 138.10): "Church congregations are like comprehensive public schools where the pupils are distinctive in being of both sexes and of all ages and social classes. In this school the less intelligent need a teacher with skills in communication; they need not only to be taught but persuaded." [54] For the stupid therefore, rather than for the highly educated élite, there is an ancillary and supportive function for eloquence, which Augustine tersely defines as the use of language appropriate to the subject, the audience, and the circumstances.[55]

The *Confessions* insist that in the Church rich and poor, noble and low-born, are all equal (8.9). On no account may slaves be scorned or treated with inhumanity (13.22). In mind and intellectual power men and women are entirely equal, even though the woman's biological destiny is physically determined and gives her a subordinate and less public role (13.47). Moreover, spiritual judgment is exercised no less by spiritual laity than by the clergy. The perception of God's will for his Church is not only granted to the ordained but to all spiritual members (13.33). Congruent with this proposition is Augustine's profound antipathy toward a clericalized conception of the Church. Though usage applies the word *sacerdos* to bishops and presbyters, all Christians share in the one priest who is Christ (*Civ. Dei* 20.10). The name *pastor,* Shepherd, provokes equal coolness: there is only one shepherd, Christ himself, who is "bishop of bishops" (*Trac. Joh.* 123.5; *S. Guelf.* 32.8). Augustine censures Donatist language about the bishop in apostolic succession as exclusive mediator to God (*C. epist. Parm.* 2.8.15f.) or about the holy clergy obtaining for unworthy laity gifts they could not obtain for themselves (*C. litt. Petil.* 2.105.240f.; *Enarr.* 36.2.20).

The truth of the preacher's message is grounded in the word of God conveyed, not exclusively, but in a special degree (*Serm.* 12.4) through the Scriptures which the Church accepts as its guiding rule or canon. The numerous difficulties which the sacred texts present are a signpost to the hidden mystery which they contain. That inner meaning is found only by grace, and therefore the young but undocile Augustine, stirred by his readings in Cicero's *Hortensius* to pick up his Latin Bible, found that once he had put it down, he could not pick it up again, repelled by the barbarous style and the translationese of the Old Latin version (3.9). Even at the time of his conversion at Milan, he found incomprehensible the prophet Isaiah recommended to him by Ambrose: "I put it on one side to be resumed when I had had more practice in the Lord's style of language" (9.13).

Ordination required deeper study. During his five years as a layman he had continued writing on the liberal arts; the Cassiciacum dialogues censured in the *Confessions* (9.7) for the literary tone which some readers found too sophisticated and élitist (*De gen. c. Manich.* 1.1), too reminiscent of his old lecture room (though they were more Christian than Alypius thought appropriate); his first attempt at an anti-Manichee exposition of Genesis on creation; his assimilation of much from Porphyry in *De vera religione.* His direct engagement with the exegesis of Scripture remained superficial, and he knew it. His non-literal exposition of Genesis picked on two points important in the Manichee debate—first, that *In principio,* "In the beginning," is not to be taken in a temporal sense, but refers to Christ, and secondly that the matter created by God was "unformed," form being imparted as a second stage. Both themes were to be restated in the *Confessions.*

The African churches included many simple believers who took Genesis to be a handbook of creation science.[56] They were uncomfortable if they were told that the first chapter of Genesis was not intended to bear any literal sense. So two years after his ordination to be presbyter Augustine began an unfinished literal commentary, composed with more than half an eye on literalists in the Church. The stress of the commentary lies on the uncertainty of the precise meaning of the creation narrative, and on the caution which is necessary in the interpretation of the text, provided that, where the essentials of the faith are concerned, there is no skeptical suspense of judgment. Even so, Augustine was also confident in this commentary that the matter created originally by God lacked form.

In the *Confessions* (12.17f.) we meet sharp polemic against Catholic critics of his exegetical work. The critics evidently thought that the clever presbyter of Hippo had expelled the Manichees at the price of inviting in the Platonists. Augustine retained lasting gratitude for what he had learned from the books of the Platonists. But he discerned a special hidden providence in the fact that he had read the Platonists first, before turning to his codex of Saint Paul. Had he read the Bible first and then gone on to study Plotinus and Porphyry, the experience might have disturbed his faith—for the Neoplatonists were in effect proposing an alternative and rival metaphysic which in Porphyry was intended to exclude Christianity. But the Platonists who saw the goal from a great distance did not know the road that gets one there. They knew nothing of "the price of our redemption"

(Augustine's regular phrase for the eucharist)[57] nor the need for humility and confession (*Conf.* 7.26–27).[58]

Neoplatonism was an important bridge in his conversion from a Manichee understanding of the problem of evil, which Mani had solved by limiting divine power to eliminate it. Neoplatonism helped him toward a Catholic acceptance of the world as a manifestation of divine power and goodness stamped with rationality and mathematical order. In the last four books of the *Confessions* Augustine would no longer look back on the path which had brought him to conversion and the realization of Monica's hopes and tearful prayers. He reached the point of describing his state of mind in the present, when he is writing as a recently consecrated bishop. Astonishingly there are few writings of Augustine more deeply impregnated with Neoplatonic themes, even to the extent of incorporating at one point a substantial piece of Neoplatonist exegesis (perhaps Porphyry's) of the last section of Aristotle's categories, discussing the multivalent concept of priority (12.40). Many Platonizing assumptions are made about the relation of mind and matter, which affect his evaluation of the sacraments in Book 13. At the same time he restates his exposition of the first chapter of Genesis, insisting against his critics that there is room for more than one correct interpretation of the sacred inspired text, subject to the proviso that the essentials of the apostolic faith are affirmed (12.27).

The duties of a city presbyter or bishop are not conducive to the contemplative life after which Augustine's soul always yearned. Rachel and Leah, Mary and Martha, symbolize the contemplative and the active; and in this life we are all Marthas who have to wait for the life to come to join Mary sitting at the Lord's feet. The nature of the pastoral ministry, however, means that if no time at all is devoted to meditative contemplation, the task becomes an intolerable burden.[59] So something of the monk's longing came through in the practical vision of the urban clergy.

Monks and urban clergy were frequently at odds; yet, they shared important concerns. The narrative in the *Confessions* leaves the clear impression that by a series of providential accidents Augustine ended up unmarried. When he was young Monica had done nothing to encourage him to find a wife, not in the least because she foresaw a future bishop in her gifted son but because the wrong partner—perhaps the only class of wife that could be expected for the son of a small-time farmer in rural Thagaste—might obstruct the success of his secular career (2.8). So she tolerated his cohabitation with Adeodatus's mother as a temporary way of containing his sexual drive. The time came at Milan when Augustine's partner blocked his ambitions and had to be sent back to Carthage. Monica found for him a well-to-do bride, but providentially she was too young for a wedding to take place. Chest pains enforced resignation from his Milan teaching post, the work which he in any event had come to find mountingly uncongenial. The decision in Verecundus's garden at Milan in July 386 was to abandon his pursuit of a secular career financed by his bride's dowry—a reversal of intention which would have made him a very unattractive son-in-law in the eyes of his fiancée's parents.

There is a temptation to suggest that it is part of Augustine's justification of his decision for celibacy that he consistently represents his relation with Adeodatus's mother in very carnal terms, as merely self-indulgent lust in which thoughts of disciplined responsible parenthood played no part. The bond of love which both parents of Adeodatus felt for their originally unwanted son (4.2) suggests that there was more to the relationship than physical appetite. And the deep pain of their separation also suggests that the cohabitation was congenial even if her lack of education meant that she could not be his sparring partner in scintillating conversation[60]—a pleasure for which Augustine turned to his male friends like Nebridius. The portrait of his sexual relations with her looks part and parcel of his picture of his past life as so alienated from grace as to partake of the very nature of sin. For Adeodatus "the son of my sin," as for himself and Alypius, baptism at Easter 387 washed all this soiled past away (9.14).

The monk and the presbyter shared the Bible, but it was more his pastoral calling in ordination which taught him to devote himself to Scripture studies with a vehement dedication. This can only have seemed extraordinary to his former secular colleagues, offended by his renunciation of literary pursuits (1.22) which, on the opposite wing, were offensive to puritan Christians (9.3). One recalls Ponticianus's amazement at finding a codex of Saint Paul on the table of the city professor of rhetoric and literature (8.14). Augustine's confession of praise to his Creator includes the line "You are not irritated by the burning zeal with which I study your Scripture" (11.28). We may reasonably deduce that, though God was not irritated, some human contemporaries were. Are they to be understood as those Catholic exegetes to whom Augustine's expositions of Genesis were hard to take? or pagan *literati*? The latter are perhaps more likely.

If so, we may suggest that in the *Confessions* there is an undercurrent of apologetic addressed to a critical pagan intelligentsia, in whose eyes the Church was a collection of largely uneducated people. In the preface to *De doctrina christiana* Augustine frankly observes that the intellectual capacities of bishops in North Africa are low.[61] Congregations often consisted largely of elderly women.[62] A powerful court official like Ponticianus who often spent time praying at the church was surely exceptional (*Conf.* 8.14). The plebs whose voice was still influential in the choice of their bishop preferred wealthy candidates with low educational and spiritual qualifications rather than poor men with high qualifications (*Epist.* 167.18, written to Jerome). Admittedly, important cities liked bishops whose sermons showed rhetorical abilities.

No work by Augustine is composed in a more sophisticated Latin than the *Confessions*. Without being obsessed with rhyme, he certainly liked assonances and indulged himself with antitheses. It seems characteristic that in this prose-poem the passage most like poetry and least like plain prose is the "Tolle Lege" scene in the garden (8.29), when a major turning point in his life is written up in high style with literary echoes of Persius's *Satires* and Plotinus's *Enneades*.

The pagan intelligentsia who mocked the Christians for their lack of high culture were assuredly infuriated by the conversion and then the ordination of the most acute intelligence in the Latin West of their time. Augustine's writings are not normally decorated with literary allusions to Vergil, Terence, Sallust, and Cicero unless he is expecting to be read by readers who would appreciate these allusions. I would therefore submit that there are latent in the *Confessions* elements both of self-vindication in relation to anxious Catholic critics needing reassurance about his past life and also of protreptic exhortation to conversion. By his ordination (as he was abrasively to inform the young Dioscorus who asked him for instruction in philosophy), he abandoned his teaching of those "arts which pagans call liberal and Christians call secular."[63] Ordination liberated him to be blissfully independent of the patronage system, the humiliating toadying of the powerful which was the only route to any considerable office of state, and even the toadying route had to be oiled with cash. He could view with a touch of detachment his old ambition for a career dependent on rich senators who could easily fall from power at the next palace revolution. That very precariousness was one of the factors that induced disillusion about a secular career (*Conf.* 8.15: "In that position what is not fragile and full of dangers?"). He despised the worldly values which priced a racehorse far higher than a skilled slave[64] and confused ends with means.[65] The *Confessions* speak always in an idealized way about clergy and about the ascetic "servants of God," and express scorn and accusation of the values of pagan society.

By implication, therefore, no work by Augustine reveals more about his understanding of the high calling of the priesthood, even though ordination is never a subject under discussion in the book.

Notes

1. *Serm.* 355.2.

2. *De coniugiis adulterinis* 2.22 (*CSEL* 41.409.15). It would be unsafe to use the riot of the Hippo poor which was intended to force ordination on the wealthy Pinianus as a basis for arguing that Augustine also came of a rich family, and so was economical with the truth in describing his family estate as relatively poor, "a few acres" (*Epist.* 126.7). However, the fact that Augustine recalls the admiration people felt for his renunciation of his inheritance no doubt implies that the farm was more substantial than a peasant's small holding. It was simply not comparable with the great estates of his patron Romanianus.

3. *Qu. in Hept.* 4.54.

4. *De fide et op.* 32; cf. *Serm.* 339.

5. Aurelius of Carthage at a council of 16 June 401 bewailed "the great shortage of clergy, many churches being so deserted that they are found to have not even one deacon, and that illiterate" (*Conciliae Africae,* ed. C. Munier, *CCSL* 149, p. 194). Augustine (*Trac. Joh.* 57.5 and *Epist.* Divjak 22+) bears this out. The Catholic community in Numidia was painfully short of Punic-speaking clergy who could be entrusted with ex-Donatist congregations: hence, the dreadful affair of Antoninus,

consecrated for such a church at Fussala on the edge of the Hippo diocese and then turning out to be a disaster. On the desperate need for Punic-speaking clergy, see Augustine, *Epist.* 84.2; 209.3.

6. This attitude is strikingly expressed to Sidonius Apollinaris by a church which desired a new bishop "more competent to intercede with an earthly judge for our bodies than with a heavenly judge for our souls" (*Epist.* 7.9.9). Augustine observed that the mass movement to join the Church in his time was motivated by hope for temporal aid, not for eternal life (*Enarr.* 46.5). Cf. *Trac. Joh.* 122.7 on mass conversions with unreformed morals.

7. *Epist.* 173.2; *Sermo ad Caesariensis ecclesiae plebem* 8 (*Bibliothèque Augustinienne* 32.443).

8. See the Life of Saint Daniel the Stylite 42. Text in H. Delehaye, *Les Saints Stylites* (Brussels: Société des Bollandistes, 1923), 38f.; English translation in Elizabeth Dawes and Norman H. Baynes, *Three Byzantine Saints* (Oxford: Blackwell, 1948), 31f.

9. *Cod. Theod.* 16.2.6 of 326, a law which proposed the impossible rule that a man could be ordained only as a replacement for one who had died. Basil the Great had to cope with men wanting to be subdeacons to avoid military conscription; they did not want to be deacons or presbyters (*Epist.* 54).

10. Cyprian (*Epist.* 39.5.2) speaks of "honorem presbyterii"; cf. 1.1.1 "conpresbyteri nostri qui nobis adsidebant."

11. Possidius, *Vita Augustini* 4, following Augustine, *Epist.* 21.

12. For sermons by presbyters, see *Serm.* 20.4; 137.11 and 13; *Epist.* 41; 63.2–5; 65; 251. In the absence of the bishop, the presbyters would preside at the eucharistic offering (*Serm.* 227). Possidius (*Vita Augustini* 5.3) records that until Augustine was ordained by Valerius in 391, it was quite contrary to African usage for a presbyter to preach in his bishop's presence. Pope Celestine (*Epist.* 21, *Patrologia Latina* 50.528–529) warns the bishops of Provence against presbyters taking on themselves unauthorized teaching roles, forgetful that the disciple is not above his master.

13. *Epist.* 23.3. Cf. *Serm.* 23.1.

14. That it was common for a young man to take a consort from the lower classes but then to separate from her is attested explicitly in Firmicus Maternus's handbook of astrology (*Mathesis* 5.3.16). Cf. the attack on the practice by Caesarius of Arles, *Serm.* 43 (*CCSL* 103.190f.).

15. *De moribus* 2.63; *C. duas epist. Pelag.* 4.4 (all procreation is the work of the prince of darkness). The Manichee demand for sexual continence was admired by Alypius who felt revulsion from sex after an adolescent experience (*Conf.* 6.21f.). To Hearers, however, sexual intercourse was allowed during the "safe" period of the menstrual cycle (*De moribus* 2.65).

16. Porphyry's maxim was that, for the higher life, "one must flee from everything bodily": *omne corpus est fugiendum* (*De regressu animae* cited in *Civ. Dei* 10.29; 12.27; 22.12.26–28; *Serm.* 241.7; criticized in *Civ. Dei* 13.17). Porphyry's principle is stated in his letter to his wife Marcella (35) quoting a Pythagorean maxim "Never use your bodily members merely for pleasure" (paralleled in the *Sentences* of Sextus 232).

17. *Conf.* 1.31; 4.30–31.

18. *Trac. Joh.* 5.1 (cited by the Council of Orange, 529, canon 22); *Enarr.* 58.1.19; 44.7; 126.4; *De doctr. christ.* 2.25.39; *Serm.* 32.10 (remove sin and what you see remaining in man is of God); *Serm.* Denis 18.2 (p. 92, 11 Morin) "Non esse in nobis nostrum nisi peccatum"; *Serm.* Mai 101.2 (p. 352, 25 Morin) "Homo sine Deo nihil potest nisi peccare." *Civ. Dei* 14.4.1; and elsewhere.

19. *Conf.* 9.14.

20. *Enarr.* 36.3.19: "People know my evil past, especially here in Carthage" (probably preached at the end of 403).

21. *Conf.* 1.26.

22. *Epist.* 21.

23. *Conf.* 6.6.

24. For orphans (*De pecc. merit.* 3.13.22; *Serm.* 176.2). Foundlings (*C. duas epist. Pelag.* 2.11; *Epist.* 98.6). *Matricula Pauperum* (*Epist.* Divjak 20.2). On later developments, see M. Rouché in Michel Mollat, *Études*

sur l'histoire de la pauvreté (Paris: Publications de la Sorbonne, 1974), 83–110.

25.   The best discussion of Augustine on poverty remains that of H. Rondet in the volume *S. Augustin parmi nous* (Le Puy, 1954). Typical exhortations are *Serm.* 25.8; 178.4; 259.5 (share in a common humanity). I discuss patristic notions of "humanity" in the *Reallexikon für Antike und Christentum,* article "Humanität" (1993).

26.   *Civ. Dei* 5.17.

27.   *Epist.* 151.2 to the prefect Caecilian; cf. 155.11 to Macedonius.

28.   Possidius, *Vita Augustini* 20.1 ". . . quod multa suae famae contemplatione amicis non praestitisset." I am not aware that the maxim is otherwise attested. The saying cited in *Vita Augustini* 19.2 is found in, e.g., *Gnomologium Vaticanum* 150, ed. Sternbach (Berlin: de Gruyter, 1963), 65. Its occurrence in Diogenes Laertius i 57 is noted by M. Marin in *Vetera Christianorum* 17 (1980), 119–124.

29.   On Monday arbitrations (*Didascalia Apostolorum* 2.47, p. 111). Connolly = *Apost. Const.* 2.47. The bishop's judgment was regarded as invalid unless confirmed by the presence of his clergy (*Statuta Ecclesiae Antiqua* 14, p. 81, Munier).

30.   *Enarr.* 61.16; cf. 72.12.

31.   *Serm.* 14.5.

32.   *Enarr.* 32.2.12. A bishop became cordially hated by whichever party lost the case under his arbitration (*Serm.* 125.8).

33.   *Trac. Joh.* 30.8.

34.   Ambrose, *De officiis* 2.24.124ff.

35.   Bishops were instructed by African canon law that if Church property was claimed by someone else, the clergy were not to yield (evidently in the hope that abdication of rights might make the Church more popular); see *Conciliae Africae,* p. 49, Munier. Augustine regretted that the plebs expected the clergy to neglect their pastoral office, even to the extent of being absent for a year or more, so as to combat attempts to

deprive the Church of its due revenues for feeding the poor (*Epist.* 21.5).

36. *Serm.* 355.

37. *Epist.* 124.2.

38. One lengthy sermon includes a prayer that God would give them physical strength to hear him to the end (*Enarr.* 49.29).

39. There is a partial collection of Augustine's evidence in Jean Gaudemet's article, "Asylum," in the *Augustinus Lexikon.* Asylum in churches was not legally recognized at the time of the writing of the *Confessions,* but was nevertheless respected by the authorities: so *Serm.* Denis 19.2 (p. 99, 28ff., Morin). Augustine defended the necessity of this kind of sanctuary (*S. Guelf.* 25, p. 529, Morin) but not inviolable asylum for acknowledged criminals and perjurers (*Epist.* 1+, Divjak). He was sad that the intervention of the Church was seldom effective: only "very few" cases were successfully defended (*Epist.* 22+, Divjak). On runaway slaves (*Trac. Joh.* 41.4). In the case of the debtor who sought the "help" of the Church (*Epist.* 268.1), Augustine paid out seventeen solidi for which he asks reimbursement. In 399 the Council of Carthage sent two bishops to ask the emperor Honorius to enact the right of sanctuary in churches (*Reg. eccl. Carth.* 56, p. 194, Munier).

40. Basil, *Epist.* 72–73; *Epist.* 112 requests the release from prison of an admitted criminal, and perhaps the letter survives because the improbable application was successful. Augustine, *Epist.* 22+, Divjak. Too many judicial decisions were determined by class or improper influence and bribery, as Augustine complained (*Trac. Joh.* 27.10). He held up the model of Alypius's integrity in *Conf.* 6.16. It was a delicate matter when Macedonius, vicarius Africae 413–414, responded to Augustine's intercession on a man's behalf by saying that he felt able to be lenient only when asked by entirely reliable intercessors and that interventions by bishops could prevent justice being done (see *Epist.* 152–154). Synesius (*Epist.* 121) refused intercession for an adulterator of wine.

41. *Serm.* 302.17. Synesius, writing as a layman, found excessive and burdensome the crowd of petitioners asking for his intercession with the governor Pentadius, and wrote to Pentadius telling him to shut the door in his face when he came on behalf of the petitioners. Only so could he and the governor have any respite (*Epist.* 29). *Epist.* 30 shows him

being more positive. As bishop he was sharply rebuffed by the governor Andronicus (*Epist.* 42, Garzya = 58 Hercher). At Milan, Macedonius, Master of the Offices to Valentinian II, resorted to locking his door to repel intercession by Ambrose. He was to regret that when he himself sought asylum after Gratian's murder (Paulinus, *Vita Ambrosii* 37).

42. *De opere monachorum* 29.37. Augustine there observes that his social and secular responsibilities left him no time for his real tasks. *Epist.* 213.5 records how the plebs at Hippo solemnly undertook in writing to allow him five days a week for study and failed to keep to the agreement. He used to work far into the night (*Epist.* 139.3; Possidius, *Vita Augustini* 24.11: "in die laborans, et in nocte lucubrans").

43. Possidius, *Vita Augustini* 9.1.

44. The consecration of new churches is mentioned in several passages of Augustine, e.g., *Enarr.* 29.2.6–9; *Serm.* 27.1; 116.7; 163; 336.1. Ancient evidence on the consecration of buildings is gathered in J. Bingham, *Antiquities of the Christian Church,* book 8, chap. 9, and E. Martène, *De antiquis ecclesiae ritibus* III, book 2, chap. 13; M. Andrieu, *Les Ordines Romani du haut moyen âge* 4 (1956), 359–384; P. Puniet in *Dict. d'Arch. Chrét. et Lit.* 4 (1921), 374–404.

45. *Epist.* 22+, Divjak; summary in *Journal of Theological Studies,* n.s., 34 (1983), 445. The Divjak letters are translated into English by R.B. Eno in *Fathers of the Church,* vol. 81 (1989).

46. *Epist.* 209.10 to Fabiola whose support Antoninus was enlisting.

47. On *sarcina episcopi,* see M. Jourjon in *Recherches de science religieuse* 43 (1955), 258–264.

48. Possidius (*Vita Augustini* 8.2) says that Valerius first obtained clearance for Augustine's consecration not from the primate of Numidia but from Aurelius, primate of Carthage. The move may reflect anxiety on some of the matters which Megalius was to raise. The Numidian primate may have felt himself diminished and slighted by Valerius's resort to Carthage; it was generally acknowledged that the bishop of Carthage was primate over all the African provinces (see *Concilia Africae,* ed. Munier, pp. 269–270, citing a council of Hippo in 393). Megalius's letter fell into Donatist hands (*C. litt. Petil.* 3.19; *C. Cresc.* 3.92 and 4.64). Petilian used it to flog Augustine at the Catholic/Donatist conference at Carthage in 411 (*Gesta coll. Carth.* 3.243–247, ed.

Lancel, *Sources Chrétiennes* 224, 1181–1187; and Augustine, *Brev. coll.* 3.9). In 397 news of Megalius's death led Augustine to reflect on his need to sublimate anger lest it turn to hatred (*Epist.* 38.2). Megalius's withdrawal and apology for his letter and willingness to consecrate Augustine at Hippo had not wholly healed the scar.

49. See *Serm.* 51.6, which is paralleled in part in *Conf.* 9.11. *Conf.* 4.26 records his harassment of uneducated Catholic Christians.

50. Much of the third book, *Contra litteras Petiliani*, deals with these "calumnies." On questions about his baptism, see *Enarr.* 36.3.19; *C. Cresc.* 4.54; *C. litt. Petil.* 3.28. Even if it were true that Augustine was baptized in Italy, that would not commend him to Donatists for whom the Church in Italy was polluted by compromise. That clergy were occasionally invited to perform like sorcerers to further amatory affairs is also attested in Augustine (*De continentia* 27), and in Jerome's *Life of St. Hilarion* 21.

51. Augustine's *Epist.* 147.52 and *De nuptiis et concupiscentia* 1.40 are explicit that "by Ambrose's priestly office I received the washing of regeneration."

52. *Conf.* 9.17 is explicit that he has omitted much.

53. *Conf.* 5.22. Palladas, in the *Palatine Anthology* 9.174, complains that his pupils would suddenly leave as they were due to pay their yearly fee of a single gold solidus.

54. *De ordine* 2.13.38.

55. *C. litt. Petil.* 2.73.

56. *De genesi ad litteram* 1.19.38–39.

57. E.g., *Conf.* 10.70.

58. The revulsion with which cultivated Platonists regarded the Christian penitential system may be seen in the remarks of Celsus quoted by Origen (*C. Cels.* 6.15), contrasting its humiliations with Plato's serene words about humility in *Laws* 715e. Tertullian (*De paenitentia* 11) shows that many Christians recoiled from the public shame.

59. *Serm.* 169.17; *Trin.* 1.10.20; *S. Guelf.* 29.543–549, Morin; especially *C. Faustum* 22.52–54.

60. *De genesi ad litteram* 9.9. Nebridius, well-to-do son of a freedman with an estate near Carthage, was with Augustine at Milan and an intimate friend—"a most rigorous examiner of very difficult questions" (*Conf.* 6.17). He was not at Cassiciacum, but on returning to Africa brought his entire household over to Catholic allegiance. After his premature death, Augustine published their correspondence as a memorial to him (*Epist.* 3–14). A biography of Nebridius is given by A. Mandouze, *Prosopographie chrétienne du Bas-empire* 1 (Paris: Editions du Centre National de la Recherche Scientifique, 1982), 774–776.

61. Similar warnings that uneducated Catholic bishops and presbyters who cannot cope with Manichee attacks are not to be taken as representative occur in *De moribus* 1.1.

62. *Serm.* Denis 18.6, p. 96, 18, Morin, quotes as an insult hurled at a Christian who confesses he has just been to a church service: "Are you not ashamed to go where widows and old women go?"

63. *Civ. Dei* 6.2. The testy letter to Dioscorus (*Epist.* 118) is a fascinating document of cultural confrontation: a clever young man (Augustine's term for that is "a Greek") who is not a Christian turns to the bishop of Hippo to answer some questions on philosophical points in Cicero's dialogues, so that he is not put to shame when he goes to Greece and meets experts. After a lengthy and regrettably pompous rebuke to Dioscorus for asking such questions of a bishop, Augustine concludes by actually answering his questions arising from Cicero's *De natura deorum*, but refuses to consider Cicero's *Orator* and *De oratore* as unsuitable topics for a bishop to discuss.

64. *Civ. Dei* 11.16; *Enarr.* 143.10.

65. The perversion of humanity is to use ends and to enjoy means (*De diversis quaes.* 83.30; *Serm.* 21.3; *C. Faustum* 22.28).

PART 3

Workshops

Augustine: Theologian and Bishop

Agnes Cunningham

We live in an age when bishops and theologians do not always agree, when bishops are not, usually, able to be "working theologians," and when leading theologians are not often called to the episcopacy. There once was a period in the history of Christianity when the greatest theologians were the most pastorally effective bishops. Augustine was one of these.

How was Augustine able to integrate what are often perceived as two mutually exclusive ministries? What does his experience have to say to us, today? Those are the questions I propose to explore.

AUGUSTINE THE THEOLOGIAN

Augustine is recognized as a major theologian, because of his influence on others, his use of a variety of theological methods, and his vast theological achievement. The following excerpt from a letter (*Epist.* 195) addressed to him by Jerome records Augustine's influence even during his lifetime:

> You are known throughout the world; Catholics honor and esteem
> you as the one who has established anew the ancient faith . . . ;
> and what is a mark of even greater glory, all the heretics
> denounce you.

One contemporary scholar has claimed that, in the history of the West, "theology, both Catholic and Protestant, is largely a series of annotations to his work" (Eugene TeSelle, *Augustine the Theologian* [New York: Herder & Herder, 1970]). The impact of Augustine's writings has been both positive and negative in the history of Christian thought and the development of doctrine. Often, Augustine's teaching is not known in its totality. We fail to take into account the "occasion" which prompted a given work or the role of ancient rhetoric reflected in his writings. We pass over the significance of his spiritual journey, or the evolution of his thought.

In terms of theological method—often the touchstone for evaluating contemporary theologians—Augustine must be judged by the "standards" of the age in which he lived. Like other great theologians of Christian antiquity, Augustine thought and wrote before the development of systematic theology, the Medieval synthesis, or the Age of Enlightenment—a few of the factors that have contributed to the emergence and development of "modern theology."

In Augustine, we can identify theological "perspectives," "principles," and "elements." For Augustine, theology was "the science which generates, nourishes, defends, and fortifies faith" (*Trin.* 14.1.3). The entire goal of Augustine's theological effort was: to explore each new challenge through a process of reflection and discovery, in light of Scripture and the living tradition as expressed through the authority of the teaching church, with the use of all the resources of the human mind and, thus, to arrive at knowledge of the truth.

Augustine pursued this goal in over 1,030 books, letters, and treatises listed by Possidius, his first biographer. An extant collection of over 270 letters represents a period of more than forty years (A.D. 386–430). His works include study of the Scriptures: commentaries, expositions, sermons, homilies. He wrote until the very day of his death. In the last years of his life, he often dictated one work at night and another by day. When he died, at the age of seventy-six, he left three works unfinished.

AUGUSTINE THE BISHOP

Augustine's ordination was the result of a spontaneous choice by the Catholic people of Hippo, who knew their own bishop needed a priest to assist him in his duties. Augustine always felt he had been ordained "by violence," because he was not "ready" or "worthy." In A.D. 395 he became bishop of Hippo in North Africa.

Augustine was convinced that his ministry was a spiritual one. He lived in voluntary poverty and gave priority in his life to prayer, study, preaching, administration of the sacraments, works of charity, and defense of the faith. His ministry reached beyond the church of

Hippo to the church of Africa and, even, to the universal church. In the exercise of his ministry, he was inspired, above all, by the idea that the proper expression of episcopal authority is ordered to *service*: weekly and, at times, daily preaching; catechesis; care of the poor; formation of the clergy; guidance of monasteries of monks and nuns; participation in regional councils; work for the reconciliation of Donatists and Catholics.

AUGUSTINE THE SAINT

Augustine stands on our horizon as a challenge and a model. As a theologian, he constantly emphasized the importance of faith in the theological enterprise. Through faith, we "possess" God, so to speak; through love, we abide in God. The wisdom of faith leads, through love, to contemplation, the summit of the spiritual life.

As a bishop, Augustine was committed to service: service in the ministry of the Word and the mystery of God and service that leads to Christian love which, for Augustine, was superior to martyrdom. Augustine was able to integrate the ministry of the theologian with that of the bishop, because he had learned to love. Love transformed Augustine into a saint.

Augustine the saint teaches us not to despair of seeking and finding truth. He teaches us to be "great lovers of understanding"; to study and love Sacred Scripture; to seek to know God and ourselves; to recognize the signs of God in created realities; and always to pursue truth, love, freedom, beauty. Augustine teaches us that the effort and the journey are well worthwhile—and possible.

PLATE 7. The title page from a seventeenth-century French translation of the *Confessions* done by Robert Arnauld d'Andilly (1588–1674). *Les confessions de S. Augustin,* traduites par Monsieur Arnauld d'Andilly, Nouvelle edition (Paris: Pierre Le Petit, 1675).

Augustine and the Church

Gillian R. Evans

Baptism does not involve only the individual and God. It is also an admission to membership of the community of Christ's body. That cannot take place in a community which is in no way or sense "Church." It must follow that at least some of the communities in which "heretical" or "schismatic" baptisms occur remain in some manner churches even if only partly or imperfectly "Church." This was the problem which confronted Augustine in his dealings with the Donatist sect, who were forceful and numerous in the North Africa of his day. It is also a problem ecumenically today in the post–Vatican II world where the model is no longer of a return of Christians who have left it to the mother Church of Rome, but of the uniting of Churches which recognize one another to be in some sense all truly *the* Church.

Augustine held that the sacraments could not normally be fruitful or efficacious except in unity, for love is an essential element and the breach of unity is the betrayal of love.[1] The Holy Spirit makes the sacraments not only the acts of Christ in the Church, but also of the living Church in the Spirit. That can happen only within the bonds of mutual Christian love.[2] But Augustine's position remains that, even in separation, communities may act as channels for the work of grace and the ordinary ecclesial means of grace can operate within them in an extraordinary way, if God so wishes.

In his controversy with the Donatists Augustine was obliged to work out an ecclesiology in which there remained, despite his best efforts, a number of paradoxes and imperfectly resolved dilemmas. Yet, he was faced with practical and pastoral pressures that made it impossible for him to let matters lie. He regarded these as of such great importance that it was necessary to make the concessions he did for the sake of the needs of the souls caught up in the controversy.

That in itself is a principle of huge significance ecumenically today.
The need to make "emergency concessions" for the sake of the
faithful arises again and again in Christian history, as theology is
tested against human fallibility. The concept of a community's being
"partly the Church" must perhaps fall into that category.

The great central difficulty for Augustine was to reconcile a
doctrine of the unity of the Catholic Church with the principle that
baptism performed outside it could, in duly defined circumstances, be
valid (if not efficacious) and was therefore not to be repeated. He also
found himself obliged to oppose the Donatists' attractive and
biblically founded assertion that "purity" was essential to the Church,[3]
an ecclesiology which asserted the Church to be a mixed community
in which only God can know who are really His. Both these main
thrusts of his anti-Donatist thinking have a number of implications for
the problems about communion which face ecumenists today. It
remains a stumbling-block to union that the sacraments and order of
one ecclesial body cannot be recognized by all others because they are
held by some to lie outside the true Church. It can also be a difficulty
that the visible Church is identified by some communions as
consisting in those whose salvation is sure, and who are known by
their faith to be justified in the sight of God; and by others as a mixed
community, wheat and tares growing together until harvest.[4]

The Donatists saw the true Church as a *hortus conclusus*. They
drew their interpretation of this image and its fellows—the seamless
garment, Noah's Ark, the enclosing net in the sea of the world, the
sealed spring or well—in part from Cyprian's account of them.[5] These
images have in common the notion of a Church where one must either
be "inside" or "outside," and outside it is impossible to "drink" from
the "fountain" of the sacraments.[6] The Donatist sect was also strong
in its emphasis on human capacity to recognize and even to define the
true Church; and perhaps somewhat Pharisaical in its self-confidence
and its reliance on a notion of "guarantee" in the matter of getting the
parameters right. What Augustine was to put forward was altogether
untidier, but it placed the stress on God as the agent of salvation,
working as He pleases within the Church and outside it. He could not
accept the Donatist equating of holiness with separation, nor their
contrasting of purity with treason.[7] Here he was departing not only
from what was in fact a very ancient and biblical idea of the Church
as a body of Christ's people who ought to keep themselves unspotted

from the world. He was also moving away from the position of his contemporary Ambrose of Milan, who had tended toward seeing the Church as a force in the world which will purify and transform, not setting itself apart, but engaging with the world.

Augustine was attracted by the paradox of the view he found in the *Book of Rules* of the Donatist Tyconius (who was himself condemned within his own sect for the opinion). Tyconius read many contradictory statements in Scripture, where what appears to be the same thing is cursed in one place and blessed in another. Isaiah 45.3–4, for example, says that God will reveal himself; Isaiah 29.13, that he will not be recognized. Tyconius offers an explanation in terms of the bipartite nature of the Church which is signalled in the Song of Songs (1.5): "I am dark and beautiful." He saw in the Church the mystery of the bringing together in one body of saint and sinner.[8] Augustine became convinced that it would be presumption to try to separate the wheat from the chaff in the Church before God's own time came for doing so, for it is not given to man to know who is saved, and that therefore the Church must be understood not as a pure, but as a mixed body.[9]

This line of thought necessitates the embracing of a further paradox: if the visible Church is thus a mixed body of saints and sinners, that cannot be understood to be the case with the mystical and invisible body of those God alone knows to be His own. So we have both a "true Church" which is "impure" and a "true Church" which is "pure" and holy, existing one within the other in some ultimately perhaps indefinable relation.[10]

Augustine went a significant step further here. He was able to envisage a communion in parts, an interpenetration of the true Church with that which is not the Church truly or fully. In his book on baptism he argued against the Donatists that the Donatists are in communion with the Catholic Church at all points where they are in agreement with it; they are in schism at the points where they disagree. Individual Christians may be partly in schism (that is, in those points at which they differ from the Catholic consensus), and partly in unity with the Catholic Church (1.1.2). That means that the Donatists are not wholly out of communion with the Catholics, and for this reason too their baptism need not therefore be regarded as invalid. "In virtue of that which belongs to the true Church in each of them," they may administer and participate in the true sacraments (1.10.14).

This is a very important concession in favor of the notion of communion (currently being developed in an emergency situation among Anglicans), as something which may persist even when it is imperfect, and still be in some sense true communion. It is therefore in favor of a view of communion which is of ecumenical significance today—indeed central to the contemporary ecumenical endeavor. Augustine's desire to acknowledge the remaining "partial" communion or "degree of communion" has a startlingly modern ring. It helps us over the difficulty set out by Cardinal Ratzinger, in answer to the question (posed to him at an interview) as to whether one can use the Pauline formula of the "Church of Corinth," the "Church of Rome" in a similar way to describe the "Church of Wittenberg," when that means the Lutheran church. "The answer is quite plainly no," he said. "The 'Church of Wittenberg' as such does not exist at all."[11] "Churches" whose identity is not local but denominational are not churches in the sense Paul meant. They cannot be in communion with one another in exactly the way in which the Pauline churches were. But it does not follow that they are not for that reason unable to be in communion with one another at all. This is a point to which we shall return.

Augustine also had a good deal to say about the ways in which the Church may be both one and many, and about the manner of the communion of the many churches in the one. The primary idea that the one Church is somehow the "source" or "origin" of the many appears in Cyprian. He uses the familiar images of the Trinity in a manner appropriately modified to make them apply to the Church. The sun emits many rays, but it is one light; a tree has many branches, but one trunk standing on a firm root; many streams flow from a single spring, where "numerousness" appears in the plenitude, but unity is preserved in the source.[12] It was of the first importance to Cyprian that the Church's unity should be seen in this way in its relation to and dependence upon the unity of God. But there remains the substantive difference that, whereas in God the plurality of the Persons does not diminish or alter or add to the unity of the Godhead, in the Church the model is that which is found in all creation, of the many multiplying from the one. Yet, of all creatures the Church is unique in being united with God Himself in Christ. Augustine seeks to find a way to express this type of plurality which is peculiar to the Church.

It had from the first been accepted that the one Church might be fully the Church in each place.[13] The many local churches remained one Church in this way, and no breach of communion was implied in their plurality. Nevertheless, there could be complicating factors of nationalism or tribalism or some other form of claim to regional identity and autonomy. There seems to be some such compounding sense in the case of the Donatists,[14] and Augustine saw its dangers to communion. He argues instead for a view of plurality in communion which resolves the whole into, as it were, conceptual parts or elements, some of which may be maintained in communion even where others are not. This, as we have seen, enables him to say that a Christian is in unity and communion with the Catholic Church at some points even if not at others.[15] On the other hand, he would not consider such a Donatist or other heretic or schismatic to be "in" the Church. The Church's claim to an autonomy which makes it somehow self-sufficient for salvation is, paradoxically for Augustine, precisely an indication that salvation is not to be found there.

He explains what he means with some care in a letter he wrote about the Donatist sect for his people, seeking to meet a pastoral need for a clear account of the difference between the Donatist position and their own.[16] The Catholic Church is the whole Church (*secundum totum*). Members of Christ are joined to one another by the love of unity (*per unitatis caritatem*), and they are united because they belong to the same Head who is Christ Jesus. No one who is not a member of Christ in this way can have Christ's salvation.[17] Those who dissent from the Head, even if they appear to be the Church in every respect, are not in the Church. Those who hold everything Scripture says, but who do not communicate with the unity of the Church, are not in the Church. Those who are in some error of faith dissent in such a way that their communion is not with the whole Church everywhere, but with some separated part. It is clear that these are not in the Catholic Church.[18] It is thus possible not to be in the Church, and so not to obtain salvation, by a breach of faith or of communion, and also by loyalty to a "part" of the Church (*pars separata*) which identifies itself as a distinct ecclesial entity over against the universal Church. The weight of "over against" is crucial here, for the ecclesial distinctness of churches not so identifying themselves is at war with

their being in union with the universal Church. Augustine develops
the point in the *Contra epistulam Parmeniani*. He stresses that the
Christians in the local Church of Africa must see themselves as joined
in unity with the Church spread throughout the world (*toto orbe
diffusa*) "by communion" (*per communionem*).[19] The Donatist position
is ecclesially untenable, because it cannot sustain that principle.

The test of universality is thus crucial for Augustine. How can
the Donatists be right when they stand against "so many Churches
throughout the world?" he asks.[20] In 398, in a correspondence on the
question of catholicity with Honoratus, a local Donatist bishop, he
argues that while the Catholics can clearly claim to be in communion
with the universal Church, the Donatists must hold to the unlikely
view that Christ allowed his whole Church on earth to disappear,
preserving it only in Donatism.[21] The Donatists also have to say that
the prophecy of the universal Church has been fulfilled and no longer
applies.[22] To sustain the Donatist case requires extraordinary special
pleading.

So we find Augustine, on the one hand, making a case for partial
communion or degrees of communion, and, on the other hand,
maintaining that only in full communion within the one and universal
Church can salvation be found. This contradictory position is at its
most challenging in connection with baptism. Augustine thought the
practice of rebaptism of those baptized outside the Catholic Church
a greater threat to communion than the acceptance of such baptisms
as valid (provided they had been administered in the name of the
Trinity.) The emphasis here was upon the once-and-for-all character
of the forgiveness of baptism. That seemed to Augustine wholly non-
negotiable, and to be so clearly the act of God that it could safely be
left to divine power to act even through unworthy or heretical or
schismatic ministers, when His name was invoked for the purpose of
baptism. The Church has its unity in Christ; its communion is with
him; and so all those baptized into his body are in some measure in
communion with him and with one another.

Notes

1.   Perhaps there is some departure from the Pauline principle of 1
     Corinthians 1:10ff. in this.

2. Yves Congar, *Essais oecuméniques: le mouvement, les hommes, les problèmes* (Paris: Centurion, 1984), 207.

3. James 1:27.

4. See the final section on communion.

5. Cyprian's position is well described in Jean-Paul Brisson, *Autonomisme et Christianisme dans l'Afrique romaine de Septime Sévère à l'invasion vandale* (Paris: E. de Boccard, 1958).

6. Cyprian, *Epist.* 79.11, ed. G. Hartel, *CSEL* 3 (1868–71), 808.23.

7. Cf. Optatus, *op. cit.,* 1.21 and Augustine, *C. litt. Petil.* 1.17.18, *CSEL* 52, p. 14.

8. Cf. Pamela Bright, *The Book of Rules of Tyconius; Its Purpose and Inner Logic* (Notre Dame: University of Notre Dame Press, 1988), 63ff.

9. Augustine, *C. epist. Parm.* 1.7.12 and 1.9.15, *CSEL* 51, pp. 31–35, ed. M. Petschenig (1908). See, too, Gerald Bonner, "The Church and the Eucharist in the Theology of St. Augustine," *Sobornost* 7 (1978), 448–461.

10. Pierre Batiffol, *Le catholicisme de saint Augustin,* 2d ed. (Paris: Librairie V. Lecoffre, J. Gabalda, 1920), 2 vols., p. 266.

11. Joseph Ratzinger, *Church, Ecumenism and Politics: New Essays in Ecclesiology* (New York: Crossroad, 1988; orig. pub. as *Kirche, Ökumene und Politik: Neue Versuche zur Ekklesiologie* [Einsiedeln: Johannes, 1987]), 114–115.

12. Cyprian, *De unitate catholicae ecclesiae* 5.213–214.

13. That paradox of being fully one in many exemplifications was to be developed strongly in the West in the Middle Ages in connection with the doctrine of transubstantiation. A number of authors of the eleventh and twelfth centuries stress the fact that the same body of Christ *unum et idem numero* is present in every local Eucharist. See *The Works of Gilbert Crispin, Abbot of Westminster,* ed. Anna Sapir Abulafia and Gillian R. Evans (Oxford: Oxford University Press for the British Academy, 1986), index.

174   *Augustine and the Church*

14.   Discussed by A.H.M. Jones, "Were Ancient Heresies National or Social Movements in Disguise?" *Journal of Theological Studies* 10 (1959), 280–298.

15.   *De baptismo contra Donatistas* 1.1.2–2.3, *CSEL* 51, pp. 146ff.

16.   *Epistola ad catholicos de secta Donatistarum* 2.2, *CSEL* 52, p. 232.

17.   Ibid.

18.   Ibid. 4.7, pp. 238–239.

19.   1.1.1, *CSEL* 51, pp. 19–20.

20.   Ibid. 1.2.2, pp. 20–21.

21.   See Batiffol, *op. cit.,* p. 145 and *C. epist. Parm.* 1.2.3, p. 22.

22.   Ibid.

Augustine's Political Theory: "Realism" Revisited

Robert Booth Fowler

The discussion section on Augustine's political theory began with a review of attitudes toward Augustine's political thought over the past forty years and concentrated particularly on assessments of Augustinian "realism." Augustine's political "realism" is especially important in the emphasis Augustine places on the limitations that sin imposes upon governments, dreams of world peace, and enduring earthly solutions to collective problems. Popular reaction to Augustine's view has waxed and waned. After World War II and during the period up to the Vietnam War, Augustinian "realism" received a good deal of praise among Western political thinkers and theologians. World War II proved to be extremely sobering for those optimistic about human beings and human governments. However, in recent decades there has been much more disagreement. For some, Augustine's "realism" is another term for the surrender of the Christian calling to radical transformation of the social and political order. For others, it remains a sobering and sensible analysis without which serious change will fail.

Discussion of the usefulness of this analysis was vigorous. The group had (re-) read some of the classic passages by Augustine in *The City of God,* including his considerations on human sin, the two cities, earthly versus heavenly peace, the nature of true happiness and why it cannot be achieved on earth. These and other specific passages from Augustine were cited at times. Also considered was the able and classic "realist" analysis by Herbert A. Deane in his influential *The Political and Social Ideas of St. Augustine.*[1] The group had read his last chapter which is an ardent defense of the accuracy of the "realist" interpretation of Augustine's political teachings—and an equally determined defense of its wisdom for modern politics. We explored other views at several points, for example, Peter Brown's perspective in his *Augustine of Hippo.*[2] Brown's image of Augustine as the "busy bishop of Hippo," a practical governor of church and state, drew our attention to Augustine's practical politics as distinguished from his theology of politics.

Participants were interested, however, in a range of topics concerning Augustine, his political analyses and ideals, his relationship to other religious traditions and to contemporary conditions and crises. The group benefited from its members, some of whom were distinguished authorities on aspects of Augustine's thought and all of whom seemed eager to learn and exchange ideas. Those with special expertise generously shared their knowledge of Augustine's political writings (occasionally quoting his Latin) as well as their mature perspectives on his political reflections. In addition, members of several religious traditions were active participants and provided some interesting evidence of the breadth of Augustine's influence in the broad modern world.

Among the other themes considered were the relevance of Augustine's "realism" to our own age in terms of both international and domestic politics and the attractiveness of his outlook (a topic on which there was lively disagreement). There was also considerable—and inevitable—discussion of Augustine and Reinhold Niebuhr, addressing Augustine's influence on Niebuhr and—equally inevitably—whether Augustine had a beneficial or baleful influence on Niebuhr. One of the most intriguing discussions focused on the connection between an Augustinian politics and that espoused by Augustine's disciple, Martin Luther. The group included a number of Lutheran ministers who offered thoughtful and pointed observations on that topic.

Participation was widespread and the time to end came surprisingly quickly. It seemed clear that Augustine's political theory was still very much alive—and as controversial now as it was fifteen hundred years ago.

Notes

1. Herbert A. Deane, *The Political and Social Ideas of St. Augustine* (New York: Oxford University Press, 1963).

2. Peter Brown, *Augustine of Hippo* (Berkeley: University of California Press, 1967).

Augustine and Calvin

Robert M. Kingdon

John Calvin, the most prominent intellectual leader of the second generation in the Protestant Reformation, was deeply influenced by the thought of Augustine. His debt to Augustine has been demonstrated in stunning detail by Luchesius Smits, *Saint Augustin dans l'oeuvre de Jean Calvin* (Assen: Van Gorcum, 1957). The influence of Augustine upon a single doctrine, the one most widely identified with Calvin, the doctrine of predestination, was used as a case study in this workshop.

It began with a brief analysis of the Augustinian doctrine of predestination, setting it in the context of the controversy with the Pelagians, as revealed in Augustine's attacks on Pelagius and his disciple Celeste, on Julian of Eclanum, and on semi-Pelagian communities in southern France—particularly the *De correptione et gratia,* the *De praedestinatione sanctorum,* the *De dono perseverentiae.* Certain variants in early doctrines of predestination were noted: (1) the distinction between single predestination, that God only predestines the saved to bliss, and double predestination, that God predestines the saved to bliss and the damned to torment; and (2) the distinction between infralapsarianism, that God issued His decrees of predestination only after the fall of Adam, and supralapsarianism, that God issued His decrees of predestination before the creation of Adam, before time.

The workshop then examined Calvin's doctrine of predestination, as revealed in the trial records of the cross-examination of Jerome Bolsec, who was prosecuted in Geneva for attacking the Calvinist doctrine of predestination, and in passages in Calvin's *Institutes of the Christian Religion.* These materials clearly showed that Calvin taught both double and supralapsarian predestination. It also became clear from these and other materials that Calvin thought he drew these doctrines from the writings of Augustine, particularly the *De correptione et gratia* and the *De praedestinatione sanctorum.*

Finally, the question was discussed as to whether Calvin was in fact true to Augustine. It is commonly said that Augustine taught single predestination and that Calvin hardened it into double predestination. Calvin knew that Augustine's thought on the problem had evolved, and felt that the older Augustine had repudiated the ideas of the younger Augustine. He was convinced that in the end Augustine had reached the same conclusions that he had, favoring both double and supralapsarian predestination, and cited in defense of his conviction treatises in which other scholars have found the doctrine of single predestination. Who is the true interpreter of Augustine? Several members of the workshop felt strongly that Calvin was a true interpreter of Augustine, and that the entire Calvinist doctrine can be found in the later anti-Pelagian tracts which Calvin cites so extensively. Other members of the workshop were unconvinced, and argued that while Calvin thought he was interpreting Augustine correctly, he actually misrepresented and perhaps misunderstood Augustine's position.

Augustine: On Education
and the Liberal Arts

Fannie LeMoine

Participants in this workshop examined three aspects of Augustine's views on education and the liberal arts. The first concentrated upon Augustine's criticism of the aims of education and included a comparison between ancient and modern views on appropriate educational objectives. Augustine's quest for education as spiritual enlightenment was contrasted with the more commonly held assumption, both in antiquity and in the present day, that education should lead to material success and career advancement. Selections from the *Confessions* formed the principal text for discussion of this first aspect of the topic. It served as the basis for an examination of the metaphors of buying and selling Augustine uses to denounce education designed mainly to facilitate selling the self for profit and power.

The second part of the workshop was devoted to a brief analysis of Augustine's changing perspective on the value of the liberal arts. In some of Augustine's earliest preserved writings such as the *De ordine* his aim for education may seem similar to that of other Neoplatonic didactic writers of Late Antiquity. Augustine's near contemporaries Macrobius and Martianus Capella are confidant of transcending the world of earthly experience through study of the liberal arts. Both the *De nuptiis Philologiae et Mercurii* (*The Marriage of Mercury and Philology*) by Martianus Capella and the *Somnium Scipionis* (*Commentary on the Dream of Scipio*) by Macrobius also contain lengthy descriptions of the magnificence of the universe visible to human eyes and accessible to human intellect when the mind is properly disciplined for spiritual ascent. Augustine's reflections in his early works on teaching and the liberal arts differ from these writers in two conspicuous ways. Augustine is more doubtful of the possibility of achieving spiritual enlightenment through human reason. And he is more muted in his praise of the universe and in the awe inspired by contemplation of its splendor.

In order to illustrate this point, selections from Augustine's work *On the Teacher* (*De magistro*) were set against short selections from *The Marriage of Mercury and Philology* of Martianus Capella and Macrobius's *Commentary on the Dream of Scipio.* Augustine composed the *De magistro* as a dialogue between himself and his son Adeodatus in 389, the period in Augustine's life when he was most optimistic about the possibility of the liberal arts serving as a path to transcendent truth. The dialogue deals with Augustine's theory of knowledge and the value of language as a means for apprehending reality.

Somewhat like Socrates in the *Meno,* Augustine leads Adeodatus to recognize what he already in some sense "knows." Yet, this Platonic view takes on a distinctive cast because of Augustine's insistence upon the inadequacy of human speech and thought without the inner enlightenment brought by Christ. Without divine assistance humans can neither teach one another nor themselves.

It is easy to read Augustine's view in this early dialogue as Platonic and essentialist. Such a reading fails to consider how Augustine's reflection on the Incarnation influences his understanding of the liberal arts. Augustine consistently maintains the centrality of Christ as the inner teacher throughout his later works. But his reflections on the meaning of the Incarnation give such prominence to the embodiment and the historicity of Christ that his theory of teaching comes to seem far more existentialist.

The last part of the workshop was devoted to examining this dimension of Augustinian thought. Meditation on the "embodiment of Christ" transforms Augustine's understanding of Christ's inner teaching. When he speaks of Christ as the teacher in his later works, he does not talk of "a spark of divine enlightenment" but rather of a shared experience, an understanding like the knowledge which joins parts of one body. Thus, Augustine's views on the value of the liberal arts in the fourth book of *De doctrina christiana* (*On Christian Doctrine*) need to be placed within a theory of the possibility of true knowledge which is much more consciously centered upon human experience. Augustine shifts the "place" of wonder, the starting point of knowledge, from the soul's ascent through the universe to the bond between God Incarnate and the human heart.

In order to illustrate this change, selections were read from some catechetical works, such as *De catechizandis rudibus,* and the fourth book of the *De doctrina christiana.* These selections included citation of a passage from *De disciplina christiana.* Although the authenticity of this work has been questioned, the views the text expresses are thoroughly Augustinian and effectively illustrate the continuity of Augustine's views on Christ the teacher in the Middle Ages.

In the catechetical works, when Augustine stresses the centrality of Christ as teacher of the inner person, he increasingly "embodies" his teaching in biblical narratives that reveal the qualities and actions of God to human understanding. The words and stories of Scripture act as a textual vehicle for the instantaneous and profound knowledge of God which Christ imparts.

The Augustinian material presented in the workshop spanned almost forty years, from Augustine's earliest period of extant writing on education and the liberal arts during his retreat at Cassiciacum to the fourth book of the *De doctrina christiana,* written four years before his death. It began with his retrospective assessment of the education he had himself received and dispensed as he recalls it in the *Confessions,* then moved to an assessment of his views on the liberal arts in his earlier works such as *De magistro.* Finally, later catechetical works such as *De catechizandis rudibus* were examined in order to support the argument that Augustine comes to a reappraisal of the value of words and the liberal arts through his deepening understanding of the Incarnation and the Bible narratives which reveal God's presence in history.

Thus, Augustine in the fourth book of the *De doctrina christiana* redeems the arts for Christian usage as spoils taken from the Egyptians and turned to better use. This retelling of the biblical story shifts the perspective on the arts from the transcendent to the immanent. A brief comparison with the spiritual perspective of Martianus Capella makes the difference clear. In *The Marriage of Mercury and Philology,* Martianus Capella's narrator tells a divine myth in which the liberal arts are presented as handmaidens given by Mercury to his bride Philology, the love of learning by which humans become divine. The thrust of the narrative is on the transcendent quality of the arts and the apotheosis toward which the disciplines may lead. On the other hand, Augustine interprets the biblical account of a "historical" event as an analogy for incorporating the arts within human experience, experience which already knows God and recognizes that divine revelation in Scripture and in Christ's human life is the foundation of learning.

The workshop arrived at these conclusions by a close reading of selected passages of Augustine's writings. To illustrate the nuances of the argument and the textual contexts for the summary presented above, I have included a more detailed examination of some of the passages used in the discussion.

SELLING ARMS TO INSANE DESIRES: TEACHING AS AN IMMORAL ACT

Augustine harshly criticized the classical rhetorical education he had pursued as a child and he had himself taught as a man. The sharpness of his attack and his bitter chagrin at the amount of misguided effort such education had forced upon him can easily be seen in the first book of the *Confessions.* In A.D. 397 when Augustine wrote this work, he could look back over more than forty years spent in learning and in teaching others. It therefore forms an excellent point of departure for examining the basis of Augustine's criticisms of education and for comparing how his perspective differs from more modern views.

A modern audience would certainly agree with Augustine's denunciation of corporal punishment. Augustine makes that criticism all the more memorable by recording in the *Confessions* both his fear of the beatings he received in school and his hurt at his parents' casual dismissal of such "childish" fears (*Conf.* 1.9). The beatings and his forced study of Greek were a torment to him. Even his love of Latin literature, so neatly summarized in his tears for Dido, became an occasion for regret as he recalled those seductive sirens of his youth in his more mature years.

Many modern critics would also challenge the commonplace ancient view that the primary goal of education should be to prepare students for a role among the educated élite, entrance to which required knowledge of the literary culture of Greece and Rome. Their reasons, however, differ markedly from Augustine's. Modern critics reject study of the classics either as an irrelevant waste of time, because "valuable" knowledge lies elsewhere, or as the misguided pursuit of those who wish to establish a cultural hegemony over a multicultural world.

Augustine saw education for profit, power, or career advancement as a fundamental betrayal of the true purpose of education. In the *Confessions* Augustine describes how he first accepted the view that "true" education should lead to spiritual enlightenment through reading Cicero's now lost protreptic to philosophy, the *Hortensius.*

Augustine's bitterest words about education he reserved for those, like himself, who had been consumers and purveyors of education designed solely to serve personal opportunism and career advancement. For example, at the beginning of Book 9 of the *Confessions,* he describes his reasons for leaving his teaching post with an unforgettable image of himself as an arms dealer selling to insane desires: *ne ulterius pueri meditantes non legem tuam, non pacem tuam, sed insanias mendaces et bella forensia mercarentur ex ore meo arma furori suo. (Conf.* 9.2.2).[1]

The contempt he felt for himself as a *venditor verborum (Conf.* 9.5.2), a peddler of the art of speaking (*Conf.* 8.6.9, *ego vendebam dicendi facultatem*) sums up his disgust for the type of teaching or learning where the real aims are not intellectual or spiritual enlightenment but a selling of God-given gifts.

Throughout the *Confessions* Augustine repeats this commercial metaphor for teaching and learning. He frequently applies it to buyers and sellers who have no understanding of the value of the educational merchandise in which they trade.[2] In Augustine's view, education for material advancement is tantamount to the corruption associated with taking bribes or selling yourself. The Latin word *venditor* which Augustine uses to describe his profession carries the meaning of selling your talent, your honor or your influence, for a fee.[3]

Augustine, in Book 8 of the *Confessions,* sets these corrupt "buyers and sellers of themselves" against the person "bought back" by Christ who sells all he has in order to purchase the pearl of great price. He begins the book with reference to that famous parable (8.1.47) and reinforces the parable's significance with the allusions to "selling what you have" in order to be redeemed from bondage. Augustine achieves an especially forceful turn on the commercial trope he has used contemptuously for his profession by repeating the biblical injunction (*vende omnia quae habes*) in *Confessions* 8.12.28

immediately before he lifts the book to read the passage from Paul's letter to the Romans which marked his conversion and the end of his bondage.

THE MASTER TEACHER

The focus of the major part of the workshop was on exploring how Augustine's practice and theory about teaching changes from his dialogue *On the Teacher* through his catechetical works to his manual for preachers, *On Christian Doctrine.* Augustine composed the first work, the dialogue between himself and his son Adeodatus, in 389. *Confessions* 9.6.14 records the time of its composition and Augustine's own reflection on his role as a father. In composing an educational treatise as a father-son dialogue, Augustine was following a well-established Roman practice. Roman didactic literature is filled with father-son dedications and dialogues. Roman fathers of the aristocracy and other fathers who imitated the practices of the educated élite were expected to show considerable attention to the education of their sons. They served as principal instructor and authority for the younger disciples. Many of these works follow a literary and a philosophical tradition which springs from Varro and Cicero. In this tradition the liberal arts are seen as a propaedeutic to the study of philosophy and their study is accorded real spiritual value.

Two famous didactic works by near contemporaries of Augustine, Macrobius and Martianus Capella, both use the pattern of father-son dialogues in order to expound the view that the *disciplinae liberales* can lead to spiritual truth. Both the *Commentary on the Dream of Scipio* by Macrobius and *The Marriage of Mercury and Philology* by Martianus Capella rest on the assumption that through study of things corporeal humans can reach the incorporeal and attain spiritual transcendence.[4]

Although other works which adhere to the same literary form as the *De magistro* strongly support the transcendent value of the liberal arts and even though it was composed in the period when Augustine was most optimistic about the possibility of human learning, the work still departs notably from other works in the tradition in questioning the ability of human language to correspond with reality. Language has lost its integrity; speech is painfully slow, halting, and fractured into as many objects as the human heart desires. Thus, for Augustine, the entire process by which humans attempt to find truth is called into question. If Christ is not present as the master teacher of the inner person, there is neither true teaching nor true learning.

When Augustine looks back upon his role in this dialogue in *Confessions* 9.6.14, he rejects his own role as father and teacher. Instead, he claims that Adeodatus reveals insights in this work which arise from his God-given talent rather than any gift his biological father could give him.

SCHOLA IPSIUS CORPUS IPSIUS EST

Augustine's rejection of his own "bodily" role can be seen as one end of the spectrum of the discussion. At the other end is Augustine's increasing insistence upon Christ as the master teacher who is Incarnate and One with God the Father. Thus, in the *De catechizandis rudibus* Augustine stresses Christ's Incarnation and the importance of instruction through Christ's life and biblical narratives, God's word embodied in Scripture. [5]

Many passages in later Augustinian works point to the primacy of Christ as the master teacher who teaches through his divine humility in assuming human form. Rather than cite better known texts, I prefer to end with a quotation from the conclusion of the sermon *De disciplina christiana*. Although the work is of doubtful authenticity, it sums up the major argument of this workshop concisely and illustrates the force of Augustine's concept of the embodiment of spiritual enlightenment in the words of the apostles and in the life of Christ.

> Quis est enim magister qui docet? Non qualiscumque homo, sed apostolus. Plane apostolus, et tamen non apostolus. *An uultis, inquit, experimentum eius accipere, qui in me loquitur Christus?* Christus est qui docet: cathedram in caelo habet, ut paulo ante dixi. Schola ipsius in terra est, et schola ipsius corpus ipsius est. Caput docet membra sua, lingua loquitur pedibus suis. Christus est qui docet: audiamus, timeamus, faciamus. (*CCSL* 46.14.15).[6]

In this passage Augustine uses a metaphor to transport his hearers from their immediate experience of weary and slow learning to a heavenly classroom in which what they learn is like the instantaneous and whole experience one part of the same body shares with other parts of itself. The metaphors for Christ's teaching are strikingly organic and lead to a description of Jesus' life which underscores the importance of his embodiment in flesh and in history as the means by which humans come to understand their place within God's paternity.

> Et ne contemnas et ipsum Christum, quia propter te in carne natus est, pannis mortalitatis circumdatus; propter te esuriuit et sitiuit; propter te lassatus ad puteum sedit; propter te fatigatus in navi dormiuit, propter te a facie sua sputa hominum non abegit; propter te alapas in faciem accepit; propter te in ligno pependit; propter te animam effudit; propter te in sepulcro positus est. Haec omnia forte contemnis in Christo? Vis nosse quis sit? Recole euangelium quod audisti: *Ego et Pater unum sumus.* (*CCSL* 46.14.15).[7]

In sum, Augustine's view of education from 387 onward is notably consistent but develops a special dimension through the greater emphasis he gives to the Incarnation. He rejects his position as teacher (and father) as that role would have been defined in late ancient society. He also rejects his career as a professional purveyor of the rhetorical art. Instead, he seeks to become a clear interpreter of the divine narrative embodied in Scripture and already inscribed within the human heart. Although he distrusts human speech and humans' ability to employ it without error, his conviction grows that the divine teacher, speaking through the words of the Bible, can reach wayward pupils as surely as the head instructs a healthy hand or foot.

Because Augustine believes spiritual enlightenment is embodied in Christ Incarnate and that true Christians share in that mystical body, his view of education comes to encompass earthly experience and human arts as valid, "usable" means for interpreting God-given truth. Augustine's organic imagery contrasts with the more mystical imagery of contemporary Neoplatonic didactic writers. It also contrasts with the stressed and fractured metaphors found in descriptions of education in the post-modern world.

Notes

(Translations are by the author.)

1. "[I did not want] boys who were not intent on your law, on your peace, but on the lying insanities and wars in the forum to buy from my mouth the arms to further their own madness."

2. For example, at the very beginning of the *Confessions* (1.13.36) he confronts the buyers and sellers of grammar (*venditores grammaticae vel emptores*) about the truth of their "fictive" wares.

3. See Cicero, *post Red. in Sen.* 4.10, *venditor dignitatis.*

4. James O'Donnell rightly underlines the importance of the mystical in ancient views of the liberal arts in his recent commentary on the *Confessions.* See the excursus on the *Liberales Disciplinae, Augustine Confessions. Commentary,* vol. II (Oxford: Clarendon Press, 1992), 269ff.

5. In recent years, Augustine's catechetical work has come to be recognized as an important literary influence on his other more widely known writings, such as *The City of God.* See, for example, Johannes van Oort, *Jerusalem and Babylon: A Study into Augustine's "City of God" and the Sources of His Doctrine of the Two Cities* [Supplements to *Vigiliae Christianae* 14] (Leiden: E.J. Brill, 1991). This attention to Augustine the catechist is a good counterweight to the scholarly tendency to study aspects of Augustine's views on education or rhetoric in isolation, both in terms of the topics treated and in the Augustinian works cited.

6. "For who is the master who teaches? Not just any kind of man, but an apostle. Indeed an apostle, and yet not an apostle. 'Do you wish,' he says, 'to know him who speaks in me as the anointed one?' Christ is the one who teaches: he has his chair in heaven, as I said a little while ago. His school is on earth, and his school is his body. The head teaches his own limbs, the tongue speaks to his own feet. Christ is the one who teaches: let us listen, let us respect [his words], let us do [as he teaches]."

7. "And do not despise Christ himself, because it was for you that he was born in the flesh and surrounded by the rags of mortality. For you, he suffered hunger and thirst; for you, he sat weary by the well; for you, he slept exhausted in the ship; for you, he did not wipe away humans'

spit from his own face; for you, he received blows on the face; for you, he hung on the tree; for you, he poured out his spirit; for you, he was laid in the tomb. Do you perhaps despise all these things in Christ? Do you want to know who he is? Remember the gospel which you have heard: *The Father and I are one.*"

Augustine on Grace: The Early Years

Joseph T. Lienhard

Augustine's "conversion" in 386 to ascetical Christianity should have disposed him favorably to Pelagianism. However, Robert Markus correctly calls his teaching "a defence of Christian mediocrity":[1] in opposing both Donatism and Pelagianism, Augustine was opposing perfectionism. Yet Augustine sensed in Pelagianism some of his own past. This workshop traced the development of Augustine's teaching on grace up to A.D. 412.

Pelagius believed he had to keep grace external to the person in order to defend true freedom; otherwise, rewards would be undeserved. Human nature could achieve great things, and hence was obliged to: Pelagius taught obligatory asceticism. Augustine also began his ascetical-Christian life with unbounded confidence in the ability of the human intellect and will to achieve their goals. In his early writings, he expressed the belief that he could come to a vision of God in this life that was in no way inferior to the vision of the world to come; and in the *Soliloquies* he wrote: "I commanded myself not to desire . . . a wife" (1.10.17). The man who could write that sentence seems worlds away from the later Augustine, so often condemned as a pessimist, who wrote: *Nemo habet de suo, nisi mendacium et peccatum* ("No one has anything of his own, except lying and sinning," *Trac. Joh.* 5.1). When did the self-confident ascetic intellectual of Cassiciacum become the *doctor gratiae* of Hippo Regius?

The change in his outlook took place, not in 412, as the Pelagians maintained (and gleefully quoted his *De libero arbitrio* to show it), but by 397, when he wrote *De diversis quaestionibus ad Simplicianum*. In 412 in *De spiritu et littera* Augustine presents his first complete and most balanced exposition of his teaching on grace. Augustine himself recognized the change he underwent when he wrote, in 428, of his state of mind in 397:

"I, indeed, labored in defense of the free choice of the human
will; but the grace of God conquered, and finally I was able to
understand, with full clarity, the meaning of the Apostle: '. . .
what hast thou that thou hast not received?' (1 Cor. 4:7)"
(*Retract.* 2.1.3, tr. Bogan).

Simplician, one of Augustine's spiritual guides, had written to
Augustine and asked him to explain Romans 9. Augustine's answer
is tortured. He obviously struggled to understand the passage—or
rather, to come to a new understanding. He concludes that Jacob's
election was utterly unmerited, and a mystery, whereas Esau's
reprobation was merited, the result of Adam's original sin and its
disastrous effects on all of Adam's descendants. He quotes 1
Corinthians 15:22 ("in Adam all die") and writes: "Carnal
concupiscence now reigns as a result of the penalty of sin, and has
thrown the whole human race into confusion, making of it one lump
in which the original guilt remains throughout" (*De diversis quaes.*
1.2.20, tr. Burleigh). Thus, the whole human race, sick with sin,
desperately needs a remedy. Not surprisingly, the metaphor of Christ
as physician recurs often in Augustine's writings. Baptism "launched
a Christian on a lifelong process of convalescence," [2] Markus writes.
And the medicine that effects the healing is grace.

When Augustine writes *De diversis quaestionibus,* he also
realizes for the first time that the *initium fidei,* the first movement of
the soul toward God, is the answer to a call of grace and not a
human, meritorious work. Thus, only in 397, he finally understood
fully what had happened in his "conversion" of 386: faith was not his
choice or his decision, but the result of the call of God's grace. Only
then was he able to write the *Confessions.*

Augustine's new understanding of Paul fits in to a larger pattern.
In the West around 350, an intense interest in Paul arose, along with
a new interpretation. Easterners saw Paul as a mystical theologian.
Westerners found the Paul who was confounded by sin and guilt and
discovered healing grace. In the half-century after 360 five Westerners
wrote commentaries on Paul: Marius Victorinus, the Ambrosiaster,
Jerome, Pelagius, and Augustine. Simplician had guided two of them,
and urged Ambrose to preach about Saint Paul. He may well have
been the *éminence grise* behind the new interest in Paul. Simplician's
importance is not always fully appreciated. Around 354 he lived, for
an extended period, in Rome, where he accompanied Marius

Victorinus on his way to Christianity, and to baptism in 354. Twenty years later, in 374, he was in Milan when Ambrose was baptized, and instructed the new bishop in Christian theology. In 386 he assisted Augustine in Milan, narrating the story of Marius Victorinus's conversion (*Conf.* 8.2.3–5).

Finally, a gradual deepening of Augustine's understanding of Paul (rather than a *volte-face,* as Paula Fredriksen suggests)[3] can be traced through Augustine's early writings on Romans and Galatians.

Notes

1. Robert A. Markus, *The End of Ancient Christianity* (Cambridge: Cambridge University Press, 1990), 45.

2. Ibid., p. 54.

3. Paula Fredriksen, "Beyond the Body/Soul Dichotomy: Augustine on Paul against the Manichees and the Pelagians," *Recherches Augustiniennes* 23 (1988), 87–114; and *eadem,* "Paul and Augustine: Conversion Narratives, Orthodox Traditions, and the Retrospective Self," *Journal of Theological Studies,* n.s., 37 (1986), 3–34.

VARIISERMONI

DI SANTO AGOSTINO,

ET D'ALTRI CATHOLICI,

ET ANTICHI DOTTORI, VTILI ALLA SALVTE DELI ANIME,

MESSI INSIEME, ET FATTI VOLGARI DA

MONSIG. GALEAZZO VESCOVO DI SESSA.

CON DVE TAVOLE VNA DE SERMONI, ET L'ALTRA DELLE COSE PIV NOTABILI.

CON PRIVILEGIO.

IN VINEGIA, APPRESSO GABRIEL GIOLITO DE'FERRARI.

M D L X V I I I.

Del monasterio di S.⁰ Andrea

PLATE 8. This Italian translation was done by Galeazzo Florimonte (1484–1567), a noted south Italian Christian humanist. Augustine of Hippo, *Varii sermoni di santo Agostino, et altri . . . utili alla salute dell'anime,* (Venice: Gabriel Giolito de' Ferrari, 1568).

Augustine and the Scientific Tradition

David C. Lindberg

It is widely believed by the educated public that the early church was an obstacle to the development of science. This view was formulated in the eighteenth century and fully articulated in the nineteenth century by John William Draper, Andrew Dickson White, and others. This workshop explored that opinion in general and Saint Augustine's role in the affair in particular.

If we are to grasp the fate of science during the patristic period, we must first understand that science was not perceived as a distinct body of knowledge, different from other kinds of knowledge, but simply as a branch of philosophy—specifically, the philosophy of nature or natural philosophy. Consequently, no educated person of antiquity had an opinion of science that diverged dramatically from his or her opinion of philosophy or learning in general. Thus, we must ask not "what was the fate of *science?*" but "what was the fate of *philosophy* during the patristic period?" The answer is that it attracted little enthusiasm. Why was that? Because it met no vital need. The Roman Empire was experiencing severe political and economic distress, and people were preoccupied with declining prosperity, the securing of peace, and the preservation of at least the rudiments of law and government. The tiny literate upper crust, which might have been expected to seek education for its children, was preoccupied with maintaining such fragments of the good life as it could and had little time for abstract, theoretical, and essentially useless knowledge about nature. Insofar as there was energy for any philosophical activity, it was directed mainly toward questions of meaning and value.

Now the appearance of Christianity and its gradual rise to power (tolerated early in the fourth century, state religion by the end of the century) did very little to change the situation. Christians had approximately the same concerns as non-Christians and approximately the same attitude toward philosophy. Or to state the case more precisely, if there was a spectrum of opinion toward philosophy among pagans, the same spectrum of opinion was found among Christians. And therefore it was not Christianity that killed philosophy, but the circumstances of ancient civilization. In this matter, Christian attitudes simply reflected those of the culture.

But is there not an objection to this line of argument? Were not Christians especially threatened by philosophy because it contradicted the Bible? Some were, and some were not—just as some pagans were threatened by natural philosophy because it threatened their sacred books, and some were not. Perhaps this is the way to put it: Educated Christians inevitably evaluated the relationship between their theological beliefs and the major philosophical systems at their disposal. There was, as we should expect, a range of responses. At one extreme, some Christians saw all philosophical systems as a threat and repudiated the philosophical enterprise. Others thought that Christianity could make its peace with philosophy; such people were naturally propelled toward the philosophical systems easiest to reconcile with Christianity. These philosophies they adopted, developed, put to use (especially for theological purposes), and disseminated. Which is to say that Christianity served a selective function: Christian theology determined, ultimately, which ancient philosophies were to prosper.

Now the ancient philosophy most readily compatible with Christianity was Platonism (or its descendant, Neoplatonism). Plato had defended a creation of the world by an artisan god, as well as the immortality of the soul. By contrast, the atomists were considered outright atheists. Aristotle described an eternal, deterministic world; he also denied personal immortality and divine providence. Such philosophies were obviously objectionable and were firmly discarded. The ultimate result was a harmonization or integration of Christianity and Platonic philosophy. Saint Augustine was one of the chief architects of this Christian Neoplatonism (though certainly not the first), and through his influence it came to dominate thought in the early Middle Ages.

Within this Augustinian tradition, what was the relationship between faith and reason? This was to become one of the central issues in the relationship between Christianity and philosophy, and it is time to confront it. The standard caricature of Augustine and the other church fathers is that every time reason (here encompassing observation) conflicted with the Bible or theological doctrine, reason was compelled to yield. The result was a crushing of the scientific spirit. The authority of the Bible wiped out the possibility of genuine philosophical (including scientific) activity—a fact to which the long dark period of the Middle Ages is ample testimony. When philosophical or scientific theory has to conform to the teaching of the Bible, you get absurdities like belief in a flat earth.

Now there is just enough truth in this caricature to give it plausibility (though it is important to note that almost no medieval people believed the earth was flat). There is no doubt that ultimate authority rested with faith (that is, the teachings of the Bible and the theological doctrine built thereon). When it came to the crunch, theology had the upper hand. But does this not mean the repudiation or destruction of genuine rational activity? Not in Augustine's view. According to Augustine, reason is not to be repudiated, but to be redeemed. Human reason is a divine gift, which distinguishes us from the brutes. However, the "fall" of humankind has darkened our rational capacities, so that they do not function to their full potential. They can be restored by submission to the discipline of faith. Faith provides a foundation and materials that make genuine rational activity possible. Understanding is the ultimate goal; only by choosing the proper starting point will one achieve genuine understanding; and that starting point is biblical teaching.

This is one aspect of Augustine's influence on the next millennium-and-a-half of Christian thought. There is another. According to that other, philosophy is *worth* pursuing only insofar as it serves higher goals—those of theology and the faith. In this perspective, philosophy (including natural philosophy) is the handmaiden of theology.

To conclude, how did all of this affect the enterprise of natural philosophy? It did not support scientific activity to the extent that it would have been supported had Augustine campaigned successfully for the establishment of a National Science Foundation, which would have poured millions of dollars into research laboratories and graduate fellowships. But that, of course, was not even a possibility in A.D. 400. More to the point, Augustine applied philosophy (including natural philosophy) to the elaboration and defense of the faith. He put it to use (extensively in his *Literal Commentary on Genesis*); and in putting it to use he preserved it and even developed it. And this was more support than it was going to get from any other quarter. Scientific knowledge was not important for its own sake; but at least it was important as the handmaiden of religion and theology. On balance, then, Christianity was more an agent of preservation than of suppression.

Deus Caritas Est

Jill Raitt

God is love. What else does the word *caritas* mean for Augustine, Bishop of Hippo? This workshop attempted to answer the question through an examination of selections from the works of Augustine. It considered *charity* from its biblical identification with the Holy Spirit through its meaning as the bond uniting Christ and Christians in one body and through its role as crown of all the virtues to its effect in human life as kindness, alms, service, etc.

Augustine's prose becomes lyrical when he writes about the love of God: "He [God] is the light, the melody, the fragrance, the food, the embrace of my inner self . . ." (*Conf.* 10.6).[1] In his *Homilies on the Gospel of Saint John,* Treatise 7, Augustine centers charity in God who is love and is the source of the grace of charity by which God's children love God in return. God first loved us. Our response, enabled by God, is love. God first loved us in Christ and the death of Christ through which Christians return to God.[2] The redemptive mysteries of Christ's death and resurrection are most intensely celebrated at Easter. It is then that baptisms were, and are, most appropriately administered to adult converts. It was on such an occasion that Augustine preached to neophyte Christians about their identity with Christ:

> The same Word assumed human nature; in other words, He took a human soul and body, became man, yet ever remained God. And since the Word suffered on our behalf, He left us His body and blood in this sacrament, in which He also included us. For we, too, have been incorporated into His body, and through His mercy we are the very thing that we receive.[3]

Augustine told his newly baptized children that they are baked in the fire of the Holy Spirit and thereby become the bread of the Lord: "There you are on the altar; there you are in the chalice."[4] As a result, Christians should love one another in mutual charity, manifesting it in fasts and good works, humility and contrition.[5]

These passages reveal the engaging Augustine. How do we reconcile Augustine's luminous insights into the love of God and of neighbor and self in God with the harsh doctrine of double predestination that Augustine developed in his arguments with Pelagius?

Because God's love is freely given, it is given to those whom God elects. Those not so elected are reprobated and not just "in general" but individually because that is the way God knows us, as individuals. Augustine develops his understanding of free will in relation to the objects of willing. Thus, Augustine says, only through the illumination of God can the mind rightly know and the will rightly seek the true good, namely God. Illumination is itself a grace and so always, the initiative is God's. Yet God has made humans in his image; humans therefore are endowed with intelligence and free will. The image, however, was so badly tarnished and its endowments of mind and will so beclouded and weakened that it no longer sees and loves God but only the things that God has made. Nor do the human mind and will understand and desire the Maker, and they fail to go beyond the beauties of creation. To redirect mind and will is the work of grace and especially of the greatest grace of all, charity, or the inpoured love from and of God, the source of all true good, including love of neighbor and self in the service of God.

Discussions during the workshop dealt with these ideas and also with Augustine's doctrine of the Eucharist as sacrifice into which the communicants are incorporated. The problem of predestination was not resolved, nor was Augustine's doctrine of double predestination accepted by most of the workshop participants. Everyone endorsed Augustine's doctrine that charity is the heart of the church and is the supreme gift of God's own self to the body of believers and to each Christian.

Notes

1. The passage is found in *Augustine of Hippo: Selected Writings,* tr. and ed. Mary T. Clark (New York: Paulist Press, 1984), 125–127.

2. Ibid., pp. 294–307. The workshop also included discussion of Augustine's treatise *On the Trinity,* Book 8, chap. 7, ibid., pp. 309–330.

3. "Sermon 11: To the Newly Baptized, on the Eucharist III," in *Selected Easter Sermons of Saint Augustine,* ed. Philip T. Weller (St. Louis: B. Herder Book Co., 1959), 108.

4. Ibid., p. 109.

5. Ibid., p. 111.

HISTORIA
PELAGIANA

& Dissertatio
DE SYNODO V. ŒCVMENICA

IN QVA

Origenis ac Theodori Mopsuesteni Pelagiani erroris
Auctorum iusta damnatio exponitur,

ET

AQVILEIENSE SCHISMA DESCRIBITVR.

ADDITIS
VINDICIIS AVGVSTINIANIS

PRO LIBRIS A S. DOCTORE CONTRA PELAGIANOS,
ac SEMIPELAGIANOS scriptis.

AVCTORE

P· M· HENRICO DE NORIS
VERONENSI

Augustiniano Sacræ Theologiæ Profesſore, & S. R. vniuerſalis
Inquiſitionis Qualificatore.

CVM PRIVILEGIO.

PATAVII

Typis Petri Mariæ Frambotti. *Superiorum Permiſſu.* MDCLXXIII.

PLATE 9. This work against heresy is by the distinguished Augustinian
scholar Enrico Noris (1631–1704). *Historia pelagiana* [etc.] (Padua:
Pietro Maria Frambotti, 1673).

Antique Modernity:
Augustine's "Liberalism"
and the Impasses of Modern Politics

Graham Walker

Modern Western thought embraces the notion that the state should be limited, a neutral arbiter among competing "value systems." The liberal state promises not merely to remain limited but to operate strictly without reference to any conception of the good or of the good life for man. It poses as a referee, a neutral arbiter among competing "value systems," remaining uncommitted to any of them as a matter of principle. This uncommitted pose is what makes the liberal state at once so serviceable and so difficult to justify. This pose also makes certain public policy disputes (notably abortion and environmental concerns) nearly unresolvable.

From an Augustinian perspective, the problem with such a liberalism is its modern tendency to make absolute what ought to remain proximate. Augustinian thought can applaud the self-imposed limits of the liberal state, because such limits respect the inescapable ontological tensions under whose shadow the state must operate. But lacking Augustine's deeper understanding of those tensions, modern secular liberalism cannot respect them. Instead, it progressively dismantles the tensions. More than that, it attempts to make the parts it arbitrarily prefers into independent wholes—even though it is impossible to do so coherently.[1] Yet, by dismantling the tensions liberalism dismantles itself. It unknowingly transforms its neutrality toward the good into antagonism, and ironically transforms its pluralistic skepticism into a dogmatic intolerance for other than nihilistically skeptical views.

---

1. See M.D. Henry, "Tradition and Rebellion," *Southern Review* 12 (1976), 50–53.

If such an analysis should prove to be accurate, it would bode ill for the modern theory of political liberalism, but not necessarily ill for liberalism's limited state. Augustine can still remind us of good reasons for a kind of proximate skepticism, for a certain semblance of neutrality on the part of political rule, and thus for the proximately neutral artifices of legality in a liberal political order. Augustine propounds a morally limited and quasi-neutral state, but not because the universe is morally empty. His reasons provide an awkwardly non-liberal kind of justification for liberalism. But that may be the best liberals can hope for. For Augustine's thought suggests both that justifying the liberal state "as is" is an impossible task, and that justifying a proximate sort of liberalism may be not only possible but the height of practical wisdom in this age.

Contributors

Gerald Bonner, Reader Emeritus, University of Durham, England (Department of Theology); Distinguished Professor of Early Christian Studies, The Catholic University of America 1991–1994.

Henry Chadwick, Professor of Divinity, Emeritus, Cambridge University, England.

Agnes Cunningham, Professor Emeritus, Mundelein Seminary of the University of St. Mary of the Lake; Distinguished Visiting Professor of Theology, Barry University, Miami, Florida.

Gillian Rosemary Evans, Lecturer in History, Cambridge University.

Robert Booth Fowler, Professor of Political Science, University of Wisconsin–Madison.

Paula Fredriksen, William Goodwin Aurelio Professor of the Appreciation of Scripture, Department of Religion, Boston University.

Robert M. Kingdon, Hilldale Professor of History, University of Wisconsin–Madison.

Christopher Kleinhenz, Professor of Italian and Chair of the Medieval Studies Program, University of Wisconsin–Madison.

George P. Lawless, OSA, Professor of Patristic Theology at the Gregorian University and the Augustinianum in Rome. During the academic year 1991–1992 he was a Member of the Center of Theological Inquiry, Princeton, New Jersey.

Fannie J. LeMoine, Professor and Chair of Classics, University of Wisconsin–Madison.

Joseph T. Lienhard, Professor of Theology, Fordham University.

David C. Lindberg, Hilldale Professor of the History of Science, University of Wisconsin–Madison.

Gerald O'Collins, S.J., Professor of Christology, Gregorian University, Rome, Italy.

Robert J. O'Connell, S.J., Professor of Philosophy, Fordham University.

Elaine Hiesey Pagels, Harrington Spear Paine Foundation Professor of Religion, Princeton University.

Jill Raitt, Catherine Paine Middlebush Professor in the Humanities; Chair, Department of Religious Studies, University of Missouri, Columbia.

Robert Alexander Kennedy Runcie, MC, DD, 102nd Archbishop of Canterbury.

Graham Walker, Assistant Professor of Political Science, University of Pennsylvania.

Index